MAKING WAVES
STORIES OF PARTICIPATORY COMMUNICATION
FOR SOCIAL CHANGE

A REPORT TO THE ROCKEFELLER FOUNDATION

BY ALFONSO GUMUCIO DAGRON
FORWARD BY DENISE GRAY-FELDER

Published in 2001 by The Rockefeller Foundation, 420 Fifth Avenue,
New York, New York 10018-2702

Book Design: Landesberg Design Associates
Cover Illustration: Cathie Bleck

Gumucio Dagron, Alfonso

Making waves: participatory communication for social change /
Alfonso Gumucio Dagron.

p.   cm.

Includes bibliographical references.

ISBN 0-89184-051-6

1. Social change—Cross-cultural studies. 2. Communication—Cross-
cultural studies. 3. Radio—Social aspects—Case studies. 4. Theater—Social
aspects—Case studies. 5. Television film—Social aspects—Case studies.
6. Internet—Social aspects—Case studies. I. Title.

303.4833 G974 2000

TABLE OF CONTENTS

Contents

FOREWORD

BY DENISE GRAY-FELDER

Capturing the essence of participatory communication on paper is by definition an illusive challenge. From the work I've witnessed, helped direct, or just monitored during a long career in communication, my observation is that the most interesting work of a participatory nature can often defy the written word. That is, when reasonably talented writers or public speakers try to explain what it is about this work that is so captivating—and has the potential to so dramatically improve lives—their words fall flat.

That is why, when I had the idea that the Rockefeller Foundation should try to catalog some of the most innovative experiments in participatory communication worldwide, only one person came to mind to write this volume: Alfonso Gumucio. What we needed was someone who could bring both poetry and imagery to his words—yet retain the objectivity of a journalist. We needed someone who could paint vivid pictures with his writing that would allow the reader to experience the type of gut-wrenching, emotional conflicts most of us feel when we visit these projects. We needed someone who could synthesise, yet not overlook. And, we also needed a writer who would devote a hugely unreasonable amount of time to this project, yet still come in on deadline and under budget!

Alfonso lived up to these expectations and more. What follows is a fascinating account of 50 experiments in empowering people—living in poor communities across the world—to seize control of their own life stories and begin to change their circumstances of poverty, discrimination and exclusion. He spent nearly one year researching and interviewing sources for "Making Waves," and has been actively involved in every phase of production. "Alfonso's voice" is evident throughout this work, and it is a tribute to what makes him the ultimate communicator: he has the soul of the good poet and filmmaker that he is, combined with an unwavering sense of justice and fairness.

Following the first introductory chapter—which explains the field of participatory communication for social change and how it is evolving—you will read 50 illustrations of the power of community decision-making and action. Many of the stories are about community radio. We hope you don't find this tedious; but our research and conversations certainly suggest that community-based radio is one of the best ways to reach excluded or marginalised communities in targeted, useful ways.

This bias towards radio also suggests that with participatory communication what matters most is the voice. I recognise that this term has been overused in the context of democracy and development. When I use it I mean the process of hearing about the lives and circumstances of the poor and excluded in words and terms that they themselves use. Radio, by nature, gives us the ability to "hear" content, context, passion and pain.

Video clearly gives us the ability to see and hear these voices, thereby allowing our emotions to be touched in ways never imagined before the advent of moving pictures. Yet, video documentation remains expensive, training is often sketchy, and equipment breaks down and cannot be repaired or replaced. Therefore, at this point, video remains out of reach for most poor villages.

We have found—through this project and the other work of the Foundation's Communication for Social Change grant-making effort—overwhelming evidence of development and aid agencies increasing support for projects that return to traditional forms of communication: drama, dance, music, puppets, drums, storytelling and dialogue circles. We have come to appreciate the true power of face-to-face and voice-to-voice communication. Every meaningful lesson or belief I've garnered in life came from someone I value explaining the issue to me and involving me in the process of **figuring out the solution**. From the mundane (learning how to brush my teeth without getting my blouse wet) to the magnificent (breastfeeding my first child), I needed a combination of face-to-face, hands-on storytelling.

I like to think this document is just another in a series of communication vehicles that the Foundation can help create for practitioners and community activists across the globe. For every case included in this volume, there are at least five complementary examples. We've only skimmed the surface, especially in capturing the successes of the oral tradition on the African continent. We've not attempted to conduct a balanced survey of the world, but rather to select cases stories that we think may help teach us all how to be better communicators.

As you read, I urge you to focus on the lives behind these stories. As I read the document, I was most often touched by the simple lines of prose: "the village schoolteacher was equipped with nothing more than a pleasant smile"; or "A four-year-old has ... taught her parents, her superiors, the basic lesson of life: joy is the first rebellion against oppressors ... a defiance of all authority that says life will be suffering."

We salute the people living these lives. They are truly "making waves" by going against cultural norms, rebelling against forces that keep them down, broadcasting tales that were previously unheard by most.

Denise Gray-Felder
The Rockefeller Foundation
New York, NY
January 2001

INTRODUCTION

S ince April 1997 the Rockefeller Foundation, through its Communications Office in New York under the leadership of Denise Gray-Felder, has been promoting a series of meetings among communications specialists to reflect on communication for social change at the hinge of the millennium.

These meetings in Bellagio, Italy, Cape Town, South Africa, and New York, New York, have helped to define the questions, rather than the models. They contributed to the creation of a position paper that has been widely distributed in print and through various Web sites, in English, Spanish and French.

Some issues discussed during the meetings—and also through e-mail exchanges between meetings—lead the group to realise that much of the ideal communication processes that involve people could be found in a number of grassroots experiences in a variety of forms in many developing countries. The need for more research that would bring to light relevant information on experiences of participatory communication for social change was clear. That is how this exercise came to life.

CASE STORIES: A HIDDEN PICTURE

This report gathers a collection of fifty "case stories," brief descriptions of experiences of communication for social change that were selected for their participatory approaches. Some of them were visited physically; for the others information was obtained through e-mail, fax and the Internet.

Despite the fact that Latin America is ahead in the number of communication experiences and that radio has been the most important medium for development and social change worldwide, the initial criteria of selection were set to achieve a balanced representation between the regions of Africa, Asia and Latin America, as well as among the media and the tools relevant to the experiences: radio, video, theatre, the Internet and others. It also aimed to select experiences with a strong component of community "ownership."

During the research period it proved very difficult to stick to the principle of selecting only those experiences where community ownership was present. There were other angles to consider. For example, some experiences had community ownership as a final objective even if at the time of the research the degree of the community's involvement in the development was still at an early stage.

Other cases proved to be important in terms of social change and participation without including community ownership of media.

The result is a collection of case stories that is important precisely because of its variety and cultural relevance to the people of each community. These examples show that the beauty of participatory communication is that it can adopt different forms according to need, and that no blueprint model can impose itself over the richness of views and cultural interactions. Which is to say that none of these experiences is perfect nor has achieved full "success." The dynamics of social struggle and social development is a process, and the accompanying communication components are also part of the process and subject to the same positive and negative influences. Some of these experiences no longer exist, but they were important for the community when they were still active. Some are in too early stages to draw conclusions about their future. Needless to say, all of them have faced constraints since their individual inceptions and have often failed to reach solutions, but they are still interesting examples to analyse.

INITIAL SELECTION CRITERIA

Although acknowledging the importance that strategies of social marketing and information dissemination have had since the 1960s, an effort was made to select experiences that moved the concept of communication for social change one step forward.

The initial criteria had to be more flexible when recognising the importance of networking projects for communication, projects that are not defined as grassroots, but nevertheless contribute to sustain grassroots efforts.

One of the main objectives was to look at experiences that were well-established at the community level, not just one-time projects with a lifespan limited by donor's inputs. The community itself had to be in charge of the communication initiative, even if the community had not originated it. The initiative should be rooted into the community's daily life. For that matter, we looked at experiences that had at least one year of development since establishment.

Ideally, the project should have been "appropriated" by the community. The foremost example in this selection describes a community that runs the communication initiative in all aspects: financing, administration, training, technical, etc. Some other initiatives included in the report aim at this objective but are still in the process of consolidating.

Another important criterion was to consider initiatives that contributed to the strengthening of democratic values, culture and peace, thus reinforcing the community based organisations (CBOs) and allowing the majority to have a voice. Cultural identity should be central to the communication experience. The community should have assimilated any new tools of information technology without jeopardising local values or language.

The research was set to look at experiences of initiatives that are innovative in the manner in which they build alliances with local non-governmental organisations (NGOs), development organisations and other institutions. Also, those experiences aim to contribute to horizontal networking and knowledge sharing.

We didn't concentrate necessarily on the most successful initiatives but also on those that, in spite of their failures, provide important lessons. Similarly, it was important to review a few initiatives that may have already left behind their most successful moments; nevertheless they had 10 or 20 years of development and often provide more valuable information than recently established successful experiences that are still protected by funding and technical assistance.

The issue of a balanced representation was key to the preparation of the report and to the final selection of case stories. All regions in the Third World are represented fairly equally in spite of the fact that Latin America has traditionally been involved in participatory communication, while Africa and Asia lag behind.

Likewise, except for print media, which is seldom employed because of illiteracy levels, almost all other media are represented here: video, radio, interpersonal, the Internet and theatre. Radio is, however, the most often utilised and successful medium for social change.

An additional effort was made to include a balanced representation of experiences initiated by different stakeholders, such as: the community, NGOs, government, international cooperation agencies, regional networks, and religious organisations.

PARTICIPATORY COMMUNICATION AND DEVELOPMENT

In Europe and the United States, the recent literature on communication for development often refers only to books and documents published in English. Thus, studies on the theory of communication development will often include in their bibliography references to the same old paradigms: Lerner, Rogers, Schramm. … and some of the new ones: Jacobson, Servaes, White, Korten, Ascroft, Schiller or Habermas, among others. There wouldn't be references to Mattelart, Freire, Agrawal, Nair, Hamelink, Flugesang or Castells if their essays were not translated to English or written in English. And definitely, the very important contributions of Diaz Bordenave, Martin Barbero, Prieto Castillo, Reyes Matta, Beltrán and others from Latin America, wouldn't be recognised at all if a handful of their articles hadn't been lucky enough to break the language barrier. However, the most substantial part of their work remains unknown by academics in the United States and Europe.

If it's true that the discussion on participatory communication has become popular since the 1980s, it is no less true that most of the existing experiences are still ignored. Much of the available literature is based on a handful of case stories, mostly drawn from countries where English is the enabling research tool. This is one of the reasons why the participatory communication experiences in Latin America—which started in the late 1940s and now count in the thousands—are taken into account far less by academics in Europe or North America.

While a much greater understanding of the role of communication in social change is now spread among development organisations, particularly in developing countries and among academics in industrialised countries, still, little is known about many concrete experiences and projects where communication has been or is instrumental in social change.

Because of the language barriers and the scarce international visibility of most of the grassroots experiences, there is much misunderstanding among development organisations, and even academic institutions, about the essence of participatory communication practices that are alive and well in developing nations. In spite of the increasing awareness about the relevance of participation in economic and social development, the concept of *participatory communication* still lacks an accurate definition that could contribute to a better understanding of the notion. But perhaps it's not so desperately needed.

Actually, *participatory communication* may not be defined easily because it cannot be considered a unified model of communication. The eagerness for labels and encapsulated definitions could only contribute to freeze a communication movement that is still shaping itself, and that may be more valuable precisely because of its variety and looseness. *"The word 'participation' is kaleidoscopic; it changes its colour and shape at the will of the hands in which [it] is held."*[1]

The experiences of participatory communication for social change are as diverse as the cultural and geographic settings in which they have been developing. In spite of participatory communication being a relatively recent topic of interest for academics, its history spans over the last fifty years, from the time *Radio Sutatenza* started in a remote area of Colombia and the Bolivian miners organised to set up community radio stations in their mining districts. Latin America has generally been the nest where the first experiences originated. Nonetheless, with the end of authoritarian regimes in Africa and Asia during the past two decades, new experiences of participatory communication for social change have also blossomed in these regions.

The diversity of participatory communication experiences has always been a sign of its healthy status. However, the linkages with development projects aimed at economic and social change have not always been successful. It looks like, at the grassroots level, the need for communication has been deeply felt by the people who took action to make it possible, while at the planning and implementation level of donor and government driven projects there has been little consciousness about change.

The two ends are eventually going to meet, because of the international cooperation for development lessons learned during past decades. Too many projects failed because of vertical planning and implementation and too much funding was channelled to developing nations that never reached the intended "beneficiaries" until donors and planners started realising that they were doing something wrong. If they had only involved the beneficiaries from the beginning. ...

Such a simple idea, involving the beneficiaries, didn't come immediately to the minds of international donors and planners, and when it did they were not able to overcome certain obstacles. One of these has been the inertia of channelling cooperation mainly through governments that are often corrupted and insensitive to the needs of their people, and the inability of getting to the real partners in development. In recent years local NGOs and CBOs have proven to be cost-efficient and trustworthy in the eyes of bilateral donors, and even governments.

Cultural barriers, as well as attitudes of arrogance about knowledge and vertical practices, have not allowed donors, planners and governments to establish a dialogue with communities of beneficiaries. Indigenous knowledge is at best perceived as an acceptable claim from communities, but rarely considered as one of the main components of development.

Communication has been neglected for too long in development projects, and still is. Even when development organisations and staff realise today that beneficiaries have to be involved, they fail to understand that without communication there can be no long-term dialogue with communities. The fact that development projects are mostly in the hands of economists and technicians impedes the understanding of social and cultural issues that are key to a communication strategy.

Too often communication was mistakenly conceived as propaganda or, in the best scenario, as information dissemination, but seldom seen as dialogue. International donors and implementers, governments and NGOs, crave communication when the objective is to gain visibility. Consequently they concentrate on the use of mass media — or worse, billboards, paid advertising in journals — and generally on media activities that have an impact in the cities, rather than in the poorest rural areas.

There has been an evolution in the concepts of development; nonetheless projects have evolved from not taking communication into account, framing it only as a propaganda or reporting tool. Massive campaigns through mass media, especially for health projects, proved difficult to sustain without permanent funding. Moreover the campaigns have not contributed to establishing dialogue with communities. Since the inception, these projects were exogenous to the beneficiaries and too general to be culturally accepted in countries where cultural and ethnic diversity is high. Development organisations from the United States, that largely promoted the marketing of social goods, had to invest additional funds in self-promotion in order to get attention in developing countries.

The concept of establishing a dialogue with beneficiaries all along the process of conceiving, planning, implementing and evaluating a project has been gradually consolidating. At first, implementers understood that beneficiaries should be involved in the activities leading to social and economic development of a community, for the purpose of building up a sense of "ownership" within the community. This was at last perceived as important especially in terms of the sustainability of the project once the external inputs ended.

Next, planners realised that the sense of ownership couldn't be promoted if the beneficiaries didn't have a word in the decisions made before a particular project started. For example, the simple issue of deciding where to dig a borehole and place a hand pump could reveal the complexity of internal relations within a rural community. Technical people that had often seen communities as a homogenous human universe went through a learning process that helped them realise that a community—as the society at large—is also a composite of interest groups, rich and poor, whose cultural complexity has to be understood beforehand.

The concept of participatory development has lead to a greater level of understanding of the role of communication for development. More projects now include communication staff and budget funds specifically assigned to communication activities. This has also revealed the lack of trained communicators for development; actually, this specialty seldom exists in universities. Among the thousands of academic institutions that produce journalists, only a very few offer training for people interested in communication for development.

It seems there are more than 300 communications schools in Latin America, training over 120,000 students. Most of these training centres aim to prepare communications professionals for the mass media, the advertising industry, the so-called business communications and public relations. There is not one single school of communications really training communicators for development, scientific communicators or pedagogic communicators. In part, that is the very reason why we find such a distressing situation in the field of communication for development. It is very difficult to understand the reason why that type of communications school and university faculties continue to proliferate while there are not enough jobs for the newly graduated. Our society needs schools that form another kind of communicator, those that do not exist right now, at least not in the quantities that are needed.[2]

—COMMENTS OF MANUEL CALVELO

Communicators for development are a rare species. Most of those that correspond to such a profile are "self-made" communicators coming from other disciplines, who turned to communications because they identified the real need by working on development projects. Agronomists, sociologists, rural extension workers and facilitators have turned into much better development communicators than journalists which are often too biased towards mass media and vertical practices.

MACRO AND MICRO, PILOT AND SCALE

One very important obstacle for including participatory communication components in development projects is the donors' need for "scale," which either paralyses cooperation or leads to gigantic and artificial projects that result in equally resounding failures. "White elephants" —as we refer in Spanish to those expensive and gigantic projects that never move—have done much more harm than good to developing countries. The issue of scale is often related to the donor's political agenda and internal administrative regulations rather than to development needs. The requirements of proving "success" in the short-term (the "annual report syndrome") or measuring a project in numbers of beneficiaries (the higher the better), while excluding qualitative aspects and long-term benefits, have lead to projects that are only "successful" while funding is available.

In a more reasonable framework for development, scale would have to do with linking communities with similar issues of concern and facilitating exchanges, instead of multiplying models that clash with culture and tradition.

The "macro" level is often a trap in a world diverse in cultures and rich in differences. Going to scale is not always the right long-term solution and massive models cannot replace bottom-up networking. The international donor community is still reluctant to acknowledge 30 or 40 years of failures and millions down the drain because of ill-planned macro programmes. The eagerness to go fast, to show short-term results, and to extend coverage to large numbers of people has actually backfired.

It has also distorted the role of communication, which has been largely misused for the purpose of institutional visibility, and seldom as a development device. Mass media has been privileged over other communication tools, with the results that we know: enormous investments, which do not leave anything at the grassroots level once the technical assistance and the funding are withdrawn.

If real changes are expected in the way communication is applied in development projects, we first need to see changes inside the donor and implementing organisations. Those changes could involve using communication strategies from the initial stages of planning a programme or project—for example, by allocating a fixed percentage of the total budget to communication activities. Also, changes are needed that will affect the profile of the project staff by incorporating development communicators rather than publicists, and sociologists rather than journalists. Maybe at some point we will all understand better that "macro" is not just a matter of "mega," but also a matter of participation of the intended beneficiaries. And participation has never been massive if it is driven from the top.

NEXT: PARTICIPATORY EVALUATION

Some progress has been made, though not enough, in terms of gradually involving beneficiaries at the planning and implementing stages of a project. However, the evaluation of programmes and projects is still a donor driven exercise, which remains external and vertical to the beneficiaries. Surprisingly enough, the whole evaluation system seems totally outdated to deal with participatory development; nevertheless it is still very strongly present. Other than the fact that institutions specialised in doing evaluations represent an industry by itself, there is another reason that explains its current predominance: by contracting private evaluators donors keep control over evaluations.

If we look at it rationally, there are important contradictions in the manner most evaluations are done today, and the main contradiction is that beneficiaries are cut off from the process, seen only as objects of study and not subjects that can contribute to the evaluation process. The following are some aspects that obscure the results of many evaluations.

First of all, the fact that donors and/or implementers sponsor the evaluations of their own projects has an impact on the quality of results; evaluators are likely to be biased to a lesser or larger extent since they depend on future contracts with the same or similar organisations.

Second, who decides on the very objectives of an evaluation? Who will mainly benefit from the evaluation: is it the beneficiaries or the organisation that contracts it? The objectives of evaluations usually respond to institutional agendas.

Third, evaluations are often done by experts with little knowledge about the cultural, political and social context, nor do they speak the language; these are mainly consultants from private companies based in the United States or Europe. Very few projects hire national or Third World consultants with a background that facilitates a higher understanding of local culture. Occasionally United Nations development agencies exchange south-south consultants for this purpose, which is already an improvement.

Fourth, the battery of evaluation instruments is usually taken from already existing models. It's usually adapted for a particular project without sufficient consultation with the grassroots communities and with little consideration of cultural aspects.

Fifth, for statistical purposes, most of the evaluations avoid open questions and concentrate on checklist type formats that aim to obtain numbers and percentages as opposed to qualitative assessments.

Finally, the timing of evaluations is habitually donor driven and has no relevance to really measuring the benefits of a project to the community. Often evaluations are done just by the conclusion of an institutional intervention, thus capturing a picture of the development process at its best moment.

The type of information that an evaluation may bring is often of more use to the implementers than to the beneficiaries. Problems of inaccuracy of information may also obscure the results and interpretation. Inaccuracy is not only related to the inputs—for example in relation to an AIDS campaign—but often with the lack of knowledge on the culture and forms of organisation of respondents. The "evidence" that evaluators are looking for, may be distorted by the existing gap between the evaluators and the community.

The bottom line is that the evaluation process should also integrate dialogue as an essential tool. The whole concept of evaluation is to be reassessed. During the past decades we have finally moved towards the concept of people-centred development and towards a people-centred communication model. It is time to move towards people-centred evaluation models.

This has happened already at the grassroots level in some of the most interesting examples of participatory communication. During their four decades of growth and development, there were no formal external evaluations of the Bolivian miners' radio stations; but the fact is that their constituency constantly and permanently evaluated the stations and actually directed the process through continuous dialogue.

Honest and useful evaluations will only be possible when donors and implementers are ready to surrender their institutional agendas. Are they prepared to do so? If they are, evaluation should become a process that involves the beneficiaries from the beginning, setting the objectives of an evaluation process.

RADIO: SMALL WAVES, GIANT CHANGES

For more than fifty years radio has been the most appealing tool for participatory communication and development. It is without a doubt the communication tool most widely spread throughout the world and has always been the ideal medium for change. Radio had much to do with the changes in the communication landscape of Europe since the early 1970s when the *radio libre* or "pirate" stations popped up by the hundreds in Italy, France and other countries of the conservative continent. Radio Tomate and the others that started in small clandestine rooms of Paris or Milan may have evolved to successful commercial enterprises over the years, but the whole spectrum of radio and television in Europe has changed since their creation.

In the mid-40s, about three decades before diversity in electronic media would spread, small and often isolated communities of *campesinos* (poor farmers) or miners in Latin America had already started operating their own stations, not only to challenge the monopoly of state media, but also to have, for the first time, a voice of their own. The social struggles of the 1960s and 1970s, the resistance to military dictatorships that were delivered to power courtesy of the CIA, contributed to the multiplication of independent and community-based radio stations by the thousands. Today, any small country in Latin America can count by hundreds the stations, most of them FM, that serve rural or urban communities with content, that is appropriate to the local language, culture and needs.

Individually, most of these radio stations, often housed in a school, a church or a union building, may not make waves that reach far, but the ensemble certainly has the power of a tsunami. They have rocked down governments and launched new populist leaders. But above all, they have served their constituency on a daily basis, without much noise, mostly open to people's ideas and voices.[3]

Asia and Africa are certainly undergoing the same process that Latin America lived through decades ago. As people repudiate the last dictators, the new voices emerge from various media, and radio is usually in the forefront. As soon as the state monopoly cracks down, small organisations and communities lift their antennas over the villages. Asia provides important examples in the Philippines, Sri Lanka and Nepal, while in Africa several countries are taking advantage of the new democratic winds, the example of South Africa being outstanding among them.

Nonetheless, participatory radio in Africa is still at an early stage of development:

> I think the term community radio doesn't apply to stations in Africa. It implies that a station has evolved from a group of people or a community, a village. That's not the case in Africa. Most private radio stations in Africa are commercial stations. It doesn't mean they broadcast commercials all day long but it does mean that they were set up with the sole purpose of making money. And most radio stations are important for the development of the country. I'd prefer to speak of development radio. More of these stations are popping up across West Africa. African culture is based on oral history. Radio now adopts the role of village chief who used to tell stories sitting under a village tree.[4]

The smallest and most precarious community radio station already makes a difference for a community. The presence of a community radio station, even if it is not highly participatory, has an immediate effect on the population. Small stations usually start airing music for most of the day, thus making an impact on cultural identity and community pride. The next step, closely associated with music programming, is carrying announcements and dedications which contribute to the strengthening of the local social networks. When the station grows in experience and skill, local production of health or education-related programmes starts. These contribute to share information on important issues that affect the community.

Community radio stations have multiplied by the thousands all over the world over the past five decades. It is almost impossible to even calculate the real numbers, as statistics do not include the many that operate without a legal license. Essentially they are important within their own community geographic and social universes, though once in a while the names of some of these stations are heard across the borders: *Radio Enriquillo* in Dominican Republic, *Radio La Voz de la Montaña* in Mexico, *Radio Animas* in Bolivia, *Radio Qawinakel* in Guatemala, *Radio Xai-Xai* in Mozambique, *Radio Tubajon* in the Philippines, *Radio Sagarmatha* in Nepal, *Katutura Community Radio* in Namibia, *Kagadi-Kibaale Community Radio* in Uganda, *Chikaya Community Radio Station* in Zambia. ...

The process of communicating through radio has gone through various stages during the past five decades. This report has selected examples that provide a view of the evolution and the new perspectives in using radio as a communication tool for social change.

Among the fifty case stories selected, no less than twenty are radio stations, which acknowledges the importance of this medium. Radio has been instrumental for social change and moreover, has invented participatory communication, as we know it today.

The first to appear in October 16, 1947, was *Radio Sutatenza*, in Colombia. Established by José Joaquin Salcedo Guarin, a Catholic priest, the station had two main objectives: to broadcast the Christian doctrine to poor farmers and to teach skills that would contribute to community development. *Radio Sutatenza* grew steadily over the decades until the powerful Cadena Caracol bought it in the early 1990s.

Participation in community radio stations varies from total ownership to different degrees of audience involvement in programming and management.

The classic example of total ownership and control of a radio station by its constituency is the network of miners' radio stations in Bolivia. Having been established since 1949, this network is one of the first experiences and one of the most outstanding examples of popular and participatory communication in the world. It is not often that we encounter radio stations that have been conceived, set up, managed, technically run, financed and maintained by the community. Furthermore, the miners' radio stations are also the paradigm of a communication initiative that is part of a larger political and social change project. Last but not least, the fact that at its peak—in the 1970s—the miners' radio network was comprised of as many as 26 independent stations, which is not negligible at all in terms of scale. Unfortunately, we won't find many other examples of this level of quality.

In recent years we have some other examples of stations where community ownership is an important feature, such as *Radio Izcanal* in El Salvador and the local radio stations in Burkina Faso, formerly known as High Volta, and Haiti. In the last two examples, the stations were actually set up with both external funds and technical assistance. In Burkina Faso the project of creating six local radio stations was a result of the vision that Thomas Sankara had when he was still Minister of Information, even before he became President and changed the name of the country. The whole project started collapsing when he was ousted and killed by his close friend and arms companion, Blaise Campaore. In Haiti in 1994, United Nations Educational Scientific and Cultural Organization (UNESCO) donated radio equipment and provided initial training for four stations in remote areas of the island, but the stations are still struggling to build their own identity in a country constantly shaken by political upheaval.

Networking has always been a challenge for community-based communication projects. Top-down networking can easily be done by commercial ventures because of the highly centralised organisation, but that doesn't work as easily when dealing with a group of independent radio stations, each one owned by a different community. Maybe the first question to answer is what defines a network? The miners' radio stations of Bolivia were not considered a network because they aired the same programmes or had a central management, but because they were capable of linking their signals when it was judged necessary, and they pursued the same objectives: to improve the life of Bolivian miners and be heard by the whole nation.

The other example of networking that is worth mentioning is *Tambuli*, in the Philippines. These stations, around twenty, were set up with the help of external technical assistance and funding from UNESCO and Danish International Development Agency (DANIDA). Some aspects of networking include exchanges of cassettes, training, meetings and overall monitoring from the *Tambuli* Foundation in Manila. But in terms of linking their signal or exchanging material in real-time, no networking is possible as the stations are spread out in the most remote places of the island and can't possibly get in touch through their low-powered transmitters. Technically, *Tambuli* is not a network, although philosophically all the stations share the same objectives and ideas.

The *Local Radio Network* in Indonesia shows radio networking is possible even when the stations that make up the network are all privately owned. Again, this is an example of the diversity that we have found during the research process. It is essential to understand the political context of Indonesia in order to appreciate the relevance of this network to communication for social change. There is simply no other community radio in Indonesia. No law provides for such, and after decades of Suharto's strong military regime, it will still take some time until new legislation on communication is established. Albeit, the need for democratic communication inspired UNESCO to support more than twenty private local radio stations, small stations with little resources of their own, and to spark a process of networking with the help of new technologies. UNESCO provided additional equipment, training and technical assistance so the stations would start producing and airing local news and locally produced programmes. Computers and Internet access enable the stations to exchange news on a daily basis, thus consolidating the networking process. In spite of threats by the army, especially in politically hot regions as Ache, the network continues to grow.

On a much larger scale, *Púlsar* is a news agency in Latin America that provides daily reports and news through e-mail and the Internet, to several hundreds of community radio stations. From a networking perspective, *Púlsar* has been successful in establishing a system of correspondents all over Latin America and the Caribbean, who provide daily feeds and news from people's perception.

Madagascar is following a model similar to the *Tambuli* stations, with its radio stations in Fianarantsoa and Morondava. These two stations—a third is likely to be established in Antananarivo—were set up with support from Switzerland's Développement et Cooperation (DDC), with the objective of serving rural communities in their respective geographical areas of influence. This may not be an example of networking because of the lack of contact among the stations, but may become an example of ownership by the community. During the first two years efforts were directed to establish the two stations as community media, the first stations of their kind in Madagascar. Next, the process is scheduled to transfer total ownership of the stations to the rural associations currently represented on the management board. However, there is much uncertainty as to what will happen when Swiss technical assistance totally withdraws.

Among the most relevant experiences of radio stations that have succeeded in establishing themselves as examples of participatory communication for social change, those originated by Catholic priests are in the forefront. From the first community radio station ever, *Radio Sutatenza* (1947), to the thousands that operate today mainly in Latin America, radio has been the most supportive medium of communities struggling for a better world. The Catholic priests behind these communication projects quickly understood that the survival and development of the radio stations had to be linked to community participation, involving the real social, political and cultural needs of the people, and not just to preaching about faith or against communism.

Again, a classic example comes from the mining districts of Bolivia. Early in the fifties a group of Catholic priests established *Radio Pío XII* in Llallagua, with the objective of "fighting communism and alcoholism" among miners, exactly as *Radio Sutatenza* did a few years before in rural Colombia. Soon after, the station moved so close to the miners' community, that it joined the network of union radio stations. In subsequent years it was often attacked by the army, and literally, under fire, exactly as the other stations and for the same reasons—defending the political and social rights of workers. *Radio San Gabriel* in La Paz, which focused mainly on its peasant constituency, has grown to become one of the most important national radio stations in Bolivia.

Jesuit priests created and are still behind one of the most interesting experiences selected for this report, *Radio Kwizera*, a station that serves the refugee population in western Tanzania, near the borders of Burundi and Rwanda. Several radio stations functioning under the umbrella of the *Tambuli* network in the Philippines, are actually supported at the grassroots level by priests and pastors, such as *Radio Tubajon* and *Radio Loreto*, both located on Dinagat Island, north of Mindanao. *Radio Quillabamba* in Peru and *Radio Huayacocotla* in Mexico, are among the group of outstanding examples of radio stations supported by progressive priests, entirely identified with the local population.

It is not unusual to find community radio stations that have been set up with support from local or international NGOs, but it is less common to find radio stations that were established by government institutions in order to serve the community. There are few of the latter and usually when these stations exist it is more often ... the result of good-willed individuals challenging the system, rather than as an expression of government policy to provide a voice for the people. What Thomas Sankara did during the early 1980s in Burkina Faso has not been replicated by other African governments, who have been too jealous to release their tight control over the media.

The Mexican government, on the other hand, does have a policy of promoting community radio, in particular within indigenous communities. *Radio Margaritas* is one of the 24 indigenous radio stations established by the Instituto Nacional Indigenista (INI), an official institution. These stations produce and air programmes in 31 local languages and Spanish, and reach an estimated six million indigenous Mexicans. As with some other interesting projects from Mexico, the stations are the fortunate result of political contradictions, and precisely because these contradictions are far from being resolved, the stations have survived through various changes of government.

Radio Kiritimati in the Kiribati archipelago in the South Pacific and *Kothmale Radio* in Sri Lanka are also examples of community radio stations that were established and are partly funded by the government, with little political interference.

Kothmale Radio is an experience worth describing because it is one of the first projects aiming at the convergence between radio and the Internet. Equipped with computers and Internet access, the station receives requests for information from the audience, searches the web for the appropriate data, and returns the results to the listeners, in local language. It is also building a database with information useful to the local constituency.

As a tool for social change and participatory communication, radio has several comparative advantages over the other media. First, it is cost-efficient in terms of investment—both for those that run the station and for the audience. Second, it is pertinent in terms of language and content—ideal for the huge illiterate population that still remains marginalised especially in rural areas of the Third World. Third, it is relevant to local practices, traditions and culture. Fourth, once the initial investment in equipment is made, sustainability is feasible, though dependent on the level of community participation. Fifth, in terms of outreach and geographic coverage radio has a strong advantage over other media. Last but not least, the convergence between radio and the Internet is providing new strength to community radio and has enormously increased networking opportunities.

Video, as a communication tool for development and social change, has always been the subject of comparisons and disputes among the film and the television industries. In order to gain its own identity, the video tool for development had to differentiate itself from the broadcasting system, which is mostly driven by commercial interests.

For many years video has been the "poor relative" of the well-established film and television industries. It has been perceived as a marginalised and low-quality desperate attempt to compete with the commercial networks. Because of the cost of running a television station, most independent projects that aim to promote culture or social issues through television are condemned to have a short life. Even in industrialised nations, the so-called "cultural networks" or "public broadcasting" has a hard life.

During the 1960s and 1970s a few attempts were conducted in Latin America to establish "alternative" television stations in countries such as Bolivia or Chile. None was successful over the years. At one point, each university in Bolivia had its own television channel offering cultural programming, debates and news from a different perspective. But it proved to be unsustainable and as soon as commercial licenses became accessible through bidding, the university television channels faded off. In Chile, as in some other countries, university television channels just had to compete commercially with the others, so little time was left for social and cultural programmes.

On the other hand, independent video networks have managed to survive by revealing a social reality that is seldom seen in television. In spite of peoples' tastes having been moulded by the commercial offerings of television and cable networks, independent video is still alive and well.

Somewhere within this process, as technology became more affordable and easier to manipulate, video grew as a separate communication tool, with its own comparative advantages over television. The uses of video in social development projects show a great deal of creativity and capacity to adapt to the changing cultural and social context. In third world countries video is now embraced in much the same manner as radio was by the previous generation, as a tool to support education, cultural identity, organisation and political participation.

Many innovative participatory video experiences have developed all over the world. *Video SEWA* in India, the Kayapo Indians in Brazil, *FAWO* in South Africa, *New Dawn* in Namibia, *Television Serrana* in Cuba, *TV for Development* in Uganda, *CESPAC* in Peru, the *Capricorn Video Unit* in Zimbabwe, *Video & Community Dreams* in Egypt, and *Nutzij* in Guatemala, among many others. The experiences selected for this report illustrate the diversity and flexibility of this communication tool.

Video SEWA (India) among the video-based experiences, is one of the best demonstrations of the participatory potential that this communication tool can unleash. It is also one of the first and long-lasting video experiences in the world. It all started in 1984 when the late Martha Stuart, an international video communications consultant and founder of Martha Stuart Communications, travelled to India and conducted a video training workshop in Gujarat for twenty women, mostly illiterate, from the Self-Employed Women's Association (*SEWA*).

The seed that was planted in the right place at the right moment has become an important tool within *SEWA*'s social and organisational work. Among the important outcomes of this experience is the fact that women with almost no formal education were capable of assimilating the video tool, and their role in society immediately changed as a result. Martha Stuart's children, Sarah Stuart and Barkley Stuart, continued the work of their late mother by supporting similar projects in Nigeria (*Action Health*, 1992) and Egypt (*Video & Community Dreams*, 1998).

Some of the earliest, best and bigger experiences of participatory video were promoted by Food and Agricultural Organization (FAO) and, ironically enough, with the acquiescence of governmental institutions. This is the case for Centro de Servicios de Pedagogia Audiovisual para la Capacitacion (*CESPAC*) in Peru in 1975, Programa de Desarrollo Rural Integrado del Trópico Humedo (*PRODERITH*) in Mexico in 1978, and more recently Centre de Services de Production Audiovisual (*CESPA*) in Mali in 1989. The three were inspired by Manuel Calvelo, a communication specialist who had enormous influence in establishing the guidelines for participatory communication projects in Latin America. Two Peruvian communicators that had been trained by Calvelo in *CESPAC*, in fact, provided technical assistance to the Mali experience. These projects are a live illustration of how individuals are determinant in defining the spirit of participatory projects: Manuel Calvelo at the field level and Colin Fraser in FAO headquarters were instrumental in supporting what may have been considered expensive and weird projects by development officials both in FAO and government institutions.

At this point it is important to underscore that among all the other United Nations organisations FAO has been the leading agency in terms of developing the concept of communication for development, followed by UNESCO which has mostly supported community radio initiatives. The United Nations Children's Emergency Fund (UNICEF), in spite of having the largest communication staff at the field level, has not been able to sustain a direction where participatory communication would be central to field activities. Following the death of former Executive Director James Grant in 1995, philosophical changes took place within UNICEF. The result was that most of UNICEF's budget now goes to fundraising campaigns and short-term impact activities. The other UN agencies barely count in terms of promoting participatory communication projects and having a long-term vision.

FAO not only supported long-term communication projects that contributed to build a national capacity, but also developed, at the same time, a conceptual framework through seminars, international meetings, and a wealth of publications. The information and communication cluster at FAO headquarters worked best under the direction of Colin Fraser and, later in the 1980s, Silvia Balit. The administrative reorganisation of FAO in the mid-90s, with the relocation of staff, departments and resources, seems to have affected the vision on communication for development that was prevalent in earlier years.

Both *CESPAC* (Peru) and *PRODERITH* (Mexico), as well as *CESPA* (Mali) more recently, are related to agricultural development and peasant organisations. The projects had a strong component of training and video which was initially utilised as a visual tool to spread technical innovations in farming and livestock management. Very soon the peasants themselves voiced the need to also focus on social needs such as strengthening community organisation. This evolution coincided with rapid improvements in video technology during the 1980s: cheaper, smaller and lighter hand-held cameras with built-in batteries and cassette tapes. Video became the ideal tool to facilitate a dialogue between the community and the technical staff, and a means to exchange knowledge horizontally. The video products (video documentaries or video lessons) still remained an important output of these projects (*PRODERITH*'s catalogue lists several thousand productions), but making the video items became increasingly important, as it involved a process of collective reflection and dialogue on each topic.

Using video as a participatory tool and emphasising the process rather than the product are key concepts in the work of *Maneno Mengi*, a group based in Zanzibar since the mid-90s. *Maneno Mengi* ("many words" in Kiswahili) is actually an NGO that specialises in low-cost digital video production, in support of social development initiatives. Its work has benefited fisher folks as well as peasants of Tanzania. *Maneno Mengi* uses the video camera as a "mirror" for communities to scrutinise their problems and find solutions. The process can last for several months, on a daily basis. The video camera participates in community discussions; the recorded segments are shown once and again to the community or to relevant authorities if needed. After several months, when social changes are already taking place, the material is edited, mostly as a summary of the whole process.

Community representatives participate in the editing sessions, which are simplified with the use of computer laptops loaded with video editing software.

Looking at the ensemble of video-based communication experiences, we can categorise three distinct perspectives: those for which the process *before* the video product is essential, those for which the video product itself is the end result, and those that emphasise the process *after* the video product is completed. Certainly these distinctions are not too rigorous, but they allow us to better understand the strengths of each communication initiative.

TV Maxambomba and *TV Viva* in Brazil, as well as *Teleanalisis* in Chile, are examples that show the impact of video after production is completed. This is not to say that these groups do not care about the production process, but they certainly are outstanding because of the way they relate to audiences.

The experience of *Teleanalisis* has long ago folded; nonetheless it had an enormous social impact in Chile during the 1970s and 1980s, under the strong Pinochet regime. *Teleanalisis* was an alternative for news systematically censored in Chilean television under the dictatorship. Aggressive cameramen went out to record peoples' demonstrations, political repression, and a variety of social problems. The material was edited in secret and copied to VHS cassettes, which were distributed through clandestine unions, religious organisations, and community groups.

TV Viva and *TV Maxambomba* in Brazil operate in a different context, a democracy where media is owned by large economic groups, among the most influential in Latin America, such as *TV Globo*. Both *TV Viva* (from Recife, Brazil, in the North), and *TV Maxambomba* (from Rio de Janeiro, Brazil), struggle to offer the marginalised neighbourhoods another image of Brazil, an image that takes into account the problems, the needs, and the overall expression of the local community. In spite of their names, neither is a television station. Their video production touches upon all kinds of issues that can be of interest to the community: politics, health, sexuality, unemployment, education, black culture, citizen's rights and the environment. Humour is an important ingredient that helps to attract audiences. In the streets and open places of Olinda or Nova Iguaçu, *TV Viva* and *TV Maxambomba* deploy their giant screens to project video shows that attract people by the hundreds. It's public entertainment and at the same time educational. Viewing is no longer a passive activity for the activists of *TV Viva* and *TV Maxambomba*.

Television Serrana, in Cuba, is a distinctive experience because it takes place in a country where the government has always had a stronghold on the media. However, it is also a country where film, video and the arts in general have enjoyed great support from the state. The main film festival in Latin America takes place every December in Havana and includes important video selections. Cuban independent video production groups have multiplied over the last decade and have their own national festival. What makes *Television Serrana* different is that the group has established itself in one of the most isolated regions of the island, the Sierra Maestra, famous for being the guerrilla stronghold during the late fifties. *Television Serrana* looks at the social situation of the peasant population and provides an opportunity for local communities to voice their concerns and expectations. Particularly successful items are the video-letters, mostly made with children and addressed to other children in Cuba and the world.

Though video, as a participatory communication tool for social change, is still at the beginning of its journey, the potential is huge particularly because of the forthcoming convergence with Internet-based visual applications. At present, the ratio between video and radio in social change experiences is, perhaps, one to fifty, but this could change over the next decade as Internet connections speed-up and hard drive memory becomes cheaper.

Video has its own comparative advantages that are worth mentioning. First, new digital technologies are making it more affordable, easier to handle, and very competitive with professional formats in terms of quality; video is no longer a "poor relative" of television. Second, the potential of using video within the framework of an interactive and dialogic process, and still having a video product at the end is an enormous advantage. The instant playback feature of video is one of its most empowering qualities; it enables continuous participation and immediate feedback. This dimension allows those who are the subject and those who operate the technology to collaborate as equals. Third, building on the classic adage "one image is worth a thousand words," the power of visuals in communication is more extensive every day. Images are trustworthy (even if we know they can be manipulated); visuals easily motivate people. Finally, the convergence with Internet-based technologies is very promising.

THEATRE: STAGING DAILY LIFE

In a world dominated by electronic media, where television antennas can be counted by the thousands even in the poorest shanty towns—and where the profiles of satellite dishes emerge even in the middle of the desert—community theatre has not only survived, but has an important role in communicating for development.

Theatre, puppets, dance and music are firmly rooted in the traditional cultural and artistic expressions of many communities in poorer countries. It is difficult to imagine a community that has completely forgotten any of these forms of collective participation and entertainment. Sometimes the tradition is only sleeping, it has been neglected because of other urgencies (like survival in the globalised world), but it can be instantly revived when a new motivation arises. The old rich costumes set aside through several generations come out from the wooden trunks where they were carefully folded; the colourful masks and puppets glow again under the sun; the drums or locally made marimbas or *balofon* regain their clear sounds. The tradition of expressing the local history and the dreams of a community through music, dance or theatre are alive and well even in the most isolated places on earth. And that is precisely why the communication projects that aim to build on traditional forms of expression have many chances to succeed.

There are several reasons for choosing theatre or puppets or dance as a means of communicating for development and encouraging community participation. The first, and more obvious, is that it's already there at the community level, and it's most appreciated by people. Another reason is that in spite of electronic media being almost everywhere nowadays, very little is there content-wise that can help communities improve their quality of life or to organise themselves better. If only entertainment were not only entertainment. At least radio, compared to television, makes a major effort to reach communities in their own local languages, but too often the contents of programming is detached from local needs and from local cultural identity overall. Many of the drama-based experiences that we know of in the world were established because the available media either were not accessible to the people, or were not responding to their needs for information and communication.

The network of popular theatre in Nigeria was born to serve areas of the country where not even national or state radio, let alone television, had coverage. In the early 1990s UNICEF realised that the investment in radio and television campaigns had little influence in zones of Nigeria where communities lived in complete isolation from any form of electronic-based information. Moreover, the very impact of the radio and television strategy over other areas of the country was in question. The establishment of small drama groups at the level of local governments greatly contributed to support health and education activities with innovative means of communication, using the most important local resources: people, culture, tradition and language. The proliferation of these groups was challenging in terms of "scale" and the impact on the population could be evaluated immediately, because of the face-to-face communication that was implemented. Scripts on the most important health issues were developed and locally adapted to each particular context.

In Nepal, the *Aarohan Theatre* has been promoting community theatre since 1988. Although the troupe is not based in a specific community, it has placed its technical capacity at the service of training local drama groups who would in turn develop scripts and plays to support local participation for social change. Over the years a network of some thirty groups have been established with the help of *Aarohan,* some in very remote areas of Nepal. Travelling theatre groups supportive of community participation and social change are also well established in the South Pacific, such as *Wan Smolbag* in the Solomon Islands or the *Awareness Community Theatre* (ACT) in Papua, New Guinea.

Theatre is also important to promote social change in urban settings. The examples of *Teatro Kerigma* in Colombia, *Nalamdana* in India and *Teatro Trono* in Bolivia are illustrative of this trend. Street theatre has a variety of forms, including one-man performances and mimes to more organised drama groups. *Teatro Trono* was initially established by street children and youths in El Alto city, on the outskirts of La Paz, Bolivia. It eventually became a larger cultural group and expanded its activities to other urban areas of Bolivia.

Puppets have also been used as a tool for social change in many countries, particularly in India and Indonesia. Among the puppeteer's groups there is much diversity of technique, topic and audiences. Adults benefit from it as well as children. String puppets, glove puppets, shadow puppets and rod puppets are some of the traditional techniques employed, but in recent years computer-controlled puppetry is being introduced in film studios and on television shows.

Various puppeteers' troupes are concerned about AIDS prevention, such as *Puppets Against AIDS* in Namibia (PAAN), active since 1995, Dadi Pudumjee in India, and Nyanga Tshabalala in South Africa. In Hong Kong, *The Kids on the Block*, a troupe of large-sized puppets, has specialised in educating children on issues of discrimination against children with disabilities.

Some puppeteer's are using television to broaden their audiences, although this has an impact on the quality of perception and participation. Using the national language, Tagalog, the *Batibot Puppet Show* in the Philippines is designed to help pre-school children from low-income families develop skills and values through entertainment. The *Si Unyil Puppet* series in Indonesia has been on television since the early 1980s. Similarly, the *Puppet Theatre* of Ardeshir Keshavarzi (Iran) and *Uncle Sargam* by Farooq Qaisar (Pakistan) are popular shows in their respective countries. It is difficult to evaluate how many of these puppet shows really deal with social change and how much of what they broadcast is plain entertainment for children. It is obvious that the ill-defined television audience forces puppeteers to address culture and content in very general rather than specific terms, without having the possibility of establishing a real dialogue with the audience.

The Lilac Tent is an amazing experience taking place in Bolivia, inspired in various performing arts and housed under a huge circus travelling-tent. The project, which aims to positively affect the sexual behaviour of Bolivian youth and prevent AIDS and STDs, is a mixture of entertainment and educational activities. *The Lilac Tent* is something like a medieval circus combined with modern educational techniques. Wherever it travels, it certainly captures the attention of the whole community. Outside the tent people can watch video documentaries on health issues, puppet performances or evening music shows; while inside *The Lilac Tent* and organised in groups of ten, the visitors have the opportunity of participating in a series of instructive activities and games. Though funded by United States Agency for International Development (USAID) and technically supported by the communication cluster at Johns Hopkins University (JHU), this project has evolved much beyond the usual social marketing model.

Theatre and puppets as tools of participatory communication for social change have comparative advantages, particularly in live perfor-mances that are not "filtered" by television. First above all, is the cultural relevance, especially when local troupes are in charge. Traditional values are preserved and strengthened, and communicating in the local language contributes to the process of community participation. Second, is cost-effectiveness and the potential of immediately having an impact—and appreciating this impact—on the audience. Third, is the advantage of establishing a live dialogue that may derive in a learning process, both for the audience and the drama group. Finally, the entertainment factor, which enables the contents to be conveyed, channels the energies of the audience, through surprise or through laughter, to the processes of comprehension and participation.

INTERNET: A PRESENT STILL TO SHAPE

Although often perceived as "the future" of communications, the Internet is already here and represents a "presence" that is still unchanged in terms of its potential benefits for social change.

Because of its own nature as the product of scientific research and intellectual development, the Internet has received much more attention from scholars than any other medium for development. While the actual experiences of the Internet as a tool for social change are only two or three years old, the number of evaluations and studies is far ahead of this reality. The willingness to make the Internet a useful tool for social development and social change leads to many assumptions and idealisations. Much is said about the potential benefits, while most of it is yet to be realised. Somehow, this competition towards defining on paper (actually, mostly through e-mail discussions and Web-based debates) what the Internet should be is a legitimate reaction to the fact that the Internet is already something which does not correspond to what we would prefer.

The very evolution of the Internet is amazing. First it was a U.S. national security project, then a noble tool for democratising information exchanges, finally a gigantic virtual worldwide super-mall. The military lost it to computer wizards and scientists at the beginning; the well-intentioned scholars lost it more recently to globalisation and advertising.

In terms of what the Internet represents for social change in developing countries, a reality check shows a mostly dim picture. The United States has more computers than the rest of the world combined. Currently, around 50 percent of the Internet users are in the U.S.; about 25 percent are in Europe; and only 12–13 percent are in Asia. South Asia, with 23 percent of the world's people, has less than one per cent of the world's Internet users. The typical Internet user worldwide is male, less than 35 years old, with a university education and high income, urban-based and English speaking— a member of a very elite minority. In a world with thousands of languages and cultures, 90 percent of Web-based information is in English. The ten other most important languages in the world are largely under-represented within the remaining 10 percent, including Spanish, which has more speakers than English worldwide.[5] The pattern is similar in terms of content. U.S. Web sites largely dominate, and consequently, the content is mainly of interest to U.S.-based users. A peasant in India or a factory worker in Brazil, just to name two important and populated countries in the Third World, will not find much of interest on the current World Wide Web, even when he or she gets around fairly well in English.

Certainly, we could say the same about television. Cable and satellite TV have flattened the landscape of television worldwide. The same concept of television, the same information, the same feature films or documentaries, the same advertising campaigns are available (or imposed) throughout Asia, Africa, Latin America, Europe and North America. Often the same television channels—or Web sites, by the way—are available in Spanish, Portuguese or Japanese, but the content is just a mirror image of the original.

Video for social change is new and radically different from commercial television. It is not yet happening on the Internet. There is only one Internet, and it is largely commercial. In terms of the social use—which up to now has been a synonym of planting computers in areas previously deprived even of telephone and electricity —the existing models are mixed and confusing.

Too many different initiatives are called by the same names, to the point that we don't know any longer what a "telecentre" is in terms of its social use. Many are just "cybercafes" for upper middle class students or tourists visiting developing countries. Other telecentres in rural areas are commercial ventures aiming to provide communication services to those that didn't have access before, which as such is not at all a bad thing. These rural telecentres or Internet cabins manage to get telephone land lines or radio and satellite links that are already benefiting community users, who often visit the place to access the phone more than the web. There is clear improvement in terms of access to communications technology, though it is not yet clear if this access will contribute to development and social change or is only a fashionable new gadget.

Many will argue that the introduction of new technologies only widens the gap between the rich and the poor, just exactly as happened in the 1970s with the "modernisation" programmes.

> While there had been some success in agricultural, health, nutrition and educational extension pro-grammes, the main beneficiaries were the better-off sections of society. There was little evidence of the hoped for "trickle down" effect. The diffusion of inno-vations that was believed to have brought about the Green Revolution, for instance, benefited the richer landowners and farmers. ... Indeed, the knowledge gap between the "haves" and the "have-nots" has widened as the elites have greater access to the mass media.[6]

In any case new technologies don't seem to frighten away anyone. The technical skills needed are not a barrier for poor and almost illiterate people to access. Knowledge of how to use a computer is not an obstacle in the Third World. Experiences such as El Limón in a small and marginalised village of the Dominican Republic or "the hole in the wall" in India show that people with no previous computer technology contact whatsoever can easily find their way using the mouse and the keyboard. "The hole in the wall" is a particularly interesting experiment conducted by Sugata Mitra from the NIIT, which is a multinational company specialising in information technologies and e-commerce: a computer screen and a control stick were placed in the wall of a poor slum. Within minutes, the children that started playing around with this mysterious object found out how hyperlinks worked, and within a week they had figured out how to write a few words without a keyboard, how to drag and drop documents, and how to browse the Internet. Of course, playing around with a magic box is not the same thing as being able to take advantage of the Internet and finding something useful while browsing the Web. The Web is not yet ready for their needs.

Shaping the Internet, or some of it, in a way that serves the objectives of development, democracy, social change and cultural identity through a participatory process may not be easy to achieve, but some are trying hard. The few Internet-based projects selected in this report are attempting to develop a critical mass of knowledge and experience, which may eventually contribute a more socially-oriented use of new technologies.

The convergence between radio and the Internet, which we have mentioned earlier, is one of the most interesting symbioses that new technologies can offer. Not only does community radio get empowered to reach new latitudes, but also Internet users learn from a participatory experience that has done much for social change during the past fifty years. The *Púlsar* network in Latin America, *Kothmale Radio* in Sri Lanka and the *Local Radio Network* in Indonesia are some of the relevant examples of this trend.

The Internet has a better chance to succeed as a tool for development and participation if linked to existing communication or information experiences. The *Sistema de Información Rural* (*InfoDes*) project in Peru has taken this into consideration when basing its information system on community libraries that were created in rural areas of Cajamarca thirty years ago. In Colombia, *Colnodo* is helping existing NGOs and community organisations to build Web sites and make available to others a wealth of information. Similar projects such as *Ecuanex* (Ecuador), *Cabinas Públicas* (Peru) and *Conectándonos al Futuro* (El Salvador) have recently been established. Both *Colnodo* and *InfoDes*—as *Kothmale Radio* in Sri Lanka—are aware of the need to develop a local database, designed to make the Internet useful to communities, and not so alienated from local reality. Developing local Web sites, in local languages if possible, could catalyse and renew the interest in the Internet and encourage participation.

In India, the M.S. Swaminathan Research Foundation (MSSRF) is carrying out an experimental project in villages in Pondicherry, about 160 kilometres south of Chennai (formerly Madras). Half the people live below the poverty line earning less than $1 per day. The project, known as "Knowledge Centre for Sustainable Food Security," is designed to provide information to local rural people according to their needs and demands, using both analogue wireless technologies and dial-up Internet connections. Information is tailored to local needs, especially relating to women and children. Also available to rural families is a directory of government projects, health issues, prices of agricultural produce, information on public events, local transportation schedules, crop insurance projects, and a directory of hospitals and medical practitioners.

The other important condition for success is the linkage of the Internet component to a concrete project of social development. Bangladesh is always surprising everyone with the most creative initiatives. Donors are also pleased to see that most of these are "in scale" given the size of the country and the population density. Though huge programmes such as Bangladesh Rural Advancement Committee (BRAC) or Grameen Bank may not be replicable in other countries, they provide a wealth of information that can certainly be of use.

Though not directly related to the Internet, since 1998 Grameen Bank established a *Village Phone System* that uses cellular phones to provide access even in the most remote villages. The whole project, which has a commercial component and a social change-oriented objective, is linked to the existing Grameen Bank loan system, which facilitates many aspects. Cellular phones are sold at very low prices to selected Village Phone operators, mostly women. They are in charge of managing the phones as a community service. Accessible prices have been fixed to avoid speculation, and these allow the operators to pay their monthly installments to the bank, to the phone company (Grameen Telecom) and to earn an additional income for their families.

There are various model examples of providing access to the Internet in rural areas of Africa, one of them being particularly interesting, the *Nakaseke* Multipurpose Community *Telecentre* (1998) in Uganda. Four similar units have been established by a joint UNESCO/ International Development Research Centre (IDRC)/International Telecommunications Union (ITU) project in Mozambique, Tanzania, Mali and Benin. These offer access to computers and the Internet, a fax and a photocopier, a basic library, video shows, newspapers, audio recording, and community listening. The core user groups of Nakaseke MCT are women, youth, teachers, students and local leaders.

A passive use of the Internet may only result in a more homogenised and globalised world, a huge marketplace with many consumers and few products. The potential of the Internet can only be fully explored through a process of occupying spaces and opening windows for local users.

The comparative advantages of the Internet look good on paper; however, the challenges in making the Internet a useful tool in places where safe water is unavailable, let alone electricity, are large. Wireless technologies and the convergence with community radio and video, are already signalling the way. But technology alone may not be the answer if culture and identity are not at the heart of the discussion. When new technologies are introduced to a different social setting, what is transferred is not only technology itself, but also the social use of it, a set of assumptions and practices that emerged from another context and other needs.

"If community media is the answer, what is the question?"[7] The question sends us back to our initial observations on development and participation. The answer is part of the dialogue that has to be established among stakeholders in a developmental process that aims for social change. The sole lack of dialogue already justifies the vision of community media where people will have the means to express what they think about their problems, their present and their future.

The history of international cooperation for development is plagued with embarrassing anecdotes that show the extremes reached because of lack of communication: development agents incapable of expressing their technical views and supposed beneficiaries unable to communicate their own perspective. One single example seems to capture the essence of this huge misunderstanding. Very often in health campaigns that aim to minimise water-borne diseases, women are advised to "boil the water" before drinking it. This advice, which may seem straight-forward, simple to understand, and logical from any point of view, actually symbolises the lack of sensitivity that often characterises development projects.

Radio and television spots with the message "boil the water" continue to be produced and aired in many developing countries regardless of its impact. A female radio producer in Mexico puts it this way: "I tell the ladies over the microphone to boil the water, but I know they're not going to do it, because they have no fuel, they have no wood."[8] Regardless of the distressing effects of unsafe water, when 80 percent of the rural women in the world depend on wood for cooking and often walk five or more kilometres every day to fetch dry sticks, boiling the water is certainly not a priority for them.

"If community media is the answer, what is the question?" The response may be: "the answer is the question." If the questions were more often discussed with the communities, if a permanent and nonexclusive dialogue was established among all stakeholders on local development issues, the question may not have even been formulated.

The questions and the answers on the communication initiatives have to be worked out with the community. What kind of communication does the community need, if any? Which is the communication system traditionally used in the community? What kind of communication tools can the community afford, not only in terms of funding but also in terms of skills and social appropriation of the new media? Participatory research would help to develop these questions and help the community to find the answers.

The dialogic process may also help to demystify the perception of the community as a homogenous human universe. The idealised vision of a community entirely united by its fate or history or culture is one of the first masking myths to go. Every society or community has social strata and divergent interests. Though to different degrees, every community—urban or rural—has the rich and the poor; the politician and the artist; the religious leader and the fool of the town. The cultural universe is complex and evolving permanently. Ready made recipes don't work, and technical assistance is only valid through permanent dialogue and communication. Experts in development come and go, and the ideal "expert," "has to go through these stages: indispensable, necessary, useful and—once the initial goals are achieved—superfluous," according to Manuel Calvelo.[9]

THE PROFILE OF
PARTICIPATORY COMMUNICATION

There is no ideal established model for participatory communication, and each of the case stories reviewed in this report confirms the uniqueness of every experience, both with its positive and negative aspects. All had to overcome obstacles, and some couldn't reach the point where external inputs were no longer necessary. We are learning from the virtues and mistakes of these experiences by placing them side-by-side like the pieces of a puzzle, not because at the end of this process there is the complete model for all circumstances, but because from the multiple experiences *we may draw some pieces for a new puzzle*.

If no ideal model is possible, or necessary, still there are some common characteristics of participatory communication that we would like to see more often in those projects and initiatives that claim they have participatory components.

Communication and participation are actually two words sharing the same concept. Etymologically the Latin *communio* relates to participation and sharing. Modern languages have given different meanings to the word *communication*, it is very often considered synonymous with the word information. There is confusion, mostly by English speakers, between communication—the act or process of communicating, and *communications* with an "s"—the means of sending messages, orders, etc.

When trying to design the profile of participatory communication, it is important to be conscious about the political implications of participation in development, and moreover of participatory communication:

- **An issue of power.** The democratisation of communication cuts through the issue of power. Participatory approaches contribute to put decision-making in the hands of the people. It also consolidates the capability of communities to confront their own ideas about development with development planners and technical staff. Within the community itself, it favours the strengthening of an internal democratic process.
- **An issue of identity.** Especially in communities that have been marginalised, repressed or simply neglected during decades, participatory communication contributes to install cultural pride and self-esteem. It reinforces the social tissue through the strengthening of local and indigenous forms of organisation. It protects tradition and cultural values, while facilitating the integration of new elements.

The main elements that characterise participatory communication are related to its capacity to involve the human subjects of social change in the process of communicating. The theoretical framework for participatory communication owes much to Paulo Freire. His books[10] have not only revolutionised the world of education, but also communication for social change.

Other models of communication for development, that have been implemented particularly around health issues, often fail to organise their strategy and their values from the perspective of the communities that are the end beneficiaries.

These are some of the issues that distinguish participatory communication from other development communication strategies in search of social changes:

- **Horizontal vs. Vertical.** People as dynamic actors, actively participating in the process of social change and in control of the communication tools and contents; rather than people perceived as passive receivers of information and behavioural instructions, while others make decisions on their lives.
- **Process vs. Campaign.** People taking in hand their own future through a process of dialogue and democratic participation in planning communication activities; rather than expensive unsustainable top-down campaigns that help to mobilise but not to build a capacity to respond from the community level to the needs of change.

- **Long-term vs. Short-term.** Communication and development in general is conceived as a long-term process which needs time to be appropriated by the people; rather than short-term planning, which is seldom sensitive to the cultural environment and mostly concerned with showing "results" for evaluations external to the community.
- **Collective vs. Individual.** Urban or rural communities acting collectively in the interest of the majority, preventing the risk of losing power to a few; rather than people targeted individually, detached from their community and from the communal forms of decision-making.
- **With vs. For.** Researching, designing and disseminating messages with participation; rather than designing, pre-testing, launching and evaluating messages that were conceived for the community, and remain external to it.
- **Specific vs. Massive.** The communication process adapted to each community or social group in terms of content, language, culture and media; rather than the tendency to use the same techniques, the same media and the same messages in diverse cultural settings and for different social sectors of society.
- **People's needs vs. Donors' musts.** Community-based dialogue and communication tools to help identify, define and discriminate between the felt needs and the real needs; rather than donor-driven communication initiatives based on donor needs (family planning, for example).
- **Ownership vs. Access.** A communication process that is owned by the people to provide equal opportunities to the community; rather than access that is conditioned by social, political or religious factors.
- **Consciousness vs. Persuasion.** A process of raising consciousness and deep understanding about social reality, problems and solutions; rather than persuasion for short-term behavioural changes that are only sustainable with continuous campaigns.

None of the experiences selected for this report can claim to have a profile that comprehends all the above strengths of participatory communication, but they all contribute to some degree to shape a collective profile, which gives much hope for the future of communication, participation and social change.

FOOTNOTES

[1] Shirley A. White: "The concept of participation: transforming rhetoric to reality," in *Participatory Communication: working for change and development*. SAGE Publications, 1994.

[2] Translated from: *La Formación de los Comunicadores para el Desarrollo* by Manuel Calvelo.

[3] Unfortunately in recent years new radio stations operated by obscure religious denominations, mostly evangelic, have contributed to the exact opposite, dividing communities, thus affecting their social and cultural tissue.

[4] Johan Deflander from PANOS Mali, at <http://www.rnw.nl/realradio/community/html/panos281198.html>.

[5] According to Ethnologue (February 1999): 885 million speakers of Mandarin, followed by 332 Spanish, 322 English, 189 Bengali, 182 Hindi, 170 Portuguese, 170 Russian, 125 Japanese, 98 German and 77 million of Wu.

[6] "Communication Approaches to Participation and Development: Challenging the Assumptions and Perspectives" by Keval J. Kumar, in *Participatory Communication: working for change and development*. SAGE Publications, 1994.

[7] Alfred E. Opubor of New Africa International Network (Zimbabwe), at a UNESCO seminar on Promoting Community Media in Africa, Kampala, June 1999.

[8] Lucila Vargas, *Social Uses and Radio Practices: the use of participatory radio by ethnic minorities in Mexico*. Westview Press, 1995, Boulder, Colorado (USA).

[9] Manuel Calvelo has been one of the most creative communicators in Latin America, his philosophy about participatory communication is behind important experiences such as *CESPAC* (Peru) and *PRODERITH* (Mexico).

[10] From *Education: The Practice of Freedom* (1967) and *Pedagogy of the Oppressed* (1970) to *Education for Critical Consciousness* (1973).

RADIO SUTATENZA

(1947) Colombia

....

TITLE:	Radio Sutatenza—Escuelas Radiofónicas
COUNTRY:	Colombia
FOCUS:	Literacy, informal education
PLACE:	Bogota, Medellin
BENEFICIARIES:	About 8 million illiterate adults
PARTNERS:	UNESCO
FUNDING:	General Electric Corporation, Misereor, USAID, World Bank, Inter-American Development Bank
MEDIA:	Radio, print

SNAPSHOT

From the square of Sutatenza you look over an immense landscape of green slopes, broken here and there by other white villages, each with its church steeple. The landscape rolls on and on over ridge after ridge, each higher than the last, until the skyline is blocked by a towering mountain range, majestic and brooding. ...

Even today, the road to Sutatenza is unpaved and full of potholes, so in August 1947, it must have been horrendous, as a rattling, gaily painted bus ground upwards towards the village. Salcedo was among its passengers. Seated with the peasants dressed in their ponchos, and with their baskets of farm produce, chickens and the like, he seemed to come from another world. ... He was very tall, with a pale complexion inherited from his Anglo-Saxon ancestors. Penetrating dark eyes were set among his bony features, and he always wore the intense expression of a man with a mission, which he was going to fulfill at all costs.

Salcedo arrived in Sutatenza with his 16-millimetre film projector; and about a month later, a primitive amateur radio transmitter built by his brother also arrived. Sutatenza was a community of about 8,000 people, many of whom lived on isolated farms scattered up and down the slopes of the valley, often a long and arduous walk from the village. Salcedo had been sent to Sutatenza as assistant to the village priest, who was a very traditional cleric. His prime activities were to make sure his church's coffers were kept replenished and to scold his congregation during interminable Sunday sermons, which he sprinkled with Latin and Greek phrases to show his erudition before his ignorant flock.

Salcedo soon fell out with his superior. One Sunday not long after his arrival, the senior priest invited Salcedo to preach a sermon. Salcedo accepted, but once in the pulpit, he told the congregation that he did not intend to give them a sermon; instead he wanted to open dialogue with them about improving life in the community. ... the more daring among the congregation began to speak up about the problems. ... Salcedo proposed that they all get together to build a theatre; he would provide a film projector and the films. ... The response was literally overwhelming. ...

—Excerpt from "The One That Died" by Colin Fraser and Sonia Restrepo.

DESCRIPTION

An amateur radio operator, José Joaquin Salcedo Guarin realised radio was the most effective way to bring educational instruction to the far-flung rural adults of Colombia. His dream was realised when *Radio Sutatenza* began educational broadcasts using a 90-watt transmitter. He conducted transmission tests for about a month until October when he got a temporary broadcasting license and the prefix "HK7HM" from the Ministry of Communications of Colombia.

On October 16, 1947, the first cultural programme was broadcast: music performed by farmers of Sutatenza. Thus *Radio Sutatenza* was born. Immediately it got a lot of attention from all sectors of society. The President of Colombia himself formally inaugurated the station in early 1948, and Pope Paul VI visited it in August 1968 and blessed its new premises in Bogotá.

"The invisible professor," Father José Salcedo initially broadcast to his parish with his homemade transmitter. The government provided a legal license to operate in 1949, and very soon *Radio Sutatenza* was broadcasting educational and cultural programmes over a radius of 1,000 kilometres.

At first there were but a few battery-operated receivers but the audience quickly grew, and so did *Radio Sutatenza*. In 1948 the General Electric Corporation donated a 250-watt transmitter and 100 radio receivers. The U.S. company continued supporting the experience for many years. A new 1,000-watt transmitter and 150 more radio receivers were donated along with antennas and other accessories.

Radio Sutatenza eventually moved to Bogotá, added more transmitters to meet regional needs and became the most powerful radio station in Colombia, covering other major cities such as Cali, Barranquilla, Magangue and Medellin. Salcedo headed one of the world's largest programmes of adult education by radio. At its peak, the organisation had one thousand paid staff. Funds came from Germany and from Catholic Church groups in Europe. Eventually financial institutions such as the World Bank and the Inter-American Development Bank became involved.

The station had become part of Acción Cultural Popular (ACPO), which was created to expand the activities of distant education to provide the eight million rural adults of Colombia with the means to assume the responsibility for their own development. *Radio Sutatenza* aimed at reaching the people with a programme of instruction based upon the five basic notions: health, alphabet, numbers, work and spirituality. Programme topics included hygiene and basic health care, reading and writing, simple arithmetic, increasing productivity, and the recognition of personal dignity.

The station activities were supported and reinforced with a printed journal called *El Campesino*, as well as rural libraries, schools and training programmes for farmers. Other publications included *Cartilla Basica* (Basic Knowledge of Alphabet and Numbers); *Nuestro Bienestar* (Our Health); *Hablemos Bien* (Let's Speak Correctly); *Cuentas Claras* (Clear Mathematics); and *Suelo Productivo* (Productive Land).

Radio Sutatenza operated two different programming formats simultaneously. The "A" programme, a general purpose format mixing entertainment and sports coverage with educational instruction; and the "B" programme concentrating on instruction with frequent repeat broadcasts of lessons for the convenience of the students.

Around 1990, *Radio Sutatenza* ran into financial and administrative problems. The station was closed down and most of the facilities were sold to the commercial Caracol Network of Colombia.

BACKGROUND & CONTEXT

The Tenza Valley is a fertile, subtropical area in the department of Boyaca.

> In fact "valley" is not really the right name. ... the Tenza Valley is topographical chaos. It is a tortured jumble of hills and ridges, serpentine valleys and side valleys, only unified by being a single watershed that flows eastwards. High on the slope above one of the valleys of that watershed sector perches the white chip of village called Sutatenza.—EXCERPT FROM FRASER AND RESTREPO.

About 80 percent of the peasants in Sutatenza were illiterate in 1947. Alcoholism-related violence and even death was frequent. The community was in total isolation from the outside world: no radio, no cinema and no distractions at all, except for getting drunk every Sunday.

It was on August 23, 1947, that the young priest, Salcedo, arrived at the parish of San Bartolomé, in Sutatenza. He found a community deeply affected by boredom, and thus alcoholism. He immediately proposed that the people build a theatre and offered his 16-millimetre projector and films. At the time the vast majority of peasants were illiterate, so he also offered them literacy and educational activities. He soon organised a chess club, musical events and sports competitions— football and basketball.

He started showing his films in the open air at the town's square, while the plans for the new cultural centre were prepared. In only a few weeks a theatre was built with the contributions and active participation from the community; 1,400 live chickens were donated and then sold in Bogotá to buy construction materials. Salcedo next began to air radio programmes through a homemade 90-watt transmitter. *Radio Sutatenza* was born.

ASPECTS OF SOCIAL CHANGE

When Salcedo put up his amateur transmitter and broadcast his first programme on the newly created *Radio Sutatenza*, no one could have imagined that many people in Chile, Brazil, Peru and other countries throughout the world would have followed his example in the next twenty years.

Although in reality *Radio Sutatenza* didn't last many years as a community-based and grassroots communication experience, the fact that it was the first of its kind has enormous merit. Its multimedia approach has been so successful, that it has widely inspired other developing nations in Asia, Africa and Latin America.

The station has been a pioneer in the use of radio for educational purposes, especially in the education of the rural adult, the *campesino*. From its modest beginnings *Radio Sutatenza* grew into a major force in the battle against illiteracy in Colombia.

Salcedo succeeded in demonstrating that education for critical literacy is a means to empower peasants and other ordinary people to be full and equal participants in development and the maintenance of just, equitable and democratic societies.

By the end of its life, *Radio Sutatenza* had broadcast more than 1.5 million hours of radio programmes. Along with this effort, by that time ACPO had printed 76 million copies of *El Campesino*, distributed more than 10 million books, and had trained 25,000 peasant leaders and development workers.

Radio Sutatenza pioneered the ideals of what was then called "integral fundamental education," a concept that emphasises the need to help people to understand their own responsibility for improvement, to recognise their own potential for progress, and to know the value of their own resources. (Fraser and Restrepo)

Over the years ACPO established objectives which included, other than literacy and arithmetic, improvements of family health, farming techniques, hygiene and environment, economic skills, development of critical capacity on social issues, community participation, human rights, ethical and religious principles, etc. To achieve the goals, an integrated multimedia and interpersonal approach was organised, comprised of textbooks, journals, records and participatory training.

CONSTRAINTS

Although *Radio Sutatenza* was the first ever community radio station and opened the path to thousands of participatory communication experiences, it was in fact a victim of its own success. The community participation components that once characterised *Radio Sutatenza* were sacrificed for the benefit of a larger influence in formal and informal countrywide education. The participatory approach couldn't be maintained as the project evolved towards an increasingly centralised model with headquarters in Bogotá, the capital of Colombia. The project gained in terms of educational outreach, but in terms of popular participation it lost its initial innovative ingredient.

The political context in the country also affected *Radio Sutatenza* over the years. In order to protect the organisation from government pressures and from a take-over attempt by an NGO (run by the daughter of President Rojas Pinilla), ACPO changed its status to that of an ecclesiastical body, which eventually exposed it to pressures from the Catholic Church, and this was to have far-reaching consequences (Fraser and Restrepo).

Not everyone was supportive of *Radio Sutatenza*'s concept of education. In 1960, Camilo Torres—the priest and sociologist who later became famous when he joined the guerrillas—conducted an evaluation of the Escuelas Radiofónicas (ACPO-*Radio Sutatenza*) and established that the programme was demagogic and harmful for the peasants. The controversy between Salcedo and Torres grew bitter. Torres accused Salcedo of being a "blind and ridiculous" anticommunist, arguing that the campaigns of *Radio Sutatenza* against communism incited hate and violence.

REFERENCES

"The One that Died—*Radio Sutatenza* and ACPO" by Colin Fraser and Sonia Restrepo-Estrada, in *Communicating for Development: Human Change for Survival*, I.NB. Tauris & Co. Ltd. 1998, New York (USA).

Sutatenza Bogota, by Takayuki Inoue Nozaki, Radio Nuevo Mundo.

"*Radio Sutatenza*," by Jim Whitehead. In *Speedx*, October 1973.

Jose Joaquin Salcedo: The Multimedia Quixote by Mauricio Salas. 1997. Film. 29 min. The film explores Salcedo's personality and ideology and features interviews, commentary, and rare archival footage of Salcedo and ACPO.

MINERS' RADIO STATIONS

BASIC FACTS

TITLE:	Radios Mineras
COUNTRY:	Bolivia
FOCUS:	Community organisation, solidarity
PLACE:	Mining districts of Potosí and Oruro
BENEFICIARIES:	Miners, Bolivian society-at-large
PARTNERS:	Network of 26 community-based stations
FUNDING:	Federación Sindical de Trabajadores Mineros de Bolivia
MEDIA:	Radio

SNAPSHOT

Back to July 1980 ... General Luis García Meza's military coup succeeded two weeks earlier; people were killed or imprisoned, many others flew to exile. The army gained absolute control over the cities. Their first target was the media: all radio stations, television channels and newspapers were shut down. Some of them reopened only under military censorship. Wait a minute: not *all* radio stations. The network of nearly twenty stations located at the mining sites in Potosí and Oruro, in the highlands of Bolivia, continued their transmission under enormous pressure. People in Bolivia turned their dials to *La Voz del Minero*, *Radio Animas* or *Radio Pío XII* to learn about what was really happening in the country since the coup. Even foreign correspondents in neighbouring countries would search for these radio stations to write their reports. But the army knew it, and day by day soldiers kept approaching the mining settlements, breaking the resistance of miners that tried to defend the stations with their own lives.

One of the latest radio stations to fall under military control was *Radio Animas*. Until the very last moment they transmitted in chain with *Radio Pío XII* and *Radio Nacional de Huanuni*. The following is an excerpt of their last dramatic live transmission: *The army is now about five kilometres from Siete Suyos and very near from Santa Ana, so we are preparing to defend ourselves ... We know about 31 people detained, who have been sent to Tupiza ... This is Radio Animas for all the south of the country ... We are living crucial moments, we are all mobilised, even our women have contributed preparing the defense ... Compañeros, we will hold until the last consequences, because that is our mission. ...*

That was near the end. Minutes after, gunshots could be heard through *Radio Animas.* The last thing the announcer could send over the airwaves was a message to the other stations to take the relay and continue the transmissions of the "cadena minera" (miners' chain, the network of stations linked in times of crisis). Several did continue, indeed, until the army shut down the last one, destroying the equipment, and killing those that defended their right to communicate.

DESCRIPTION

La Voz del Minero, Radio Pío XII, Radio Vanguardia de Colquiri, Radio Animas, Radio 21 de Diciembre, Radio Nacional de Huanuni ... these were some of the most important radio stations created, funded and managed by Bolivian mining workers.

It all started in 1949, with one radio station in the mining district of Catavi. During the next 15 years, other districts followed: they bought the equipment, they trained young people from their villages, and the workers themselves funded the experience by giving a percentage of their salary to sustain their radio stations.

Most of the radio stations started small and precariously, only equipped by very simple means. A few of them managed to get foreign support and evolved into more sophisticated radio stations, with better equipment and installations. A few, even built a theatre next to the premises, so union meetings would take place and be transmitted live through the radio. *Radio Vanguardia,* for example, had a beautiful theatre decorated with large murals narrating the story of the Colquiri mining centre. One particular scene on the mural depicts the attack by Bolivian Air Force planes in 1967, when the country was under military rule.

In the early 1970s, 26 radio stations were in operation, all of them in the mining districts of the highlands of Bolivia. At that time the miners' unions in Bolivia were still very powerful and considered among the most important and politically advanced in Latin America.

In times of peace and democracy—not very often—miners' radio stations were integrated into the daily life of the community. They became the closest and most effective replacement for telephone and postal services.

People would get their mail through the stations and post messages of all kinds, which were read several times during the day: calls for a meeting of women from the Comité de Amas de Casa (Housewives

Committee); messages from the union leaders about their negotiations with the government in the capital; messages of love among youngsters; announcing a new play by *Nuevos Horizontes* drama group (often staged on the platform of a big truck, with workers illuminating the scene with their own lamps); announcements of sport activities, burials, births and festivities.

In times of political upheaval the union radio stations would become the only trustworthy source of information. As the military captured newspapers, radio and TV stations in the capital and other cities, the only information available would come from the miner's radio stations. All of them would join the "cadena minera" until the army would penetrate the mining camps and assault the stations, which were usually defended to the death by the workers. A film by Bolivian filmmaker Jorge Sanjinés, *The Courage of the People,* re-enacts the attack on the mining district of Siglo XX by the army in June 1967.

In times of political and social crisis the miners' radio stations would link to air reports on the political situation; they would also link for live transmissions when an important sporting or cultural event took place in the mining district. Other than that, each station had full independence from the next.

Certainly, miners' radio stations were important because miners were already important. But also, Bolivian miners were more influential than ever because during several decades they had powerful means to communicate their ideas. As the importance of mining in Bolivia declined in the 1980s, the unions were weakened and some of the radio stations disappeared along with the mining districts.

BACKGROUND & CONTEXT

Even before Bolivia was a Republic, mining had a huge importance. When the Spaniard conquerors discovered silver in Potosí, they never thought there was so much of it under the cone of the "silver mountain." Bolivia's exports were traditionally based on mining, first silver and later tin, until its economy changed during the last three decades of the 20th century.

During three centuries they took the silver to Spain, until the mountain lost its original shape and gradually collapsed. It is said that six million Aymara and Quechua Indians, and a high number of African slaves, died in the mines during that period. Potosí was by that time one of the dream cities of the world. In 1625 the city had a larger population than London or Paris, and more churches than any other city in America. Though isolated in the highlands at 4,200 metres of altitude, it was easy to find in Potosí the most luxurious items imported from Europe.

Since the independence of Bolivia in 1825 until the mid-70s, mining continued to be the principal income generating activity of Bolivia. Silver became less important, but the country became the 2nd largest producer of tin. In the mid-50s minerals amounted to more than 70 percent of total exports.

The few thousands of miners working in the twenty main mining centres were largely responsible for sustaining the economy of the country and its 5 million people. No government could afford to ignore their political opinions, moreover since the miners' unions were among the most democratic and more politically advanced in Latin America.

ASPECTS OF SOCIAL CHANGE

Radio stations played an important role to strengthen the social power of the miners' unions and to achieve unity. All unions were affiliated with the Federación Sindical de Trabajadores Mineros de Bolivia (FSTMB), which during four decades (1946 to 1986) had been the vanguard organisation of the powerful Central Obrera Boliviana (COB). It is not by mere coincidence those miners' unions and radio stations would be sharing premises in most mining districts, and that the Secretary of Culture of the union would generally be the director of the radio station.

The impact of miners' radio stations on social change is also important in terms of building cultural identity among miners' and nearby peasant communities. On a daily basis, the radio stations were permanently open to participation. Visits to the stations were very frequent, whenever people needed to express themselves on any issue affecting their lives.

The main innovations of the miners' radio stations concern community participation. As simple as it looks when we describe it, it was as revolutionary in the 1950s, as it is today: clearly, very few participatory communication experiences have reached the point of total ownership of media in terms of technology, management, contents and service to the community.

One of the most interesting aspects of social change is capacity building. The miners' radio stations have trained several generations of journalists. Training was done locally most of the time, in partnership with other organisations. Many local journalists and announcers that were trained to work at the miners' stations later became renowned broadcasters when they migrated to the cities.

Miners' radio stations formed the principles of participatory communication even before the term existed. At all stages of their development they were independent, self-sustained, self-managed and faithfully served the interests of their communities and the interests of the Bolivian society-at-large. In terms of ownership they symbolise the most advanced example of participatory media. They were planned and conceived by the miners, the equipment and infrastructure funded by the workers themselves, they were managed and technically run by the miners who learned how to do it, and the programming was created and produced locally.

There are not many examples in the world where media for democracy has played such an important role simultaneously at a local and national level. There are fewer examples of communication experiences totally under control of the community. If that were not the case, it wouldn't have been possible for the miners' radio stations to have such a political and social influence in Bolivia.

CONSTRAINTS

Although radio stations were driven by the ideology of the union, this was not an obstacle for democratic participation, because the union responded to the will of the workers. Traditionally, unions elected leaders from the various political parties and encouraged ideological alliances, which reflected in the radio stations programmes.

The real challenge for the radio stations was political repression, the same as affected the miners' community as a whole. Some of the stations were destroyed by the army six or seven times in their life-time. A few chose to preserve the scars of resistance on the outside walls of their buildings: the holes of gunshots. New equipment was bought once and again because miners, as poor as they are, would give one day's salary for their station.

On a more technical note, radio stations suffered from scarcity of materials. Equipment was very basic though adequate for the job, but because of the scarcity of funds to pay the salaries of producers, not much was done — content wise — in terms of high quality production of educational programmes. Technicians were generally hired locally and were capable of repairing the equipment with few instruments and lots of creativity.

What really drove miners' radio stations off the spectrum in the 1980s was the abrupt change of the economy. Mining was no longer important in terms of exports, and the cost of producing tin was higher than the international price. As the government shut the state-owned mines, miners migrated to the cities leaving behind phantom villages. Miners' unions got weaker and less influential. Only a few radio stations survived towards the new the century.

REFERENCES

Las Radios Mineras de Bolivia, by Alfonso Gumucio Dagron and Lupe Cajías CIMCA, La Paz, 1989.

The Voice of the Mines (film) directed by Alfonso Gumucio Dagron and Eduardo Barrios. UNESCO, 1984.

Short essays: *Las Voces del Coraje: Radios Mineras de Bolivia,* by F. Lozada and G. Kúncar (1984). In English: *The Bolivian Miners' Radio Stations* by Alan O'Connor (Ohio State University).

RADIO HUAYACOCOTLA

1965 Mexico

....

BASIC FACTS

TITLE: Radio Huayacocotla

COUNTRY: Mexico

FOCUS: Community organisation, education

PLACE: Huayacocotla, Chicontepec
(State of Veracruz)

BENEFICIARIES: Peasants, rural population

PARTNERS: Asociación Lationamericana de Escuelas
Radiofónicas (ALER), World Association of
Community Media Broadcasters (AMARC),
INI, UNESCO, Radio Educación

FUNDING: Catholic Church

MEDIA: Radio

SNAPSHOT

The cocks are singing, it's 6 a.m. The sun is already up but it is still cold outside. Juan and Ana live in a small wooden house near Huayacocotla; they have six children. Ana was up at 5 a.m., silently, she put on the fire avoiding waking the others. She boiled water for coffee, cleaned the nixtamal and grinded maize. She prepared the salsa, strong and spicy, and the tortillas for Juan to take to work.

Just as she awoke she turned on the old and dusty radio hanging in a kitchen corner. At first sight it may look impossible for such a radio to provide any sound, but it works. At 6 o'clock she turns the needle in search of Radio Huaya. Mexican music and a soft voice announcing the hour: Radio Huayacocotla, The voice of peasants is on-the-air. *The sound of huapangos — music from Veracruz, invades Ana's soul. She is almost compelled to follow the rhythm with her feet.*

At 6:30 a.m., when the news starts, Ana wakes up Juan who washes, dresses and sits to take his coffee while listening to the local news: the group of potato producers didn't get the financial support that was offered by the Rural Credit Bank, the meeting of delegates from the Unidad de Producción reached the following agreements. . . . The national and international news follow. Juan leaves for work.

Ana keeps the radio on while preparing breakfast so her children won't go to school with an empty stomach. By 7 a.m., the announcer dedicates Las Mañanitas (birthday song) and reads the list of saint's days: "Today we celebrate Saint … and we congratulate those that bear that name." He reads letters of congratulations sent by relatives from nearby communities.

At 7:15 a.m. starts "On the Mountain Paths." The programme is devoted to local festivities; Ana participated, so she is very attentive. She wants to hear what she said, how her voice sounds on the radio. She chuckles happily. By 8 a.m., the children's programme starts: songs, tales and the voice of the announcer saluting and counselling children. At 9 a.m. Radio Huayacocotla *ends its morning transmission and Ana walks down to the river carrying a bucket of soiled clothes and a bag of soap for the washing.*

—Excerpts from "Radio Huaya, Cada Día" by Aurora Velasco.

DESCRIPTION

Radio Huayacocotla started airing in October 1965 with a 500-watt transmitter, on the 2390 kHz frequency. It was the first radio-school of México, and aimed to provide basic education to zones of difficult access. From the beginning *Radio Huayacocotla* transmitted in short-wave, which ensured its coverage of the rural population of Veracruz and other Mexican states such as Querétaro, Hidalgo and Puebla, where other radio-schools were eventually set up.

The story of *Radio Huayacocotla* is made of several phases. The first includes its swift expansion which culminates in 1969 with 126 established radio-schools in the network. During this period a consistent methodology was developed, including training, materials production, and coordinating activities.

A second phase was prompted by an internal institutional crisis, which practically resulted in the crumbling of the project by 1973, the number of radio-schools being reduced to six. The Servicio de Escuelas (SER) of México intervened and placed the project under the responsibility of Fomento Cultural Educativo, a non-governmental association founded in 1970. The new orientation promoted community participation and education as a process for holistic development.

This transition phase included an ambitious research plan; the results were instrumental for designing the new programme and activities. In 1975 it was decided that the station would concentrate its coverage on two nearby municipalities, Huayacocotla and Zacualpa. The geographic proximity enabled a better knowledge of local social phenomena and increased interaction with the rural population.

A third phase started in 1977, with restructured, diversified and participative programmes, further integrated into the community daily life:

Music programmes: Various entertainment segments alternating songs and brief messages. Preference was given to Mexican music (*ranchera*, *huasteca* and *norteña*), though additional slots were established to promote Latin American songs and local music, often with live participation.

Training programmes: Aiming to recover traditional knowledge from the rural folks, for the benefit of the local community. The segment included information on farming techniques and forestry, legislation on the Agrarian Reform, education and culture, and the recuperation of oral history and local traditions.

News programmes: Included the already famous *Noticiero del campo* ("News from the Field") and a segment analysing recent events.

Children's programmes: The early morning *Open Doors and Windows* included songs, tales and advice on health, hygiene and ethics. *Entering the World of Children* was a live segment aired in collaboration with teachers assigned to the local schools.

Other than the above the station aired soap operas with social and educational contents—produced by *Radio Educación*—as well as mini-series, promotional spots, *comunicados* of interest for the community, programmes produced by social-service students and by community groups.

The fourth phase in *Radio Huayacocotla*'s development started in the 1990s, when the station was increasingly involved in defending the peasantry against the abuses of local landlords and political bosses. This increasingly committed stand brought to the station threats of censorship and suspension.

BACKGROUND & CONTEXT

Huayacocotla is a small town of Chicontepec, a region in the State of Veracruz, which includes several municipalities of predominantly indigenous population (Nahuatl and Otomi). The word "huaya-cocotl" means "place of high *ocotes*" in Nahuatl. *Ocote* is a variety of resinous pines preferred to make fire. The surrounding landscape, made of high woods, rivers and hills is rich in kaolin and precious woods that have been irrationally exploited during the past decades. The timber companies that invaded the region in the 1970s left nothing in place for the community, except poverty and shaved hills.

During decades, this region that appears in the maps like an island between the States of Hidalgo and Puebla, has lived in seclusion and isolation. A swift process of migration towards the Mexican capital took place in the 1960s and 1970s, because the farming would only occupy the rural population for five months every year. Telephone and electricity was atypical and no local television or radio stations existed at all. The only option for the local population was listening to the stations from neighbouring states.

This situation of isolation and poor available services motivated the creation of *Radio Huayacocotla* in 1965, as a radio-school. This happened to be an initiative developed by Hector Samperio, the priest of Huayacocotla parish, who in turn received support from the Universidad Iberoamericana in helping to clear legal matters with government institutions. Based on the model of *Radio Sutatenza*, which had proved enormously successful in Colombia, *Radio Huayacocotla* promoted the idea that underdevelopment, poverty and injustice were mainly a result of lack of education.

ASPECTS OF SOCIAL CHANGE

Radio Huayacocotla has grown to be very popular among rural folks. The station is extremely influential in the process of informing, forming opinions and training. Its programmes make the effort of recovering the culture, the music and the philosophy of peasantry in the region. The messages in Otomi, Nahua or Tepehua on lost livestock, of solidarity with a poor family that has no means to take a suffering patient out of the community, and the complaints against the abuses of local bosses, are part of its daily programming.

Radio Huayacocotla has helped to re-evaluate the local culture by spreading the news about achievements and struggles, making the microphones available to the voice of the native communities. Although the participation of rural people took much time and effort to be achieved, by the mid-80s. groups of peasants were already familiarised with the use of microphones, recorders and even studio hardware.

The presence of *Radio Huayacocotla* in the regional communication landscape resulted in the weakening of the hegemonic position of commercial and government media. Moreover, it provided to large sectors of the peasantry and the indigenous population the possibility to access a communication environment linked to their interests, problems and needs.

From its original objective of supporting literacy programmes, the station evolved to supporting communities in their struggle against the stripping of their natural resources, towards a model of sustainable and self-managed development. The systematic denunciation of repression and violence contributed to generating a collective consciousness on human rights, according to Carlos Cortez Ruiz's paper "La Información y la Comunicación en la Democratización de la Sociedad Rural: Posibilidades y Limitaciones" which was presented at the Latin American Studies Association (LASA) XIX International Congress, September 28–30, 1995 in Washington, D.C., U.S.

As a station devoted to support the concept and practice of radio-schools, *Radio Huayacocotla* had developed not only specially designed methods to meet its educational objectives, but also counted on trained staff, materials and infrastructure adapted to the need of each of the member radio-schools for follow-up. Every six months coordinating meetings are held with instructors, who regularly receive supplies, textbooks and brochures on literacy, grammar, arithmetic, health, improving housing conditions, etc.

Its content and format define the nature of the station. The format enables the most deprived people to express their points of view, in particular rural workers and the indigenous population. Through the content of its programming *Radio Huayacocotla* strives to analyse local issues and regional processes, positioning them in the larger context of their relationship with the national social reality. Thus, the content is characterised by a continuous and open questioning of local and regional power structures, and by its support of social organisation activities seeking to accomplish the social, cultural and political objectives. (Cortez Ruiz)

CONSTRAINTS

The fact that *Radio Huayacocotla* transmits in short wave makes it difficult for some regions to get the signal. The most common radio sets available in the local markets lack short-wave capability.

The identity of the station as one in favour of peasants and indigenous people of the region has provoked reactions by the local political bosses too used to manipulating the surrounding villages. In the Huayacocotla mountain range, the power in the local municipalities has been passed down for decades from generation to generation in the same families and has always been employed to control the indigenous people.

In March 1995, inspectors from the Secretariat for Communications and Transport (SCT) of Mexico abruptly suspended the transmission of *Radio Huayacocotla*, arguing "technical deficiencies." The station was accused of transmitting "coded messages" promoting violence in support of the Zapatista struggle in Chiapas. It turned out that the "coded messages" consisted of community messages in the indigenous languages of the *campesinos*: Nahua, Otomie and Tepehua. Eventually the station was authorised to operate again within a month.

During many years *Radio Huayacocotla* has been fighting to obtain an AM frequency, which would allow the station to be heard on normal radio sets. However, the Mexican government, under pressure from local landlords, has repeatedly denied the license to the station.

REFERENCES

México: Radio Huayacocotla, *una Emisora Campesina* by Aurora Velasco. Cuadernos de Comunicación Alternativa N° 3, CIMCA 1985, La Paz (Bolivia).

La Información y la Comunicación en la Democratización de la Sociedad Rural: Posibilidades y Limitaciones by Carlos Cortez Ruiz. Universidad Autónoma Metropolitana-Xochimilco. Latin American Studies Association (LASA) XIX International Congress, September 28–30, 1995. Washington, D.C., U.S.

RADIO QUILLABAMBA

1969 Peru

....

BASIC FACTS

TITLE:	Radio Quillabamba, Centro y Medios de Comunicación Social (CEMCOS)
COUNTRY:	Peru
FOCUS:	Rural development and community organisation
PLACE:	Quillabamba, La Concepción province
BENEFICIARIES:	Indigenous and rural population
PARTNERS:	ALER, Coordinadora Nacional de Radio (CNR), Comunidades Cristianas Campesinas (CCC)
FUNDING:	Misereor, Adveniat, Santa Infancia, Misión Cuaresmal Suiza, Misiones Dominicanas de España
MEDIA:	Radio

SNAPSHOT

Beginning one's day by sharing a radio programme with farmers in the Quillabamba valley makes the world seem a much smaller place and makes a cold December morning in the Midwest of the United States a little warmer. Most overseas listeners understand little Spanish or Quechua. Yet, the pacing of the programme and casual chat of the announcer provides a warm authenticity that is lacking in mass-market commercial radio in the developed world. The highlight, though, is the music. Long-time short-wave listeners cannot only tell the difference between Peruvian huaynos and Ecuadorean pasillos, but even know if the style of the huayno is more typical of northern or southern Peru.

My experience with Radio Quillabamba *began in 1974 when I was a high school student studying Spanish. In my early morning listening, I came across their hauntingly beautiful Peruvian melodies. I had written to few radio stations, and none in Peru, but I felt a need to write this station and tell them of a far-off listener who had found them, listened to them, and been moved by their broadcasts. In the years since, Peruvain stations like* Radio Quillabamba *have continued to be my favourite early morning listening targets.*

Radio broadcasters such as Radio Quillabamba *are vital in educating, informing and providing a voice to their local audiences. Yet, in many cases their influence extends much further. If, as does* Radio Quillabamba, *the broadcaster uses short-wave, it also has an audience of hundreds, perhaps thousands, of short-wave enthusiasts (DXers) in the USA, Japan, Europe and Australia.*

Receiving small distant short-wave stations requires a good receiver and antenna. But, even more so, it requires a burning desire to connect with far away places. The best time to hear Peruvian radio in North America is in the early morning hours, around 4 a.m. in the Midwest. Only that burning desire gets dozens of distant listeners out of bed at that hour.

— WRITTEN BY DON MOORE, AN EXPERIENCED DXER.

DESCRIPTION

Radio Quillabamba is the station with the largest coverage over La Concepción province. It started as an initiative of Dominican missionaries from the Puerto Maldonado Roman Catholic Vicariate, who in 1966 bought a small station that already existed in Quillabamba, and transformed it over the years to the innovative project of communication for social change that we know today. This process, however, didn't occur immediately; first the station had to develop its technical capacity. By 1969 new equipment and a 1000-watt transmitter were bought to replace the old one, which only had 300 watts. Later, with the support of Adveniat, Misereor and other Roman Catholic organisations, a 5-kilowatt transmitter and additional hardware contributed to extending the coverage considerably over most of the Andean South of Peru.

The philosophical evolution of the station could be encapsulated as follows:

> At first the station emphasised the "religious" pro-
> grammes; later on, there was an attempt to provide
> training and "formal education" to poor farmers; then
> we saw the need of becoming the "voice of the peo-
> ple" and we put radio programmes under the responsi-
> bility of popular organisations and groups working on
> massive concientisation. Finally we concluded that the
> most important thing was to become a centre of com-
> munication and participation for popular organisations.
>
> — FROM AN ARTICLE BY ENCINAS AND LOBO.

Thus, radio programmes evolved over the years as *Radio Quillabamba* increasingly committed itself to social struggle. Between 1972 and 1975, "human and religious education" dominated programming, while content-wise it didn't relate to formal education programmes nor to popular education concepts. Between 1975 and 1978 "formal education" programmes were produced, aiming to develop the reading habits of the new literates. From 1978 on, the station committed to "popular education in support of organised people." Part of the 16 daily hours of programming was allocated free-of-charge to social organisations such as the Provincial Peasants Federation, Workers Federation, Municipal Council, and Human Rights Committee among others.

The most popular format is the radio-magazine, which includes segments of information (news and interviews), education (analysis), communication (messages), entertainment (participation) and music (dedications). The majority of programmes are transmitted live. The music dedication slot is one of the most successful, since the messages are read in Quechua, the local language.

Over the years, a network of volunteer correspondents built up naturally around the station. Letters arrive from very remote places of the province, informing the station on events that the national media is not aware of, such as the clashes between the army and the Shining Path guerrillas.

It has been the policy of *Radio Quillabamba* from its inception, to let the constituency cover the ordinary expenses of the station, while reserving external funding for investing in infrastructure. Employees' salaries, office rent and services, such as telephone or electricity, are taken care of through commercial advertising, social messages and music dedications.

Commercial advertising is strictly regulated and limited to fixed time slots and days of the week. Institutional messages of social interest are aired with no cost, but individuals sending personal messages to their families have to pay a minimum rate, which allows the station to generate additional funds for ordinary expenses.

BACKGROUND & CONTEXT

La Concepción province, in the Cuzco Department, is one of the most diverse of Peru in terms of its geography, as it extends from 6,300 metres of altitude in The Andes, towards 300 metres in the Amazonian basin. Quillabamba, the capital city, sits in a valley at 1,050 metres high and is inhabited by 20,000 members of the 130,000 population of the province, the majority of which are Quechua peasants who live in rural areas producing coffee and coca leaves.

Since the 1950s, peasants established their own cooperatives, unions and political organisations, which survived repression from local landowners and various military regimes. During the 1980s the region became a stage for the violent confrontation between the army and the Shining Path guerrillas.

Radio has traditionally been the most important medium in rural areas. It often substitutes for telephone, mail and other conventional means of communication. The story of popular and community radio in Peru is closely related to the action of progressive Catholic priests who had been, since the 1960s, involved in the struggle of the poorest and most forgotten segments of society.

The experience of the Dominican missionaries from the Vicariate of Puerto Maldonado in the operation of Radio Madre de Dios made them aware of the significance of a communication tool that responded to the social needs of the communities surrounding Quillabamba. Thus, the decision was made to create a new station.

Quillabamba already had a small private radio station, though of limited reach because of its low power and its lack of clear objectives. However it already had a legal license and its own frequency to operate. The Dominican priests bought it in 1966 and started developing a new communication experience.

ASPECTS OF SOCIAL CHANGE

Similar to what happened with *Radio Pío XII* (Bolivia), *Radio Huayacocotla* (México) and many other Catholic stations, *Radio Quillabamba* evolved while getting closer to the social reality. During the first years its objectives were merely religious and educational, but after 1978 the station took a clear stand "for a popular education and in support of organised people," which meant a political definition in favour of the poorest and most excluded communities. We can actually measure the social impact of this strategy by the number of sabotages and attacks that the station suffered since then.

The power of its transmitters extends the area of influence of *Radio Quillabamba* over the totality of the Cuzco Department, and also over neighbouring departments in the Andean Southern of Peru.

The station acts as a post office, telephone booth and telegraph for most of the peasants in the province, who often visit the radio station to pick up the letters they have received from other cities. Upon reception, the station normally airs a courtesy message signalling the arrival of each letter.

The most representative local popular organisations prepare and conduct their own radio programmes, often live broadcasts of massive meetings and demonstrations. Though these transmissions may last for five or six hours, they definitely have the support of most listeners.

Over the years *Radio Quillabamba* has developed a comprehensive "Doctrinal Framework" which covers the ensemble of its activities. The document recognises the social, cultural, economic and political nature of the region as the baseline for its philosophical option.

Community participation in *Radio Quillabamba* takes place through the most representative local social organisations. Unions and cooperatives are in charge of radio slots on the local social reality, thus expressing the critical voice of the majority on issues such as social discrimination, injustice and violations of human rights. Each organisation is responsible for preparing an annual work plan including objectives, structure and people in charge of the production of the programmes.

The selection of staff for the station is mainly based on criteria of social commitment and identification with the regional needs. All candidates have to be bilingual and show, above all, a great will of working in harmony with the social organisations of the province. Technical training is provided once the above conditions have been met.

In terms of coordinating with others, *Radio Quillabamba* participates in the effort of strengthening the alternative communication networks, through its presence in various progressive organisations: the National Radio Coordination (CNR), the Campesino Christian Communities (CCC), and ALER at the international level.

CONSTRAINTS

Though at the very beginning *Radio Quillabamba* had a license to operate, 1971 government provisions compelled the station to start all over again to obtain a new operating license.

Due to its commitment to the people, *Radio Quillabamba* has been often the victim of threats and violent attacks. An attack with explosives destroyed the transmitter in June 1975 and forced the station to work for several years in precarious conditions until the new equipment was mounted in May 1986.

The station suffered two other attacks in 1987 and May 1988. A violent intervention incited by the local and national government in January 1989 resulted in the closure of *Radio Quillabamba* until April of the same year. In December 1989 a heavy rain prevented another explosion from doing more harm. Each of these attacks against freedom of expression interrupted the activities of the station, but no attack was able to silence it or to frighten the people involved in running it. On the contrary, *Radio Quillabamba* grew and got stronger with the support of the peasantry.

REFERENCES

"*Radio Quillabamba* y la Educación Popular" by P. Alfredo Encinas Martín and P. Rufino Lobo Alonso. Cuadernos de Comunicación Alternativa No. 8, CIMCA (Centro de Integración de Medios de Comunicación Alternativa), Bolivia, 1990.

"*Radio Quillabamba*, Peru" by Don Moore, *The Journal of the North American Shortwave Association*, February 1991. Web site <http://www.swl.net/patepluma/south/peru/quilla.html>.

"La Radio: Actor Clave en el Desarrollo Humano" by Anouk Hoeberichts and Miguel Lopez, in *Sustainable Development Dimensions*, FAO (Rome), January 1999. Web site <http://www.fao.org/sd/spdirect/CDan0023.htm>.

CESPAC

(**1975**) Peru

....

BASIC FACTS

TITLE:	Centro de Servicios de Pedagogía Audiovisual para la Capacitación (*CESPAC*)
COUNTRY:	Peru
MAIN FOCUS:	Rural development
PLACE:	Several rural areas in Peru
BENEFICIARIES:	About 550,000 peasants
PARTNERS:	Ministry of Agriculture, Centro Nacional de Capacitación e Investigación de la Reforma Agraria, Peru (CENCIRA)
FUNDING:	FAO/UNDP, Friedrich Ebert Stiftung (FES)
MEDIA:	Video

SNAPSHOT

It seems there are more than 300 communication schools in Latin America, training over 120,000 students. Most of these training centres aim to prepare communication professionals for the mass media, the advertising industry, the so-called business communication and public relations. There is not one single school of communication really training communicators for development, scientific communicators or pedagogic communicators. In part, that is the very reason why we find such a distressing situation in the field of communication for development.

How can an education process ever be efficient, in human and financial terms, where the teacher is only sending one-way unintelligible messages to a passive receiver, and where the whole process of learning is ignored?

How can the messages devised for development projects be adequate to a particular context if they are usually designed by people specialised in manipulating through commercial advertising?

How can messages that carry scientific information be socially appropriate if people that prepare them ignore the specificity of scientific language and only value as news those that are spectacular and unusual?

How can the population be informed if the informers are not informed and yet they produce messages that nobody understands, out-of-context, inappropriate, biased and with no utility for the people?

It is very difficult to understand the reason why that type of communication school and university faculties continue to proliferate while there are not enough jobs for the newly graduated.

Our society needs schools that form another kind of communicator, those that do not exist right now, at least not in the quantities that are needed.—Excerpts from "La Formación de los Comunicadores para el Desarrollo" ("The Training of Communicators for Development") by Manuel Calvelo, the founder of *CESPAC*.

DESCRIPTION

CESPAC was created in the early 1970s with support from FAO. This is one of those projects that was successful partly because of the motivation, dedication, deep involvement, clear objectives and stubbornness of one person. The person is Manuel Calvelo, a Spaniard that has been working in Latin America for decades, and has positively influenced many of the most innovative communication processes for rural development.

By 1975, the first group (27 staff members) was trained in seven months. It was decided from the beginning that everyone should be acquainted with all stages and skills of video production: research, scriptwriting, camera operation, sound, editing, production and dissemination. This was the first activity as well as the first mistake of the project: the training was too heavy on theory and too weak on direct experience in rural areas.

The process of recording, interacting with peasants, and conducting training sessions at the community level had to take into account the agricultural cycles and the availability of peasants during the day. For this reason the duration of videotapes was kept down to an average of 15 minutes.

A team of two people would normally stay in the community during the process of recording the video lessons that would be used for training. The same team had previously developed a script, which was reviewed by technical staff. Once the recording was completed, the team returned to *CESPAC* headquarters in Lima (the capital city of Peru), and produced a draft editing, which was again submitted to specialists on the subject matter, before returning to the field level for testing with peasants. Their comments and criticism would be the basis for a final editing.

The themes covered by the video lessons are as varied as the range of topics associated with rural development. For practical purposes *CESPAC* divided them into fewer categories: farming, livestock, natural resources, health and habitat, forestry and fish farming, and mechanisation.

CESPAC started operation with black and white video cameras and open-reel recorders until 1978, when U-Matic (3/4-inch video) became available and facilitated recording and editing in colour. A few years later, when Betamax (Sony) and VHS (JVC) formats invaded the consumer markets, *CESPAC* acquired the technology and used it mainly for reproducing and distributing. In order to transport and protect the near 120 units used for showing videos at the village level, *CESPAC* built wooden cases to hold monitors and VCRs. Even with the lightest technologies of the early 1980s, the load was still 63 kilograms. Video projector technology had not yet improved as it has in the 1990s.

The project produced a series of manuals for trainers and for trainees, to orient the process of *capacitación* (training) by providing sets of questions and answers, and practical activities. The guides were fully illustrated to facilitate comprehension, and copies remained with participants for future reference.

CESPAC's principle of gathering, preserving and reproducing indigenous knowledge, and adding to it modern scientific knowledge, facilitated the emergence of open flows of communication in many directions, linking communities with rural development technicians, or communities with other communities. Communication tools became familiar in rural areas largely deprived of electricity and telephone lines.

BACKGROUND & CONTEXT

Peru has gone under important changes in the last few decades. In the 1950s the majority of the population were native Indian— mainly Quechua and Aymara, who lived in rural areas. The process of migration towards the cities in search of jobs altered the correlation in the following years: 60 percent of the population is currently living in urban areas, mostly incorporated in the slums around Lima. The capital city alone has six million of the twenty million people in the whole country.

Rural areas in the highlands, the coast or the Amazonian forest are deprived from basic services and investment. Agriculture has gradually diminished its importance; only 3 percent of the land is productive. Poverty in rural areas is pushing people into the cities while deeply affecting the social and economic structures of those rural communities.

The populist military government of General Velasco Alvarado launched an ambitious agrarian reform in 1969, aiming to eliminate large and unproductive properties and redistribute land to small peasants—with the objective of encouraging the establishment of rural cooperatives in view of increasing agricultural production to meet the national needs.

In those years, FAO and UNDP backed the creation of CENCIRA, a centre of training and research for the Agrarian Reform. The design of CENCIRA included a component of communication for development aiming to train and orient the "beneficiaries" through the process. Peasants with very low levels of formal education were now in charge of running the cooperatives; it was imperative to mobilise and train them.

About 42 percent of the men and 67 percent of the women in rural Peru were illiterate in the early 1970s, so a very innovative approach was needed to face the challenge of improving the educational level and sharing the knowledge about agricultural modernisation. Based on the experience that FAO specialists had developed in Chile during the government of Salvador Allende, the choice of video was almost immediate. By 1975 the project started its activity under the name of *CESPAC*.

ASPECTS OF SOCIAL CHANGE

The success of *CESPAC* has had enormous influence in planning and developing rural development programmes. The use of video tools for training is now widely accepted by governments and international cooperation agencies in Latin America. The rich experience of *CESPAC* was the main reference for the creation of *PRODERITH* (Mexico) and *CESPA* (Mali). In both projects the leading staff had worked before with Manuel Calvelo in *CESPAC*.

The programme outputs are impressive and show the extent of the achievements: 150 Peruvians were trained as video producers, 200 more learned how to use video programmes for rural development activities. More than one thousand video programmes were produced. By the end of the project in 1986, approximately 550,000 peasants had benefited from the video training sessions. Each training period lasted an average of six days, with peasants attending three hours every day. By 1980, 48 percent of the trainers were women.

According to Manuel Calvelo, *CESPAC* activities should not be evaluated in terms of cost/benefit, but rather of investment/results. The final cost of the training per person was only of US$24. "We put together a highly efficient system, not only from the financial point of view, but in terms of the pedagogical achievements."

MEDIA & METHODS

Training is an essential condition for rural development. Many studies have given proof that rural productivity is directly related to knowledge about agricultural techniques. Lack of information often leads to lower performance of cultivated land. A programme that contributes to inform, organise and empower rural communities, as *CESPAC* did, can obviously make a difference, especially if the effort has been sustained over the years.

CESPAC is about *capacitación*, a Spanish word already incorporated in the development jargon; it refers to training but goes far beyond. No single English word can synthesise or translate the meanings of *capacitación*. The concept is not limited to acquiring technical skills or improving knowledge through information dissemination. It also relates to inducing individuals and communities to organise to transform their reality, to empower themselves through a process of appropriation of the tools and concepts that they can apply to development.

One of the methodological breakthroughs of *CESPAC* was to incorporate the original knowledge and practices of peasants, instead of bluntly discarding their culture and treating them as "ignorant." Thus Calvelo prevented the project from falling into practices of what he calls "academic terrorism."

Training was done in Quechua or Aymara, the peasants' mother tongue, and did take advantage of all kinds of cultural codes and customs that are an indissoluble part of their daily lives. The contents were heavily oriented towards having a practical value that peasants could use. The "visual pedagogy" devised by Manuel Calvelo and his team was encapsulated in "What I hear I may forget; if I see it, I can remember; if I do it, I learn."

CONSTRAINTS

By the time *CESPAC* started using video in rural Peru, technology was far behind what it is today, which makes this venture even more, revolutionary for its time. In the early 1970s only black and white video was widely available, with open reel recorders detached from the tube-based cameras. Equipment was heavy, not easy to carry, and needed heavy batteries or electricity to operate.

The project never really developed a process for the selection of staff consistent with the needs of the rural population. In many cases government imposed its choice of personnel who were not up to the tasks, not sufficiently motivated and committed, and oblivious of local language and customs. The initial training in 1975 was too long and heavy on theory, which was corrected in the following years.

As for peasant involvement in video productions, Colin Fraser asserts: "An objective analysis would demonstrate that there hasn't been enough peasant participation; the project has developed under so much pressure to survive that it has been unable to provide suitable attention."

SOURCES & REFERENCES

"Un Nuevo enfoque para la comunicación rural: la experiencia peruana en video para la capacitación campesina," a case study. FAO 1987.

"Video y Desarrollo Rural," by Colin Fraser. Chasqui N° 33, Quito 1990.

E-mail exchanges with Manuel Calvelo provided additional information.

PRODERITH

$$\boxed{1978}$$ Mexico

....

BASIC FACTS

TITLE: Programa de Desarrollo Rural Integrado del Trópico Húmedo (*PRODERITH*)

COUNTRY: Mexico

MAIN FOCUS: Rural development in tropical wetlands

PLACE: San Luis Potosí, Yucatan, Chiapas

BENEFICIARIES: 800,000 peasant farmers

PARTNERS: Facultad Latino Americana de Ciencias Sociales (FLACSO), Instituto Mexicano de Tecnología del Agua (IMTA), Secretaría de Agricultura y Recursos Hidráculicos, Mexico (SARH), Comisión Nacional del Agua, Mexico (CAN)

FUNDING: FAO, World Bank, Gobierno de México

MEDIA: Video

SNAPSHOT

The charismatic old man, with his white hair and white beard, sat cross-legged in front of a video camera for hours on end. He held forth about the past, about the Revolution, about the greatness of Mayan culture and about life today. He deplored the decline of such Mayan traditions as the family vegetable plot, explained how he cultivated his own maize, and complained that today's young people did not even know how to do that properly. He accused the young of abandoning all that had been good in Mayan culture; they would sell eggs to buy cigarettes and soft drinks, and so it was no wonder that diets today were worse than they were in his youth, and so on.

Scores of people sat in attentive silence in the villages as these tapes were played back. In the evening, under a tree, the words in Mayan flowed from the screen, and the old man's eloquent voice and emphatic gestures spread their spell. For many, it was the first time they had ever heard anyone talk about the practical values of their culture. It was also the first time they had seen a peasant like themselves on "television," and talking their own language. Frequently they asked that the tapes be repeated again and again.

The desired effect was achieved: the people began to take stock of their situation and think seriously about their values. Thus, the ground was prepared for when PRODERITH *began to discuss development proposals.*

There is also a good example of the communication system helping to create participation. In one project area the technicians had proposed a drainage plan to cure the regular flooding that occurred in a particular place. A peasant thought that the plan would not work because, in his opinion, the technicians were wrong in their analysis of the cause of the flooding. The peasant was video-recorded as he explained his reasons, scratching a diagram in the soil with a stick to illustrate his point.

This tape was shown to the technicians. They studied the situation again, and they found that the peasant had been right. —FROM FAO CASE STUDY ON *PRODERITH*.

DESCRIPTION

The Programme of Integrated Rural Development in the Tropical Wetlands (*PRODERITH*) had two distinct phases: from 1978 to 1984, and from 1986 to 1995. From its inception *PRODERITH* received full technical support from FAO and loans from the World Bank. Institutionally, it depended initially on Mexico's SARH, but this evolved during the following years, as government institutions suffered political and administrative changes.

The objective of *PRODERITH* Phase I was to increase agricultural production in the tropics, improve the living standards of poor farmers and conserve natural resources. The activities included building roads, soil conservation, credit and social participation of peasants. Ultimately, community participation became the overall goal and although a Rural Communication System was created within the project, the *PRODERITH* acronym actually became a synonym for the communication and, in particular, video activities.

The overall development strategies can be encapsulated as follows: First, it was to be a learning process by generating practical field experiences extreme enough to be later replicated on a larger scale; secondly, it aimed to achieve active participation of all involved, peasants as well as project staff; and thirdly, it was meant to foster coordination between the various institutions involved in rural development at the community level.

The initial rural universe of the pilot experience included 3,500 peasant families on 54,000 hectares of land in three separate project areas. For the second phase these figures were largely increased, which may have had a negative impact on the quality of results.

Training with video as a tool was the main activity conducted at the community level. In the years 1978–84, close to 345 videos were produced, along with supporting printed material. Cameras were available in the project areas, but the editing was centralised at the project headquarters in Cuernavaca. Initially 3/4-inch U-Matic video equipment was utilised for recording and editing, but later in the 1980s new technologies were adopted, including the use of computers for animation.

The economic crisis in Mexico during the 1980s led to structural adjustment programmes that affected government development projects, including *PRODERITH*, which lost up to 70 percent of its qualified field staff. Thus when the second phase started in 1986, it had bigger ambitions but less human resources to deal with the increased problems that the economic crisis had brought to rural areas.

An untimely effort to decentralise and gradually give more power to the peasant organisations followed; five regional communication units were established in San Luis Potosí, Yucatan (two) and Chiapas (two). Under these, new local communication units (LCUs) were created, as well as "communication committees" made of local people. The LCUs were equipped with a loudspeaker system complete with cassette recorders and amplifiers, plus a covered area for meetings and video screenings.

The rural communication system absorbed 2.2 percent of the total cost of *PRODERITH*, which is in fact not negligible considering that the added investment for the two phases was US$292 million. Out of the US$5 million utilised by the communication system, 1/5 was spent on equipment. The average cost of producing a 15-minute video programme was estimated at between US$3,000 and US$5,500.

BACKGROUND & CONTEXT

Mexico's policy in agricultural development during several decades was dominated by the goal of expanding irrigation in its arid areas. Nevertheless, during the 1960s the need to increase food production and the high cost of continuing focus on the development of irrigation projects lead to granting more attention to the potential of tropical wetlands and rain-fed areas which make up 75 percent of cultivated land, particularly in the coastal plains.

The first major attempt of switching to the new strategy resulted in a big failure to accomplish the ultimate objectives. The Plan Chontalpa initiative was successful in installing infrastructure in a vast area in the State of Tabasco, providing credit and technical assistance to farmers, but failed to conquer community participation. It was totally a top-down intervention for which there was no prior consultation with the beneficiaries. The peasants never identified with the project and never did use or maintain the infrastructure properly.

Given the importance of the tropical wetlands (23 percent of total area) for the future of Mexican agriculture, the government decided to continue developing the new policy in spite of the Plan Chontalpa failure. This time the strategy would call for a communication process to ensure active participation of the local people, and in doing so would ensure that proposals would be appropriate to the situation and agreed to by the communities.

A period of research took place in 1977, during which a video camera was used to help peasants analyse their situation and problems, to record meetings and use playback throughout the process of discussing future plans. Video proved to be an excellent tool for motivating peasants and bringing them into the planning process. As a result, a specific project was designed, with an important communication component, and specifically, with video as the centrepiece of the communication strategy. That is how *PRODERITH* came to life in 1978.

ASPECTS OF SOCIAL CHANGE

During the two phases of *PRODERITH*, more than 700 training videos and accompanying printed materials were produced, and no less than 800,000 people participated in the training sessions. These had no doubt great impact on the daily lives of peasants, as the topics covered farming, fishing, livestock, health, nutrition, environment, water, community organisation and every other possible topic related to the needs of rural population. At its peak of productivity in 1981, the communication team was able to produce one hundred videos in one year.

Peasants often show difficulty in articulating their views of their reality, and they seldom share with outsiders their individual perceptions. *PRODERITH* has contributed to rural development by enabling the articulation of the collective perception within the community, on the local situation, its problems and options for improving it. The video methodology prompted internal debate about history, culture and future perspectives of the communities involved in the communication process.

In a broader perspective, *PRODERITH* is an example of communication becoming instrumental to move forward a major rural development programme. It shows how communication at its best can be fully integrated if the need has been identified from the inception of the programme. "The Rural Communication System developed by *PRODERITH* was uniquely imaginative and effective," according to FAO assessment.

As many rural development reports will assert, improved knowledge and skills in all areas of rural life are the key for better productivity and better standards of living. To meet these needs *PRODERITH*'s Rural Communication System adopted a methodology based on video with supporting printed materials, the whole forming so-called "pedagogical packages." A package covers a subject broken down into a series of videos, each one constituting a single lesson of the course. A printed guide for the technicians who will be using the material provides them with additional information on the subject and how best to use the package.

The methodology was primarily based on field units, small teams of technicians and *promotores* (development or extension workers) who worked at the community level. They used video to promote discussions on issues relevant to the community, and to facilitate the participatory process of developing a Local Development Plan that would enable *PRODERITH* to take concrete steps.

The video methodology was also used for the training of project staff and to complement reports and evaluations.

CONSTRAINTS

The very high cost of the experience makes it very difficult to serve as an example for replication. The programme could only be sustained with the constant flow of cash borrowed from the World Bank, and could only happen in a large borrower-country such as Mexico.

For the same reason, the decentralisation process and, moreover, prospects of transferring the experience to the community was an unrealistic and untimely move. Furthermore the initial project had based its structure on a highly centralised structure and was very heavy on technical and specialised staff.

During *PRODERITH* I, which was the first phase, no real attempt was made to transfer control of the communication system to the communities, or at least to decentralise it. During *PRODERITH* II, the phase of crisis, the decentralisation could only mean an attempt to decentralise the cost and responsibility of the crisis on the shoulders of the communities. It could not work on a large scale. The attempt at decentralisation was too late to be accomplished.

The institutional changes in a country that is so marked every six years by political revamping also affected *PRODERITH*; being a government agency it was not spared at all. The five existing regional communication units that resulted from decentralisation were facing an uncertain future by the end of 1995; their chances of survival without proper funding were, at the least, very bleak.

REFERENCES

This chapter is mostly based on:

"Comunicación para el Desarrollo Rural en México: en los Buenos y en los Malos Tiempos," a case study, FAO, Rome 1996.

Colin Fraser and Sonia Restrepo-Estrada. *Communicating for Development: Human Change for Survival*. I.B. Tauris, London-New York, 1998.

TEATRO KERIGMA

1978   Colombia

....

BASIC FACTS

TITLE:	Fundación Teatral Kerigma
COUNTRY:	Colombia
MAIN FOCUS:	Knowledge, cultural development, participation
PLACE:	Bosa
BENEFICIARIES:	Population of Bosa, Usaquén, Ciudad Bolívar, Soacha, Kennedy
PARTNERS:	Colnodo, Centro de Investigació y Educació Popular, Colombia (CINEP), Corporación Raíces, Universidad Central, Programa por La Paz, otros
FUNDING:	Netherlands Organisation for International Development Cooperation (NOVIB), DIAKONIA, Ministerio de Cultura, Instituto Distrital de Turismo
MEDIA:	Theatre

SNAPSHOT

Far in the border between Bogotá and the Soacha Municipality where the city ends, survives a neighbourhood that looks impersonal at first sight: La Despensa. Its houses built by segments seem to have no regard for aesthetics. Brick over brick their facades resemble, giving the general impression of pitiable and monotonous architecture.

The shops offering homemade curative potions, the road mechanics repairing old trucks from the time of World War II, and the night stands selling hot dogs are part of the local landscape. However these streets have witnessed the growth of strong bonds of solidarity, friendship and affection. It is in this neighbourhood where the experience of Fundación Kerigma started 22 years ago and has developed on the basis of a network of human relations that is more important than ideologies and personal or economic constraints.

Kerigma started as a youth group that held its meetings at the parish, in homes or even in the streets. Soon after, they got a small communal room that was too often flooded with water. Finally one day they were able to rent a place, which they used for rehearsals, exhibits, as well as drama, music and dance workshops.

In 1988 Kerigma received a house as a donation. With the support of the Librovía programme the house was revamped and new rooms were added in 1991. Today, the three-story building is full of kids, full of dreams and smiles, full of rehearsals, public and visitors. It is now the headquarters of the Casa de la Cultura (the House of Culture) with a small theatre, a library, various workshops, and room enough to keep the video and photographic equipment, the theatre props, and to house a computer unit that provides training and community access to the Internet.

Certainly, we haven't had time to get nostalgic, because things are very much alive around here. What we do have, and lots of, is time to fall in love. — Excerpts from an article by Jairo Chaparro Valderrama, president, Corporación Raíces.

DESCRIPTION

 Kerigma is a cultural NGO that started in 1978 as a group of young people eager to promote theatre in the locality of Bosa, in Bogotá. Since the first Bertold Brecht's *The Exceptions and the Rule* staged by *Teatro Kerigma* in 1979, other plays have been added to Kerigma's repertoire. The theatre troupe has produced its own scripts or has adapted plays to the local context, increasingly relating the contents to community needs, social analysis and citizen participation.

In terms of the audience and the methodology of work, Kerigma makes the distinction between plays performed in theatres and those performed in open spaces, in the streets. Around twenty plays— mostly by well-known authors as Brecht and Tennessee Williams— have been staged in theatres during the first years. However Kerigma has increasingly taken advantage of Latin American authors and gradually developed its own collective creations directed by Enrique Espitia León and Camilo León Mora. Although Kerigma now has its own theatre for 100 people, with a 64 square metre stage, in recent years the troupe has increasingly developed performances in open spaces, thus showing a major interest in community work.

In spite of theatre being the most dynamic factor within the ensemble of activities of Kerigma, the organisation has evolved in a number of other areas. Part of Kerigma's activities to promote community awareness and participation relate to training. Every year new training activities are conducted, mostly workshops on art, skills and training on alternative media skills for young journalists.

Every year Kerigma organises the "Muestra de Arte Popular" ("Popular Arts Festival") which has already reached its 20th anniversary in 2000. The participation at this event has increased steadily. When the first festival took place in 1981 only four groups performed; however, more than 30 groups participated every year since 1995.

Other than the performances and events, Kerigma has a series of publications and audio-visual productions. Even before Kerigma formalised itself as an independent foundation for cultural development in Bosa, the group produced several booklets, such as *Cartilla Raíz* (1979) or the *Boletín de Casa de la Cultura* (1987). But since 1992 Kerigma has published its own news bulletin "Notas de Encuentro," which is now a regular page on its Web site. The video tools concentrate on documenting Kerigma's activities, mainly those related to community development in Bosa and citizen participation. These videos were produced in partnership with other NGOs and development agencies.

In 1997 *Teatro Kerigma* was selected along with Fundación Pepaso and Fundación AVP, to house one of the Neighbourhood Information Units (Unidades Informativas Barriales — UIBs), a project promoted by Colnodo with support IDRC (Canada). Colnodo established the UIBs for reassessing local knowledge and facilitating access to it. "Each human being is living knowledge, moving information, generator of communication bits, which makes him or her, a potential actor of development." The programme plans to collect people's knowledge and organise it so it will be useful for citizen participation in development. Computers are used to gather and stock the information, while Internet and e-mail services are offered to the community.

The collaboration with Colnodo, an organisation that promotes the use of Internet for community development, has expanded the horizons of Kerigma. The organisation has gained visibility while developing a new line of community work. The *Teatro Kerigma* Web site is now a window for the world to peek into the activities of this theatre group and cultural organisation.

BACKGROUND & CONTEXT

Bosa is one of the 20 localities of Santa Fe de Bogotá, the capital city of Colombia. Though formerly inhabited by Chibcha indians, little remains of its ancient cultural identity. The small rural huts disappeared two centuries ago, but the area continued to be an important agricultural setting, producing wheat, potatoes and barley. By 1950 the population was still under 20,000 however unemployment and violence in rural areas pushed thousands of people to the capital and soon Bosa became one more urban locality of Bogotá.

Bosa is divided into 283 barrios, with a total of 250 thousand people. Migration sharpened social problems and poverty in Bosa as well as in other peripheral localities of Bogotá; however, Bosa benefited at the same time from institutions that started cultural and educational programmes in the locality.

The "Grupo Juvenil Kerigma" ("Kerigma Juvenile Group") has come a long way since it started in the 1970s promoting the development of community theatre. A few years later Kerigma opened a Casa de la Cultura and vigorously expanded to other activities. The motto of the festival is significant: "Cultura para la Paz y la Convivencia" ("Culture for Peace and Reconciliation").

ASPECTS OF SOCIAL CHANGE

Kerigma has had an impact in community development in Bosa, by strengthening cultural identity, encouraging citizen participation, and promoting local governance. Its activities of theatre, music, dance, community arts festivals, publications, audio-visual production, training workshops, etc., have been successful in reaching a wide audience of children, youths and adults. The organisation has succeeded in bringing together concepts of culture and society, culture and development, and culture and participation.

One of the aspects of social change that Kerigma has promoted is networking with other institutions and cultural organisations. The initiative has led to the constitution of a network of theatre groups from other localities of Colombia, such as Teatro Esquina Latina (Cali), Corporación Nefesh (Medellín), Teatro El Agora (Envigado), Grupo Teatro Tecoc (Bello), Grupo Jocrar (Medellín), and various other drama troupes from Bogotá.

The work of Kerigma has transcended the community to the international level. The organisation has participated in international theatre festivals, with plays such as *Carreras por el Poder* and *Pies Hinchados* ("Swollen Feet"), an adaptation from the classic *King Oedipus*.

One of the most important achievements, by the UIBs project supported by Colnodo, was to take computers and Internet access to low-income and working class neighbourhoods, thus breaking down the typical centralism that characterises access to new technologies in the capital city of Colombia. The participatory communication experience of the UIBs, was presented at the Global Knowledge II Conference in Kuala Lumpur, in March 2000.

Cultural organisations visit Kerigma's UIB regularly to use the computers, though mainly for word processing and printing. As several of these organisations do not have their own headquarters, they find the UIB a very useful place and friendly environment for preparing proposals and researching.

The expansion of Kerigma's cultural coverage over Bosa led the organisation to seriously focus on the study of the social, economic and cultural characteristics of the locality. The study was developed in collaboration with Universidad Central and the participation of various local institutions. Colnodo contributed by publishing the research results on the Internet.

The research methodology provided Kerigma with very complete information on the social interactions within the Bosa locality, thus strengthening the style of work once designed on the basis of empirical knowledge. The study comprises a "cultural map" of Bosa, as well as specific data on social, economic, institutional and geographical aspects.

The task of incorporating the tools of new information and communication technologies has been challenging for Kerigma. The group has explored innovative ways of conducting training activities for adults and children, using participatory approaches to build and organise knowledge collectively.

CONSTRAINTS

The most recent constraints deal with the establishment and sustainability of the UIB. In spite of Kerigma's longstanding reputation as a well-established cultural institution, the introduction of new technologies has been met with the indifference of most of the intended beneficiaries.

"To date, the UIBs have no routine visitors either from within the organisation or from outside. It is only the unit coordinators who make regular use of e-mail and the Internet" according to Luis Fernando Baron from CINEP.

The lack of articulation between the UIB and the general activities of Kerigma at the community level partly explains the cultural resistance and the prejudices of local people against the use of computers and the Internet. Students and organisations aiming to improve the look of their documents and presentations mostly use the services. Word-processing and printing are in high demand, while e-mail and the Internet are seldom utilised, which seems to point to the fact that the initial purpose of making knowledge accessible to the community was defeated. Nonetheless, the process is still young and changes may occur in the next two or three years if adequate strategies to promote the UIB are implemented.

The numerous communication breakdowns caused by the poor quality of telephone lines and the frequent power blackouts represent additional obstacles.

REFERENCES

Information for this chapter was provided by Marcya Hernández and Sylvia Cadena through e-mail exchanges.

Kerigma's Web site: <http://www.uib-kerigma.colnodo.org.co>.

De la Educación y la Participación Ciudadana en Colombia by Marcya Hernández, Fundación Kerigma. Bogotá, 1999.

"Experiments in community access to new communication and information technologies in Bogota" by Luis Fernando Baron, CINEP. Telecentre Evaluation: A Global Perspective. International Development Research Centre (IDRC), 1999.

TEATRO LA FRAGUA

1979 Honduras

....

BASIC FACTS

TITLE:	Teatro La Fragua
COUNTRY:	Honduras
FOCUS:	Raise community consciousness, cultural creativity
PLACE:	El Progreso
BENEFICIARIES:	El Progreso, Northern coastal zone of Honduras
PARTNERS:	The Jesuit Community
FUNDING:	Misereor, Trocaire and Accion Cuaresmal Suiza (40 percent), individual donations (50 percent) and ticket sales (10 percent)
MEDIA:	Theatre

SNAPSHOT

Three actors, two musicians, bare stage. A deliberate entrance, a strong introduction, and the sudden hush of an audience involuntarily seized by the power of electric performers. The physical presence grabs the room and doesn't relent. Most of the audience has never known the human element to be capable of such raw personal power, power that comes from vision, inspiration, and much work. Raw, unfettered power that emanates from the soul and not from a gun. The power of hope, not of fear.

The audience at first is not sure of this presence. A nervous uncertainty grips the crowd; the actors feel it, and their rhythms are rigid. Then the children save it: the honesty of children who don't know their hope has been hocked to a foreign lender.

An icy-clean four-year-old's laugh slices through the night; the scald of oppression eases, and adults join the little girl. Actors struggle to maintain character; one musician can't suppress a grin as the single shiver of laughter continues above the rest. A child has saved it. A four-year-old has revealed an impulse in every person, has taught her parents, her superiors, the basic lesson of life: joy is the first rebellion against oppressors, the wildly revolutionary act, a defiance of all authority that says life will be suffering. This is raw, gritty, tough theatre in a land beset by hurricanes, deforestation, corruption and poverty. Theatre that finds it as important to train its audience as it does to train its actors; theatre that competes for its audience with cockfights, machete duels, floods, harvests, and a cultural illiteracy that has robbed these people of their proud Mayan heritage. Tenacious theatre that refuses to concede defeat in the face of washed-out bridges, tenuous funding, and moonscape highways.

Why do we do theatre in a country as desperately poor as Honduras? Why do we do theatre in the midst of all the needs that are so obvious? Theatre is never going to lower the infant mortality rate. Theatre will not save (nor even ease the pain of) a child dying of malnutrition. Theatre is never going to change the world. But a child's laugh reminds us that theatre can fulfill another need perhaps as desperate: theatre can make a child laugh. Perhaps it can even give a child a spark of hope. — WRITES JACK WARNER S.J., FOUNDER AND DIRECTOR OF *TEATRO LA FRAGUA*.

DESCRIPTION

Teatro La Fragua, "The Forge Theatre," is a theatre group based in El Progreso, Honduras' third largest city. Its goal is "to forge a national identity by means of the people's own expression" and "awaken the creativity of the people with the help of theatre, to find solutions to current problems." Jack Warner, a Jesuit priest, has been its artistic director since he created it in 1979. The company consists of fourteen Hondurans who not only perform, but also do the maintenance and public relations. *Teatro La Fragua* started in 1979 in the remote eastern town of Olanchito, but quickly moved its base to El Progreso, which is more accessible to major population centres like San Pedro Sula, the economic capital of Honduras. The building that is now the theatre had fallen into disrepair, much like El Progreso itself. It was once the social hall of the banana company's country club, a place where executives and their families enjoyed dances and parties.

To address social issues and to achieve their mission of creating a Honduran national identity, *Teatro La Fragua* has adopted a strategy that includes: 1) staging of dramas often featuring Latin American writers; 2) performing religious plays, such as *¡El Evangelio En Vivo!* (The Gospel Live!); and 3) dramatic adaptations of Honduran stories, myths and folklore.

They have created a varied body of work: explorations of Central American history and traditions; dramatisations of biblical stories in a Honduran context; adaptations of theatre classics; and theatre for children. *Teatro La Fragua* performs in plazas, churches and schoolyards, primarily for poor and working-class audiences—illiterate with little access to the sources of official culture, who otherwise might never see a play. It has dedicated itself to the principle: "If people can't come to the theatre, then theatre must come to the people." Actress Nubia Canales notes, "the small villages we visit always turn out to be our most enthusiastic crowds. They treat us like we're really important."

Other than creating dramatisations, La Fragua conducts training workshops in Honduras, Nicaragua, El Salvador, Costa Rica, Cuba, Guatemala and Belize, and it has toured in the United States, Mexico, Spain and Colombia. More than 600 youngsters are involved in drama classes and workshops. It has also invited Honduran guest artists to perform in its theatre, including El Teatro Latino (puppeteers), Son Cinco (modern dance) and Guillermo Anderson (a singer-songwriter who fuses jazz and reggae with the rhythms of Honduras' Caribbean coast).

La Fragua operates under the auspices of the Jesuits, who own the complex on which the theatre is built. The troupe devotes six months of the year to religious plays associated with the Christmas and Easter seasons, while reserving the other half of the year for works of a more secular nature. Many of the troupe's members have joined through their involvement in church-related youth activities, including the drama classes that the company sponsors. The religious connection offers the group a network of support and a public legitimacy in a society where most secular institutions, both public and private, are characterised by inefficiency and corruption.

A group of international "friends" of La Fragua provides 50 percent of the funding. Misereor, Trocaire and other religious agencies also help (40 percent), while local contributions and selling tickets for performances makes up the rest.

Teatro La Fragua has survived public indifference, economic setbacks and political repression to become one of the most stable and enduring popular theatre troupes in all of Latin America.

BACKGROUND & CONTEXT

Honduras suffers from a long history of dependence and under-development. Still dragging the leg irons of a feudal past, this is a country where the majority of its peasantry can neither read nor write; chronic malnutrition and disease make surviving very difficult. *Campesinos* farm on steep and rocky slopes not far from the immense and fertile plantations of multinational fruit companies. The country typifies the concept of a "banana republic." During many decades it has been under the occupation of the multinational United Fruit Company, and has served as a military base for U.S. troops during the decades of guerrilla activity in Nicaragua, El Salvador and Guatemala. Statistically it continues to trail even its war-torn neighbours in terms of life expectancy, unemployment and per-capita income. All this in spite of an unprecedented decade of United States military and economic aid, including millions of dollars funnelled through projects sponsored by USAID, as well as one of the largest Peace Corps programmes in the world.

Honduras seems to be in search of its historical and cultural identity. In Mayan times its sparse indigenous settlements were but outposts of an empire centred in the Guatemalan highlands and the Yucatan lowlands. In colonial days, Honduras was but a remote province of the Spanish Kingdom of Guatemala. By the time of Honduras' independence, British imperial interests controlled large sections of the country's sizable Caribbean coast, logistically remote from the capital of Tegucigalpa. This century, the international fruit companies have enjoyed an economic sovereignty over this same coast.

ASPECTS OF SOCIAL CHANGE

In contrast to the occasional nature of most *campesino* theatre in Honduras, *Teatro La Fragua* constitutes a year-round, professional attempt to use theatre as a means of empowerment. What La Fragua seeks to do—address socio-political issues, explore Honduran history, teach literacy, and stimulate personal and group autonomy—is similar to what the other Honduran *campesino* groups seek to do.

The theatre group has cultivated a form of performance that sees a relationship between theatrical and spiritual values. It performs for a community that sees no distinction between the two, like the audiences of the medieval passion plays.

Through its work La Fragua has challenged the values of the political and economic establishment in a land where doing so means risking political persecution. While director Warner eschews propagandistic theatre, he still views La Fragua's feat as political: "It's political in the sense of being from the point-of-view from which one sees the world. We're trying to create a theatre in which the point-of-view is precisely that of the dispossessed." Teatro acts politically by giving Hondurans the opportunity to see themselves reflected on stage and to hear their own language.

As another avenue for making theatre a vital part of Honduran society, La Fragua places high emphasis on developing children's theatre. They stage "Historias Exactamente Así," from Rudyard Kipling's Just So Stories. The adapted story, "How the First Letter Was Written," conveys the importance of learning to read and write, a theme that strikes a particularly resonant chord in a country where approximately half the population is illiterate.

In 1989, Edward Burke, Ruth Shapiro and Pamela Yates directed the documentary *Teatro!* focusing on La Fragua; the film was seen on public television in the United States, bringing the group's work to the attention of English-speaking audiences.

According to Harley Erdman, the religious core of La Fragua's work, has led the troupe to forge a theatrical style that may be termed "neo-medieval," appropriate for a country with a feudal past, where the majority of its peasantry can neither read nor write. In this neo-medieval society, the church, gracing the central plazas of its far-flung towns and villages, remains for many the central focus of life. A major part of the work of *Teatro La Fragua* is focused on the development of a community tradition of theatrical expression. The model for this is taken from the cycle plays of medieval Europe. The members of the troupe are continually involved in workshops, which use as their base youth groups in the rural parishes.

La Fragua eclectically mixes the didacticism of Brecht's "epic theatre" with Grotowski's actor-centred "poor theatre" to create stylised pieces which rely heavily on gesture, pantomime, dance and music. Says Jack Warner: "Images matter much more to non-literate audiences than the written word." This emphasis on images comes through in all of La Fragua's work.

Although it places a primary emphasis on movement, the group maintains a healthy respect for text. The group prefers plays written in verse, accessible in a greater extent to rural audiences. "It's easier for our audience to understand verse," Barahona, an actor, explains. "It's the rhyme, I think. Prose is the hardest thing for people with no education."

CONSTRAINTS

To understand the difficulties La Fragua has faced, one must understand something of Honduras, which usually ranks among the hemisphere's poorest countries. The early years were difficult for a number of reasons. Support from the local community was not forthcoming. "A lot of people thought we were crazy, especially because of all the physical exercises we do," Barahona recalls. Questions that had to be answered included: How to find an audience in this country where lack of education and years of foreign domination have created a cultural vacuum? How to "forge" a Honduran cultural identity?

As Honduras was suffering from the repression, disappearances and cases of torture in the early 1980s, La Fragua's social commitment bothered some authorities. In one instance, during a performance inside a church, they learned that the building had been surrounded by armed troops who eventually dispersed, having made their point. In another case, an actor was detained for four days, for no apparent reason.

REFERENCES

This chapter is mostly constructed with excerpts from articles available at *Teatro La Fragua*'s Web site <http://homepages.infoseek.com/~fragua/fragua.html> and e-mail exchanges with Jack Warner.

Harley Erdman: *Taking It to the Streets—A People's Theatre Thrives in Honduras.*

Carlos M. Castro: *El Progreso, Yoro en Honduras: Clay and Hope.*

Jack Warner S. J.: *Plank a passion.*

John Fleming: *Forging a Honduran Identity: The People's Theatre of Teatro La Fragua.*

Teatro! documentary film on *Teatro La Fragua* produced in 1989 by Edward Burke, Ruth Shapiro and Pamela Yates.

VIDEO SEWA

(**1984**) India

....

BASIC FACTS

TITLE:	Video SEWA
COUNTRY:	India
MAIN FOCUS:	Women and community organisation
PLACE:	Ahmedabad
BENEFICIARIES:	Grassroots women
PARTNERS:	Self-Employed Women's Association (SEWA)
FUNDING:	USAID, John D. and Katherine T. MacArthur Foundation
MEDIA:	Video

SNAPSHOT

Leelabehn Datania's background is a unique preparation for at least one aspect of film-making: carrying the equipment. She had never switched on a light or watched television before she started to learn her new trade, but these things, along with the fact that she cannot read or write, have not deterred this remarkable former vegetable vendor from the slums of Ahmedabad from becoming one of the leading lights of a remarkable film-making [video-making] collective.

Video SEWA *is a collection of women from varied backgrounds who have produced over one hundred films [videos], thirty-nine of them complete and available to the public. Because of the extraordinary women who make them, the films [videos] have a tendency to teach you extraordinary things which you would not learn anywhere else. Where else but on the* Video SEWA *training video on smokeless stoves, would you find out that women who use ordinary kerosene stoves inhale as much smoke daily as they would if they smoked a packet of cigarettes?*

"I know all the symbols," says Leelabehn, who is about 50, fondly touching the buttons as she recites, "Fast-forward, rewind, pause ..." Since she could not take notes during the workshops, she committed everything to memory before making her first film [video], Manek Chowk. This is an impassioned documentary about the women like her who sell vegetables and

fruit on the pavement, and their harassment at the hands of the police.
SEWA used this film [video] *as part of the campaign for recognition of the*
vendors' status, and now all the vendors of Manek Chowk have licenses.

Leelabehn punches the Play button and the screen fills with green peas, red
tomatoes and purple eggplants. A woman raises her voice and shouts, "Vatana
Lo!" (Buy Peas!) A familiar sight, given new urgency on film [video] *as*
we are drawn into the problems and triumphs of vegetable sellers. . . .
—WRITTEN BY SOHAILA ABDULALI, A FREELANCE WRITER WITH A SPECIAL
INTEREST IN WOMEN AND DEVELOPMENT.

DESCRIPTION

In 1984, the late Martha Stuart, an international video communications consultant,
came to Gujarat from New York and held a
three-week video production workshop at
SEWA (Self-Employed Women's Association).
Twenty women, most of them illiterate, took
the workshop and began to make videos. The
group included women of all ages, some Muslims and some Hindus,
vendors from the market, as well as senior organisers from SEWA.

For three years they had no editing equipment or expertise, so
they shot their video productions in sequence. A second installment
of equipment and training, including editing equipment and training,
was introduced in 1987. A new training was held in 1994; 15 grassroots women were taught to handle the video equipment, in preparation for starting village-level communication centres in the rural
areas. By 1999 there were four permanent staff members at *Video
SEWA*, but many women take part as they are needed.

Video SEWA has been making simple, appropriate and modern
video technology available to SEWA members, SEWA organisers,
policymakers and planners at regional, national and international levels
and to the public in general. Videos on issues of the self-employed
are shot, edited and replayed by workers themselves.

The women who produced these tapes can conceptualise a script,
shoot, record sound, and edit, though many of them cannot find the
tape on the shelf when they need it, because they cannot read or write.

Screening videos has become an important part of workers' education classes at SEWA. They give new members the opportunity to see
and understand issues pertaining to their own and other trade groups.
Watching tapes helps new members feel a connection with a larger
movement. Video can aid by bridging barriers of distance, class and
culture so that people of very different backgrounds can grasp and

empathise with each other's concerns. Sometimes video messages can help to make understanding in situations where a face-to-face meeting would not.

The video team members are nonprofessionals who use sophisticated technology effectively. They can make a short documentary edited "in camera," as well as a broadcast-quality documentary, depending on the need.

Sometimes their target audience is one person (e.g., a local authority) and sometimes the target is hundreds of thousands. For the 1991 census *Video SEWA* produced *My Work, Myself*, a fifteen minute programme addressed to Gujarati women, which reached an audience of approximately a half-million women through cassette playbacks and was broadcast on state television.

SEWA videos are used for different purposes. Some, like *Manek Chowk*, was an advocacy tool that helped to raise consciousness. Others are training productions, such as the videos about oral rehydration therapy and building smokeless stoves.

The women record significant events at SEWA, as well as outside, and their news clips have been used nationally and internationally. They hold regular training courses and have an ambitious plan for communication centres all over India.

Video has become an important instrument for SEWA and has contributed to the strengthening of the organisation.

BACKGROUND & CONTEXT

The Self Employed Women's Association is a trade union formed in 1972 in the city of Ahmedabad in Gujarat, India. Under the auspices of TLA, SEWA began to fight for the rights of the majority of women workers in the city—those involved in the self-employed sector of the economy.

SEWA is both an organisation and a movement with each strengthening and carrying forward the other. As a Sangam or confluence of three movements, the labour movement, the cooperative movement and the women's movement, it especially enhances the SEWA movement. Gandhian policy is the inspiration for SEWA. The poor self-employed SEWA members organise for social change through the path of nonviolence and truth. SEWA organises women to enter the mainstream of the economy through the twin strategies of struggle and development. The struggle is against the many constraints and limitations imposed on them by society and the economy; while development activities strengthen their bargaining power and offer them new alternatives.

The union carries out the struggles on behalf of its members. These struggles are at the level of exploitation faced directly by the members; at the level of implementation of laws and dealings with officials; and at the level of policy and legislation formulation. First development takes the form of helping members to create their own cooperatives and groups. The cooperatives move towards early self-reliance, thereby offering an alternative, nonexploitative method of employment to the producer. Social security is another form of development, where the member is able to gain access to such social services and benefits as health care, childcare, savings and insurance.

Any self-employed woman in India can become a member of SEWA by paying a membership fee of 5 Rupees per year. Every three years the members elect their representatives to the Trade Council, who in turn elect the highest decision-making body, the twenty-five member Executive Committee. Four committed and experienced SEWA organisers are also elected to the Executive Committee. This body represents the major trades and occupations of SEWA members.

ASPECTS OF SOCIAL CHANGE

Over its more than fifteen years of existence *Video SEWA* has shown that even an apparently sophisticated technology, like video, can be tackled and used effectively by workers. And the power of the medium and its potential for organising the poor by raising awareness and bringing issues to the forefront is beyond doubt.

Besides having been successful in creating visibility for the issues of self-employed women and influencing policymakers, and other than contributing to empower new community leaders, *Video SEWA* has made important contributions as an internal training and orientation tool. Video activities have been instrumental in supporting SEWA's legal actions, explaining how to build smokeless stoves, how to treat diarrhea, or how to use SEWA's savings and credit services.

When organising in rural villages and urban slums, video productions can act as a magnet for people to meet and start discussions on the issues portrayed.

Thanks to *Video SEWA* a leader of vegetable vendors can produce a video, which directly affects her constituency and which, is an effective tool encouraging participation and enabling awareness building and empowerment.

After the initial training, the video team practised and experimented with the skills they had learned. SEWA union did not pressure the team to produce results immediately. Video producers were given functional literacy in twenty video words, which has enabled them to operate any piece of equipment. For the first three years they operated without editing equipment, the editing was done "in-camera" by shooting the sequences in order.

SEWA uses video to motivate, mobilise and train their existing members, to organise new trade groups and new members in the existing trade groups. Their productions are used for teaching, informing and orienting. *Video SEWA* members lead and facilitate group discussions when their programmes are used.

The instant playback feature of video is one of its most empowering qualities; it enables continuous participation and immediate feedback. This aspect allows those who are the subject and those who run the technology to collaborate as equals.

CONSTRAINTS

The effects of their new careers on the lives of *Video SEWA* staff are no less profound. They have had to deal with astonished husbands and neighbours who disapprove of their late hours. "I would get up at three o'clock every morning so I could do all the housework before I went to work, so then my husband could not complain," says Darshana P. "Still he used to get angry at me. Now that some of our videos have come on TV, he shows off to people about me: 'my wife uses a camera!' "

The group has enough challenges to keep complacency at bay. Technical know-how is at a premium, as it is hard to find people to help them. They recall a time in a remote village where they were shooting a scene when the portable tape deck stopped functioning. Afraid of lost time, money and opportunity, Darshana P. brought out a screwdriver, took everything apart, and put it back together in perfect working order.

They have had to face the prejudices of the local experts on video equipment, who refuse to hold workshops for illiterate people. They have dealt with the vagaries of the national television network, which uses their videotape sometimes, and censors them for bizarre reasons at other times.

REFERENCES

The power of video in the hands of grassroots women, by Sara Stuart and Renuka Bery.

"These women call the shots," by Sohaila Abdulali, in *People & the Planet* Magazine, Volume 4, N° 3, 1995. Web site <http://www.oneworld.org/patp/pap_profile.html>.

SEWA's Web site <http://www.soc.titech.ac.jp/icm/sewa.html>.

A profile of SEWA at <http://www.soc.titech.ac.jp/icm/makiko/sewaE6.html>.

Communication for Change Web site <www.c4c.org>.

KAYAPO VIDEO

BASIC FACTS

TITLE: Mekaron Opoi D'joi

COUNTRY: Brazil

FOCUS: Cultural identity, social, economic and political struggle for land and political rights

PLACE: Amazonian State of Pará

BENEFICIARIES: Kayapo indigenous community

FUNDING:

MEDIA: Video

SNAPSHOT

In 1985 we started the first project of indigenous media in Brazil, enabling members of the Kayapo to familiarise themselves with video technology. As the experience developed the Kayapo understood and explored the possibilities of a video camera. Initially they used it as a tool for preserving their traditional culture, their rituals, dances and songs, for future generations:

> *In the past, many photographers came here and took our pictures, but they never gave us anything in return. They never attempted to teach anything. Now we, the Kayapo, we are recording our rituals for our children.* — KREMORO, METUKTIRE-KAYAP CHIEF

> *We are learning the Brazilian culture, the things of the Brazilians, in order to hold our land and protect our own culture.* — MEGARON, LÍDER METUKTIRE-KAYAPO

> *My name is Noyremu. I speak for all the chiefs. I had a vision of our land as one united country. We have to protect our woods for our women, who guard our children in their arms. My words have been straight and honest. I will be expecting your answer.* — NOYREMU, CHEFE METUKTIRE-KAYAPO FROM KUBENKOKRE VILLAGE

Our children and grandchildren will be able to look at these images. Even the white people will watch the images of our culture, and that is how we will remain Kayapo.
—MEGARON, LÍDER METUKTIRE-KAYAPO

This project of indigenous media made us understand how the Kayapo reconstructed their cultural identity by combining elements of their traditional practices with appropriations from modern culture. The video camera adds itself to corporal painting. Whereas the televised and printed media illustrate the modernity of the Kayapo, they—masters of their own history and creators of their own representation—are leading us towards a strategy of pluricultural audio-visual representation, characterised by the diversity of voices.—EXCERPTS ARE FROM MONICA FROTA'S ARTICLE AND INTERVIEWS WITH THE KAYAPO.

DESCRIPTION

 In 1985 a young Brazilian photographer and filmmaker, Monica Frota and two anthropologist friends started the indigenous video initiative *Mekaron Opoi D'joi*, which means "he who creates images" in Gê language spoken by the Kayapo. During two years they worked with two groups of Kayapo: the Metuktire and the Mekrangnoty. Once the Kayapo had the video cameras in their own hands, initially they used it for the preservation of the cultural memory of the community, motivating the recording of their rituals.

Afterward, video was utilised to communicate among villages and its chiefs, enabling relatives to see each other after many years. "Our observation of the use that the Kayapo did of radio, lead us to suggest that the video project—originally limited to the Metuktire-Kayapo group—could be expanded to other Kayapo groups living in the southern land of the State of Pará, thus stimulating the exchanges of video messages among villages," recalls Monica Frota.

The Kayapo had been exchanging messages between villages and documenting their own rituals and dances. However, they soon started to exchange political speeches and to document their protests against the Brazilian state.

The political dimension of the project was a logical development. The Kayapo showed a high level of understanding of how media interacted with public opinion. For example, they used video to document the agreements signed with government representatives and their demonstrations in front of the Presidential Palace. Their image of "hi-tech" indians quickly gained the front pages of important journals, including a cover of *Time* magazine when they denounced the construction of a hydro-electric dam in Altamira that would flood their land.

The Kayapo became much more conscious of their own "culture" as an important component of their identity as a social group and a valuable political resource. Although in some cases they reinvented the content of that culture to appeal to nonindigenous allies.

Representation has played a fundamental part in the Kayapo political and ideological offensive. To understand the ways the Kayapo have used representation it is necessary to understand Kayapo cultural notions of representation, above all the idea that representation is creative of the reality it represents. For the Kayapo, the moral force of social solidarity or the power of strong leaders to compel consent and obedience is created and conveyed by symbolic performances, such as communal ceremonies or chiefly oratory, and imbued in the symbolic acts, images and verbal expressions of which they are constructed. Representation, in sum, is not merely mimetic, but creative and compelling; and the act of producing representations is itself imbued with the power to create and compel. It was thus extremely important to the Kayapo to acquire and learn to use potent contemporary technologies of representation such as video, and moreover to make sure that their video camerapeople were on prominent display on occasions like political demonstrations and ceremonies being staged for Brazilian or international audiences and documented by nonindigenous TV or video crews, according to Terence Turner

One important source of support was the increasingly positive evaluation of non-Western cultures, that was associated with anthropological teaching, and multicultural movements. Another source of support was the growing movement in defense of human rights. Most important of all was environmentalism, also according to Turner.

BACKGROUND & CONTEXT

The Kayapo indians are one of a group of indigenous Gê-speaking tribes that inhabit the Amazon River Basin of Brazil. Their territory in the State of Pará, made up of tropical rainforest, is mostly contained in six reserves that cover a combined area of some 100,000 square kilometres, about the size of Portugal. Their villages lie all along the upper tributaries of the Xingu River. As of 1993 there were about 14 Kayapo villages left, with a total population of approximately 5,000. The name Kayapo means "resembling apes"; it wasn't picked by the tribe itself, but rather given to them by the neighbouring indian tribes; most likely given because of a ritual they practice where the men perform dances in monkey masks.

Since gold was found in their land, the Kayapo's contact with the outside world has increased, leading to more dependence on consumer goods. This has led some of the Kayapo to abandon their fields, which have always been a central part of their traditions. In an effort to preserve their tribal culture the Kayapo also began, by 1985, to use portable video technology to record their rituals.

The Kayapo had already integrated into their daily activities various tools and practices from the modern surrounding societies, such as managing medical instruments for basic treatments. Young people, duly trained, had been acting as health promoters. They also used radio to communicate with other Kayapo groups living within the Xingu Indigenous Park.

Instead of just being subjects of documentary films, the Kayapo quickly understood the advantages of video technology as a communication tool for transforming their social and political reality. Thus, the appropriation of video tools by the Kayapo strengthens the notion that people can master their own history, as long as they can master their own representation in the media. The control of the Kayapo on the manner they are represented, as "hi-tech" Indians, is also a culturally valid statement on their identity, as they conceive their culture both from the point-of-view of permanence and transformation, according to Frota.

During the early 1990s the Kayapo used video for numerous social struggles. They successfully sought political and financial support—from nonindigenous public opinion, NGOs and governments, both in Brazil and abroad—to compel the Brazilian state to legally recognise their territory and their rights to control its resources. They have accomplished this by various means including: political lobbying of Brazilian governmental officials from the President down, demonstrations in major Brazilian cities, alliances with the environmental and human rights movements, and extensive coverage of Kayapo actions in print media and radio.

By maximising the use of audio-visual communication they have managed to project representations of themselves, as well as appeals for political and monetary aid, partly through videos shot and edited by them, which have gained wide attention from global audiences in the First World. The assimilation of Western ideas of culture through the interaction with the anthropologists and the use of modern technology like the camera gave the Kayapo a means of preserving their own culture in the face of opposition by the Brazilians. The Kayapo performed their "culture" as a strategy in their increasingly confident opposition to the state, according to Turner.

By the 1990s the Kayapo had obtained videos, radios, pharmacies, vehicles, drivers and mechanics, an airplane to patrol their land, and even their own missionaries.

In third world countries, video has been embraced in much the same manner as radio was for a previous generation, as a technology for training, information gathering, political agitation and cultural preservation. The appropriation of video has been seen as a key way for economically deprived communities to gain some measure of democratic control over information and communication sources now controlled either by the state or multinational corporations. The term "indigenous media" is generally employed to cover those aspects of visual representation over which "indigenous" people and others have direct control.

Media helped the Kayapo people to get their message out to the rest of the world. The Kayapo people turned video around into a tool to make the public see their side of the situation. "As an anthropologist I had become a cultural instrument of the people whose culture I was attempting to document. How could this be done by people who many of us view as underdeveloped and inferior? Have we not underestimated their intelligence?" states Turner.

The determination of the Kayapo to use video to document their own culture made them re-enact ancient dances and rituals that most of them had not seen. Thus video became the tool for perpetuating and reaffirming their cultural values. The technical potential of video enabled them to immediately see the recorded material, and to strengthen the identity and the cultural bonds within the community.

During their political struggle, the Kayapo recorded everything that was said, done, promised and agreed upon. The government wasn't able to deny any promises made because the Kayapo had a record on video. "From the moment they acquired video cameras of their own, the Kayapo have made a point of making video records of their major political confrontations with the national society," says Turner.

CONSTRAINTS

By bringing Western technology into their villages, the Kayapo are also allowing some of the western culture that they resist to infiltrate their own culture. The danger of losing their culture will increase for future generations who become more acclimated to western culture. Yet, it is not the introduction of video that started that process; the Kayapo had already been exposed to several other aspects of modern life. In reality, the video project contributed to reaffirm the cultural identity that was at risk.

Some Kayapo leaders sought to mask the extent of Kayapo involvement in ecologically destructive activities, such as mining and logging, to avoid alienating international support, particularly among environmental organisations. Issues of the "authenticity" of some aspects of Kayapo self-representation inevitably arise, and represent serious political problems for the Kayapo.

REFERENCES

Taking Aim e a Aldeia Global: A Apropriação Cultural e Política da Tecnologia de Vídeo pelos Índios Kayapos by Monica Frota, at
<http://www.mnemocine.com.br/osbrasisindigenas/frota.htm>.

Self-representation, Media and the Construction of a Local-global Continuum by the Kayapo of Brazil by Terence Turner. Web site
<http://www.uiowa.edu/~anthro/fulbright/abstracts/turner.html>.

Indigenous Media: Is it Hurting More Than It is Helping Their Cause? by Nafeesa T. Nichols. Web site <http://wcw.emory.edu/ECIT/vis99/nafeesa/indigenous2.htm>.

TV MAXAMBOMBA

1986 Brazil

BASIC FACTS

TITLE:	Projeto Vídeo Popular—TV Maxambomba
COUNTRY:	Brazil
MAIN FOCUS:	Community organisation
PLACE:	Nova Iguaçu (Rio de Janeiro)
BENEFICIARIES:	Grassroots communities
PARTNERS:	Centro de Criaçao de Imagem Popular (CECIP)
FUNDING:	NOVIB, World Health Organization (WHO), International Labor Organization (ILO), UNESCO, UNICEF, Catholic Agency for Overseas Development (CAFOD), Trocaire, Christian Aid, War or Want, Comité Catholique conte la Faim et pour le Développement, France (CCFD) and others
MEDIA:	Video

SNAPSHOT

"The land is generous: she gives back, multiplied many times, what you give her." Cristiano Guedes is a tall, strong peasant, the father of ten children, grandfather of 30 and great-grandfather of eleven. *"They all come here and take what I get from this land, working all by myself. When I first came here, there was nothing around. I liked the place and decided to cultivate it. I made a tent over there,"* his finger points somewhere among the banana trees, *"and lived for six months, clearing the land of thorns and weeds. I planted black beans, corn, manioc, bananas and some vegetables. When the land started to return what I gave her, I bought a small cart and started selling my things around. I have faithful customers, because I'm a good farmer. My stuff is better and cheaper than what you get in the supermarket in town.*

"Then one day a man came up, with a big gun, and said to me, 'Nigger, what are you doing? I don't want anyone planting here, you understand?'

He had a big gun. So I said, 'Yes sir, I won't plant any more, just these things I have here for myself.' Now, I said that but as soon as he would leave I'd start planting again. And so I stayed. This is my life, see?"

Now when Guedes' image appears on the television screen in sessions we hold at church grassroots communities, local residents' associations or schools, people listen attentively.

"Another man came up recently, saying he wanted to make a deal with me. My rights would be respected, he told me, 'but the others came much later; they have no rights.' They think that because I'm illiterate, I'm stupid. He wants to get rid of the others and then get me. So we all stick together, shoulder to shoulder, united like the fingers of a hand." The audience laughs as Guedes runs his fingers through his grey hair. "The man is illiterate, but his words make more sense than the president's," someone says. This testimony on video is part of the popular video project established in 1986 in Nova Iguaçu.— As described by Claudius Ceccon, Centre de Imagem de Criação Popular, Brazis (CECIP), executive secretary.

DESCRIPTION

TV Maxambomba is a project of CECIP. It was created by 1986 as the Popular Video Project, but changed its name to *TV Maxambomba* by 1990. Maxambomba was the name given to the slaves who once carried farm products to boats heading for the capital. Not only has the name changed, the project has also developed a larger presence in the region, a better understanding of social events, and an opening towards community participation in the communication process.

TV Maxambomba—as had *TV Viva* in Recife during the 1980s— spends more time in the streets, in public squares, schools and open markets, in every place where 200 to 300 people gather to watch the public screenings. Aided by a video projector and an old Volkswagen mini-bus—bought with support from NOVIB the main funding agency, *TV Maxambomba* increasingly became a people-driven project.

TV Maxambomba uses video to record the experiences of local people, appraise what is done by grassroots or community orga-nisations, and brings information necessary to the understanding of people's rights. It also produces videos on local culture and programmes for children.

Some of the projects are video documentaries on special issues. One of the most famous produced by CECIP is *The Debt Game*. A key scene shows two well-dressed couples dining at a fancy restau-rant; they laugh while eating sophisticated food and drinking French wine. One man notices a beggar nearby and asks the waiter to give him the leftovers of the meal. The beggar is delighted with the food and eats with his bare hands. The couples leave and the waiter brings the bill to the beggar, remarking with irony: "Why, didn't you participate at the banquet?"

Humour and short animated subjects helped *TV Maxambomba* clarify the meaning that was hidden by a jungle of figures, the complex issue of Latin America's international debt was conveyed to the general population. To facilitate discussion during and after the show, it was decided to split the one-hour video into five segments, so that after each segment a discussion could take place.

As many as 100 video documentaries have been produced since 1986. Various relevant social issues have been treated, such as democracy, citizen's rights, education, gender, environment, black culture, health and sexuality, as well as the production of programmes for children. *TV Maxambomba* also entertains people with mini-soap operas and parodies on political Brazilian personalities.

The subjects portrayed in video and discussed at the community level make a list that never ends. Examples such as the creation of a small factory to employ jobless youth; a health centre built by the community; a national women's meeting; and many other issues are ignored by the private television system.

Working in Nova Iguaçu is challenging every day. In September 1992 *TV Maxambomba*'s van, video projector, giant screen and sound equipment were stolen at gunpoint in the very centre of the city. Performances by artists and celebrities raised funds so the project could replace the stolen items, but above all they learned how much solidarity they were able to inspire.

In terms of funding, CECIP and its pet project *TV Maxambomba* have received support from a large number of international cooperation agencies, both from the United Nations sphere and from individual European countries.

BACKGROUND & CONTEXT

Per capita income in Brazil is around US$2,000 a year. However the real distribution of this income is extremely uneven. Only 36 percent of the population have jobs; 70 percent of people who work earn less than US$100 per month. The wealthiest 10 percent of Brazilians have 51 percent of the national income.

Television in Brazil reaches 80 percent of the population. More than 90 million people watch television, while the total number of printed newspapers doesn't reach five million copies a day. Commercial television in Brazil—e.g., Rede Globo, Rede Bandeirantes—is controlled by powerful political and economic interests, which do not provide the immense mass of the population with the information and participation necessary to lead to social changes in the direction of democracy.

A group of people concerned about the fact that no real changes in Brazil can happen without the active participation of the majority of the marginalised population decided to do something. They created CECIP, an independent, nonprofit association dedicated to producing educational materials using video and graphic media, aimed principally at an audience of poor sectors of the Brazilian society.

CECIP is located in Nova Iguaçu, an area on the outskirts of Rio de Janeiro. Nearly two million people live there. Fifty years ago it was an agricultural area, and its population was ten times smaller.

There is an almost absolute lack of infrastructure and services in the neighbourhoods farthest removed from the centre of the municipality: only 35 percent of the houses receive water. Nova Iguaçu has one of the highest rates of infant mortality in the country.

Nova Iguaçu is a microcosm of Brazil: crowded, unequipped urban centres and vast, empty, unproductive rural areas. It is one of the most violent regions, because of the combination of poverty, disease, unemployment, corruption and government neglect.

ASPECTS OF SOCIAL CHANGE

In *TV Maxambomba*'s videos people express themselves articulately, defending their points of view, saying things with all the flavour, irony and humour characteristic of them. This fact alone would justify the project for its political and humane contribution to the self-esteem of the people.

The open discussions on- and off-camera—in both cases prompted by the video production process—have certainly contributed to find concrete solutions to many of the problems faced by people in Nova Iguaçu.

Visual aids, such as video, have helped the large majority of those who had difficulty reading to participate in social and political life, as they had never done before.

Nurseries have been created in Nova Iguaçu to take care of babies while their mothers are working. People are more confident in the choices they make when its time to participate in elections or other democratic activities.

Overall, their capacity to develop a critical view of Brazilian society and to better organise to achieve their goals as a group, have notably improved. Video has been instrumental in contributing to strengthen local organisations.

TV Maxambomba videos increasingly involve the participation of the people for whom they are done. They are shown in the communities as an alternative source of information and communication. Watching the videos is a collective experience, considerably different from watching TV at home. The videos prompt people to discuss local problems. The examples of what was achieved in other places spark new ideas and show that is possible to take a situation in their own hands.

No off-camera voice explains the images on the screen or paraphrases what people want to say. Their productions have the eloquence of those who have been silenced for much too long and can tell their truth now.

The nature of delivery of media is of vital importance. The medium is the message. *TV Maxambomba's* street screenings bring neighbours together and build communities where presently none exist. In a country where less than four percent of the population read newspapers or magazines, video is a most effective means of communication.

TV Maxambomba avoids communicating with a popular audience adopting simplistic forms. People are accustomed to watching sophisticated productions shown by the big television networks, and demand creative efforts. The information is organised in such a way that it corresponds with the language, the experiences and the real problems faced in their everyday lives. Group discussion produces new knowledge, resulting from collective participation.

CONSTRAINTS

Materially speaking *TV Maxambomba* is an investment without return. The people have no means to pay for it; therefore it is supported through an incredible number of international and national cooperation agencies. But of course, the question of sustainability will always be there.

From an experiment of community-based screenings in public squares and schools, *TV Maxambomba* has grown into a production house respected for innovative techniques and high-quality video productions. Will this curtail the practice of keeping close contact with people at the grassroots? Will it change the participatory approach when producing videos on social reality?

REFERENCES

The information for this chapter was based on e-mail exchanges with Claudius Ceccon and:

Claudius S.P. Ceccon. "A Seed in Fertile Ground." *One World*, November 1987.

Claudius S.P. Ceccon. "Brazilian Centre Shows That Video is an Agent of Change." *Media Development*, April 1989.

Claudius S.P. Ceccon. "Learning to Reach the Grassroots." *One World*, May 1993.

Percq, Pascal. "Les Caméras des Favelas," *Editions de l'Atelier*, 1998. Pp. 157.

Mayer, Vicki. "For the People and By the People: *TV Maxambomba*'s Regeneration of Popular Cinema." *Latin American Popular Culture*. Spring (1998). Pp. 223–232.

CECIP Web site <http://metalab.unc.edu/cecip/max.htm>.

RADIO MARGARITAS

(1987) Mexico

BASIC FACTS

TITLE: Radio Margaritas "La Voz de la Frontera Sur"

COUNTRY: Mexico

FOCUS: Community development

PLACE: Las Margaritas, Chiapas

BENEFICIARIES: Tojolabal, Tzeltal, Tzotzil and Mam communities

FUNDING: INI

MEDIA: Radio

SNAPSHOT

Dear announcers of the well-liked XEPUR (Cherán, Michoacán): we send you this letter from the city of the big buildings that is New York. If you can be so kind with we the absents, we work in a Japanese restaurant and we don't forget the radio station's Cultivando Amigos *[XEPUR's write-in programme]. We are from here, from Cherán, and well we wanted to see if you can please us with a pretty pirecua [Purépecha song] of the band San Francisco. We Jorge and Héctor are neighbours of the station. Well, we hope you can dedicate this song to the following people. . . .*

The letter continues with a list of 22 names, starting with the sender's wife and children. Dedicating a song over the radio, a communication practice that might be trivial in other settings, acquires a novel significance in this context.

La Voz de los Purépechas (XEPUR in Cherán Michoacán) is part of the INI network of radio stations serving no less than twenty ethnic groups, along with La Voz de la Montaña (XEVZ in Tlapa, Guerrero), La Voz de la Mixteca (XETLA in Tlaxiaco, Oaxaca), La Voz de la Sierra Tarahumara (XETAR in Guachochi, Chihuaha), La Voz de los Mayas (XEPET in Peto, Yucatán), La Voz de la Sierra Juárez (XEGLO in Guelatao, Oaxaca), La Voz de los Cuatro Pueblos (XEJMN in Jesús María, Nayarit), La Voz de los Tres Rios (XEETCH in Etchojoa, Sonora), La Voz del Corazón de la Selva (XEXPUJ in

Xoujil, Campeche), La Voz de los Vientos (XECOPA in Copainala, Chiapas) La Voz de la Frontera Sur (XEVFS in Las Margaritas, Chiapas) and a handful more.

This chapter focuses on *Radio Margaritas* (La Voz de la Frontera Sur, XEVFS), but it relates to the entire INI network of rural radio stations; which constitutes an interesting experience of decentralised communication, locally adapted to the needs of the indigenous population. This is one of the rare projects where a government institution promotes and funds permanent structures of participatory media.

The INI network of stations is not the only one serving the indigenous population. There are also other independent FM stations at San Antonio Soctzil, Chemax, Yaxcopoil and Samahil, in the area of Yucatan, managed by a Mayan organisation La Voz de los Mayas. We won't deal with them in this chapter.

DESCRIPTION

Radio Margaritas (XEVFS) is located in Las Margaritas, Chiapas (southern México), a city that was seized by the Zapatista rebel army on January 1, 1994. This radio station is one of twenty AM stations created by the INI serving various indigenous communities across Mexico. *Radio Margaritas* has a transmitter of 4000 watts and airs at the 1030 frequency, covering an area of 20,000 square kilometres. Though it reaches as many as nine different ethnic groups, programming is done in the languages of Tojolabal, Tzeltal, Tzotzil and Mam. The station is equipped with a postproduction room, a recording studio, and the broadcasting studio where programmes are aired.

Programming includes nine categories: [1] music, [2] messages from the audience, [3] programmes on tradition, [4] newscasts, [5] programmes on development, [6] programmes for special segments of the audience, [7] programmes on government institutions and Mexican law, [8] vernacular language classes and language workshops, and [9] programmes produced by members of the audience.

At *Radio Margaritas*, the slots on health, agriculture, law, women, etc. are scheduled daily at dawn (30 minutes) and spread out during the afternoon (for a total of 60 minutes). Most of the rest is traditional, Mexican, Latin American and marimba music—as many as 95 songs per day. Community announcements are interspersed in between, which makes the music programmes among the most popular; *Radio Margaritas* programme *Aquí les mando mi saludo* receives about 30 letters per day. Unfortunately, newscasts are poor and irrelevant to the indigenous communities.

One of the most interesting features of INI network stations are the programmes produced with support from the station, but by members of the audience such as Alcoholics Anonymous. Audience participation in the programming has probably strengthened the bonds among Tojolabal villages. The broadcasting of *saludos* (greetings), regardless of the low informational value, indirectly furthers intervillage information flow by keeping open the channels of social networks.

XEVFS receives an average of 200 visitors per week, 130 speak the vernacular, the rest speak Spanish. And, of those speaking the vernacular, only 10 percent are women. Contrary to other INI network stations that double as phone booths and post offices, the audience of *Radio Margaritas* doesn't use the station for these purposes.

The Tojolabal Maya are the main audience of *Radio Margaritas*. They are among the most dispossessed people in Mexico. Other than their few material resources, they live with scarce knowledge about their history, their culture, and their current socio-economic conditions. Radio receivers have been a popular consumer good among Tojolabals for at least two decades. The oldest, commercial station in the area is Radio Comitán, which has broadcast since 1963 only in Spanish and is considered the station of the "rich" (the *ladinos*), as opposed to Margaritas, the station of the "poor" (Tojolabal). Evangelical radio stations have been transmitting from Central America since the fifties.

Rather than introducing a new communication technology, *Radio Margaritas*' impact has more to do with the station's format, its emphasis on traditional cultural forms, and its potential for new social uses. Under the influence of Protestant sects many Tojolabals choose not to speak their own language, prefer not to dress in their traditional costume, and are determined not to participate in traditional festivities. *Radio Margaritas* was established in the region with the specific purpose of counteracting the influence of such modernising forces.

BACKGROUND & CONTEXT

The INI was created in 1948 by the federal government to address the problems of indigenous people. The radio network is one of the numerous projects that this agency has sponsored. In the early 1990s it had 8 AM stations with an estimated audience of three million from more than twenty indigenous groups. With transmitters ranging from 500 to 10,000 watts, the area covered by these stations is as large as 30,000 square kilometres. In 1989 the average annual operating budget of an INI station was less than US$38,000.

The first station was established in Tlapa, Guerrero. By the year 2000, about twenty are functional. The stations combine Spanish and vernacular languages in their programming, which includes local ethnic music, news programmes, two or three hours daily of personal messages and institutional announcements, series on health, agricultural practices, etc.

The Zapatista movement brought extreme changes in the relationship between the State and the indigenous peoples—Mexico acknowledged that it is a multiethnic and multicultural country, where inequalities affecting the indigenous population have historical and structural bases. As a result of changing policies, the INI is currently encouraging a gradual process of transferring the network stations to indigenous communities.

ASPECTS OF SOCIAL CHANGE

Radio Margaritas has had a tremendous impact on the local flow of information. The author Lucila Vargas suggests that the station, "through its broadcasting in Tojolabal, may have had a democratising effect, especially for women, on the local community practices."

The broadcasting of *avisos* (announcements) in different vernaculars free-of-charge is probably the major immediate contribution by the INI stations to indigenous populations. This service has enabled villagers to expand and facilitate information flow in their social networks. Linked to the *avisos* service is the fact that the telecommunications infrastructure furnished by the stations can and has been used in relief efforts for natural disasters.

The efforts of *Radio Margaritas* to improve the living conditions of the Tojolabal range from the global endeavour to bolster the group's self-esteem to the individual programmes specifically aimed at remedying health and agricultural problems.

Radio Margaritas is perceived as the station of the "poor" and Radio Comitán is seen as the radio of the "rich." The station has helped to enhance and speed up interpersonal communication among villagers. It has also facilitated the spread of information from government agencies and indigenous organisations to the local level.

To the question "What do you use the radio for?" many villagers responded simply: "We use the radio for not walking. Before we couldn't find out what was going on in other villages, for example if there were problems or they were celebrating festivals, we didn't find out because we had no radio. ..." says a villager from Madero.

An audience study by Inés Cornejo Portugal and Silvia Luna (1991) which included a similar question, obtained the following results: out of 56 interviewees, 22 said the station provided companionship and distraction, 15 pointed out that XEVFS constitutes a feasible medium for fulfilling their telecommunication needs by allowing the audience to send messages, 13 claimed it helps them to find out about what goes on in other villages, and 2 indicated it offers a service to them by telling the time.

Most of the programming of *Radio Margaritas*, as of the other INI network stations is produced locally. The only programmes that have been regularly furnished to the stations are soap operas produced by the federal government's Radio Educación and news furnished by Notimex, the Mexican news agency.

Every station of the INI network has its own policy regarding multilingual broadcasting. At least half of the transmissions are done in vernacular languages, although often this percentage may include songs in Spanish. Also, announcers easily switch between Spanish and a vernacular when doing their work.

The INI network stations regularly produce a newscast with three segments (international, national and local); the news content varies greatly from station to station. The best newscast produced by the INI stations combine three elements: they rely on local reporting, they are the responsibility of a single producer, and they are not produced every day, leaving free time for the producer to do in-depth reporting at the community level.

CONSTRAINTS

A major drawback is the poor compensation given to the *mestizo* and indigenous staff. The best positions are occupied by *ladinos*, including the station manager—invariably a *ladino*. In her study, Lucila Vargas showed the existing "racist ideology at work" and the discrimination from *ladinos* towards the Maya.

The question of "status" among *Radio Margaritas* staff is also a problem. Only the General Manager of the station has visibility and is prominent, only his name is mentioned in XEVFS' broadcasts.

Visits of *Radio Margaritas* staffers to communities are not frequent; interviews with members of the indigenous population are mostly done at the station with the few visitors that can afford the cost of the trip from their community.

Nothing is more poorly done at *Radio Margaritas* than newscasts; sadly, the station relies only on newspapers for its news.

Multilingual broadcasting requires careful programme planning which depends on the availability of human resources. One of the few reasons why listeners turn the radio off or switch to another station, is when broadcasting in a vernacular language certain listeners are unable to understand.

XEVFS' selection of music constitutes a form of censorship, on the basis of aesthetic judgments made mostly by the *ladino* members of the staff.

One of the few open criticisms of *Radio Margaritas* by the Tojolabal audience refers to the station's failure to discuss the present oppression of the Tojolabal and to situate this oppression in its historical context.

REFERENCES

This chapter is entirely based on the book *Social Uses and Radio Practices: The Use of Participatory Radio by Ethnic Minorities in Mexico*, by Lucila Vargas. Westview Press, 1995, and e-mail exchanges with the author.

Additional information provided through e-mail by Inés Cornejo Portugal.

AAROHAN STREET THEATRE

(**1988**) Nepal

....

BASIC FACTS

TITLE:	Aarohan Street Theatre
COUNTRY:	Nepal
MAIN FOCUS:	Health, environment
PLACE:	Kathmandu
BENEFICIARIES:	Urban and rural poor
PARTNERS:	Network of 30 local drama groups
FUNDING:	Ashoka, UNICEF, Plan International, Save the Children, United Nations Fund for Population Activities (UNFPA), Centre for International Studies and Cooperation, Canada (CECI), World Conservation Union (IUCN), Nepal Leprosy Trust, etc.
MEDIA:	Street theatre

SNAPSHOT

A village in the remote tarai, the plains of Nepal, an area most affected by leprosy. Two thousand men, women and children gather to see a street magician performing. People here love to see magicians; but, they don't know yet that this time the magician is an actor, and that a play on the topic of leprosy is about to start.

People hate and hide leprosy. If we told them before that what they are about to see is a play about leprosy, nobody would be there. They don't want to talk and see anything about leprosy. So, we used the character of a street magician to inform about the early symptoms of leprosy, and to tell people don't hide it, go to the health post, treat it. It is a disease that can be cured if you go to the health post and take the full course of treatment. It is a disease like any other disease.

The street magician walks into the village and announces his magic tours. The audience gathers immediately, they love to see the magic. Even women, who normally are not allowed to come out in public, take their places. The magician starts with simple tricks interacting with the audience.

Slowly another character is introduced in the show and the dramatic conflict begins. The whole story builds up around the street magician, but the message is gradually delivered throughout the play. At the end the magician's assistant finds a symptom of leprosy on himself. He tells the magician and both go to the health post. The magician speaks to the audience ... don't hide it, go to the health post. No magic can cure it, only medicine can.

The play ends but the audience doesn't leave. They embrace a long discussion about their situation in relation to leprosy. They have now realised that it was a play, and the actors inquire about their reactions. Believe me, 20 to 30 people in every performance showed white or brown patches on their body (or other symptoms) and wanted to know whether it was leprosy or not. Most of the audience wanted to learn more about symptoms and treatments.

The villagers offered tea and snacks to thank us. People approached and asked if we would perform in their nearby village. They wanted to make the arrangements; they would provide the food for the day of performance. They wouldn't take a no for an answer.—COMMENTS SUNIL POKHAREL, AAROHAN STREET THEATRE DIRECTOR.

DESCRIPTION

In Nepalese language, *aarohan* means to climb, which is not surprising for a country that has a concentration of the highest mountains in the world. It also means to climb on a performing stage. *Aarohan Street Theatre* was established in 1982 though the street theatre activities really debuted in 1988. Before that, the group used to perform on-stage.

Their first street play about the problems of deaf people was called *Aawaj* (The Voice). A two-month workshop with deaf people was conducted; actors learned sign language, and some deaf people were invited in as actors. The first street play was performed in Dhulikhel, 30 kilometres outside of Kathmandu.

Many other plays were staged during the next years, among the most successful:

- *Parcha* (Pamphlet)—A play about voting rights and democracy, calling the audience to participate in the first parliamentary elections.
- *Sabadhan* (Be Aware)—A play about the relation of population and environment. It was performed over 350 times.
- *Kalchakra* (The Death Circle)—A play about sanitation, based on a famous folk story of Nepal.
- *Bishwas* (The Faith)—A play about leprosy with more than 450 performances so far.

Other topics include family planning, community development, health, poverty, forest conservation, drinking water, HIV/ AIDS, education and human rights. Plays about corruption and political issues are more successful in the cities; while in the villages the plays about environment and leprosy are much more appreciated. Performances are usually staged for very large groups; as many as 2,500 to 3,000 people in the cities, 600 to 1,200 in hilly villages and around 1,000 to 2,000 in the *tarai* (the plains).

Aarohan performs street plays in more than 55 out of 75 districts of Nepal. The drama group has been more active in certain districts such as Dhanusha (mid tarai of Nepal), Kathmandu (capital city), Sunsari (eastern part of Nepal), Jumla (far western district) and Kaski (midwestern district).

For sometime the group also conducted a programme called Aarohan Shanibar (Shanibar means Saturday), which was addressed to the intellectual audience of Kathmandu. Performances took place every Saturday followed by discussions with the audience. Apart from staging plays at the community level, *Aarohan Street Theatre* has at times staged for television.

From 1988 to 1991, Sunil Pokharel, the Director of Aarohan, got a grant from Ashoka organisation to develop the project "Social Use of Theatre." During three years, other than the regular theatre performances in Kathmandu he conducted drama workshops outside of the capital city, and developed his experiences in the social use of theatre. Aarohan also provided training to NGOs so these institutions would use theatre for creation of awareness and for community participation. During these training sessions, villagers were involved. By 1990 Aarohan started to work with street children, familiarising them with the medium of theatre.

Workshops have been conducted in more than 40 districts, training local people, youth groups, children and community members, who select the subjects, and participate in the preparation of the plays, and participate as actors during the performances. After the workshop, the new community group remains established.

BACKGROUND & CONTEXT

Nepalese people are hard to reach, especially outside of the Kathmandu Valley. Only about 70,000 receive television in the whole country, and the circulation of newspapers is insignificant. Only radio has been growing steadily over the years, since a handful of community radio stations started their operations.

By 1988 when *Aarohan Street Theatre* started, it was the time of the old political system, the Panchayat system. Freedom of expression was largely restricted and human rights were ignored. Only one political party existed, the one in power. The government was sensitive about theatre performances that would touch upon social and political issues. Instead of words, Aarohan used symbols and gestures during performances to refer to social and contemporary issues.

Street theatre was still a very new concept in Nepal, though it was already powerful in India. Still today, there is no drama school in Nepal. Sunil Pokharel studied psychology at Nepal's Tribhuvan University and later graduated in drama from the National School of Drama, New Delhi, India (1984–87), specialising in direction. He was the founder and still is the director of *Aarohan Street Theatre*.

ASPECTS OF SOCIAL CHANGE

Aarohan Street Theatre has generally contributed to creating awareness among the population on a number of issues relating to the social, cultural and political environment. Some of its interventions target long-term changes (health, education), and some have an immediate effect on behavioural change. Here are a few examples:

In the late 1990s the government prepared to pass a new law allowing the police to make arrests for 90 days without a warrant. Political leaders, writers and artists lead a movement against it. Aarohan and Sarwanam, another drama group, performed street plays in Kathmandu, with messages so powerful that they influenced public opinion and eventually the government refrained from passing the new law.

The training of eleven local groups from three districts in *tarai*, which are the most affected by leprosy, had enormous impact. More than one thousand performances of the play about leprosy were staged during 1999. Many people turned to the hospital for check-ups and treatment. The majority of patients asserted that they were prompted by the play.

Ten years before, Aarohan had conducted a two-month training workshop for street children and prepared a play with them based on their situation and stories. The street children performed in this play, which influenced people to change their perceptions about street children. For the last two years, these same street children have built an organisation named "Jagaran" ("creating awareness") to provide help to other street children. They set their goals, their programmes, and have an office.

With support from UNICEF, Aarohan conducted a communication project about sanitation in the mid *tarai* area of Nepal, inducing villagers to use latrines. Four local drama groups were trained to perform a play in the local language. After one year, the demand of subsidised materials to build latrines had multiplied five times in the areas where the play was performed.

Near 30 drama groups trained over the years by Aarohan are still active and they constitute an informal network with enormous potential for social change.

Three important traits are prominent in Aarohan Theatre's methodology: training of new groups, research for new plays and interaction, during and after performances.

The foremost feature is training, which provides the means to expand the communication activity over hundreds of villages that otherwise couldn't be reached. By regularly forming new groups and sharing the experience of the socially oriented street theatre, Aarohan multiplies the impact of this innovative grassroots communication tool. Groups of 10 to 30 participants are trained during approximately 10 days. All elements of drama technique and history of theatre are built-in, including physical exercises, games, yoga, and certainly all aspects concerning the research and development of a play. The training is generally addressed to youth groups that can concentrate on it fulltime.

In Nepal, there is a tradition of open-air performances. Folk dances and drama plays are performed with participation from the community; street plays are easily accepted by the people. Aarohan's research for new plays builds on that tradition; it is at the same time straightforward and innovative. Sunil Pokharel and his team travel to the selected areas and get a sense of both local concerns and whatever local music or dramatic customs exist. He writes a play incorporating the dramatic traditions and the contemporary social setting.

Last but not least, discussions taken place after every performance and are the keys to establishing if the communication process has been successful so far. This process ensures that the messages have been rightly conveyed.

CONSTRAINTS

Initially, when the Aarohan Theatre team used to perform by themselves in remote areas of the country, the differences of language, culture and lifestyle was a real problem. But with the strategy of training local people the difficulty was solved. Still, the challenge is to get the right style and content for each community. And the risk is always present that the play turns out to be superficial or too heavy on propaganda.

Sunil Pokharel considers that another important issue his drama group faces is that often the development agencies sponsoring a play would like to see numerous messages crammed into that single play. He thinks there should be a balance of entertainment and education in every play. On the other hand, some actors have a tendency to push too many entertainment elements during performances thus weakening the messages.

An important challenge is the follow-up after performances—which is seldom carried out because of limited resources. This should be done regularly by the concerned agencies, but isn't.

Logistic problems often hamper the quality of the work. Nepal is a hilly country and transportation is very limited to reach remote locations—which demands extra effort from actors forced to walk for many days. Moreover, restricted funds to pay actors have prompted them to leave and look for other jobs.

REFERENCES

Information for this chapter provided by Sunil Pokharel, Director of *Aarohan Street Theatre*.

CESPA

....

BASIC FACTS

TITLE:	Centre de services de production audiovisuelle (CESPA)
COUNTRY:	Mali
MAIN FOCUS:	Rural development
PLACE:	Bamako
BENEFICIARIES:	Rural Population
PARTNERS:	Ministry of Culture
FUNDING:	FAO, United Nations Development Programme (UNDP) (income-generating since 1994)
MEDIA:	Video

SNAPSHOT

In a country often so dry and austere, the garden in the middle of the *CESPA* building in Bamako looks like an oasis. Somehow it symbolises the very perspective of the project, which aims to create many oases of participatory communication in the remote, rural communities of Mali. The garden is protected by the square building surrounding it, inspired by old architectural models that make much sense considering the harmattan—the dusty winds that blow furiously during each year's winter. I've seen the skies turn dark and red, clouds of dust and sand suspended over the North of Burkina Faso, Mali, Niger, Chad and other Sub-Saharan countries. The desert is slowly but implacably extending towards the south. Every year a few metres are lost to the sand dunes that may be beautiful to see, but only signify death and poverty. The cattle perish, the few trees that are left disappear under sand, and the communities dismantle their villages and migrate. Not even the Niger River, which imposingly draws a gigantic 4,180 kilometres arch across four countries, seems to reverse the process. Though on second thought maybe its waters are the only barriers impeding a more destructive process. Mali still has a rather humid region south of Timbuktu, where the Niger River generously flows into the Faguibine, Do, Niangay, Débo and Korarou lakes, but even here the land is not willing to produce as much as needed.

Mali usually ranks at the very bottom of the list in the United Nations Human Development Report. Projects, such as *CESPA*, contribute so as to improve the economic situation of rural communities, by supporting the people to better organise for development and to develop innovations in agriculture. They can then make the best of the existing land, while fighting erosion and desertification, and protect the natural resources. The video tools utilised by *CESPA* aim to promote dialogue and develop new communication channels. If the objective were to only produce audio-visual training packages on technical issues, the long-term objective would be defeated. Only a communication process, which promotes community participation, can restore confidence in the future of rural Mali.

DESCRIPTION

By the end 1988 the government of Mali signed an agreement with FAO and UNDP to establish *CESPA*, a programme inspired in a series of experiences, methodologies and technical achievements that FAO had led in Latin America, namely *CESPAC* (Peru) and *PRODERITH* (Mexico). These had been successful in training, mobilising and organising the rural population with the use of audio-visual tools, specifically video.

The general objective of *CESPA* (Centre de Services de Production Audiovisuelle) was to expand the training of peasants in view of facilitating the implementation of the new government social development policies, based on the participation of rural communities. The project aims to use multimedia communication tools and innovative participatory approaches to facilitate the development of new techniques for agriculture, and for improving community management capability and increased participation.

Other than bringing in new knowledge and technical alternatives to enhance agricultural production, *CESPA* aims to research, gather and disseminate traditional knowledge, local development initiatives, and cultural values of rural communities. Video is perceived as a means to facilitate these exchanges and establish a fruitful dialogue between the traditional ways and the modern improvements.

During the first three years of the project, considered as a pilot phase, *CESPA* concentrated on developing its own institutional capacity to use video for training and production of educational packages. The main concern was to adapt to the context of Mali the "visual pedagogy" principles developed by Manuel Calvelo and his followers in various rural development projects in Latin America. By the end of this period, 30 "audio-visual pedagogues" had already been trained and integrated into the project. The emphasis given during the training was on participatory communication.

By 1993 a second phase started with *CESPA* becoming an autonomous entity, independent from the government and from official funding sources. The new status links the life of *CESPA* to its capacity to generate its own financial resources, thus becoming an income-generating communication service provider. To adapt to its new role, *CESPA* started by upgrading its video equipment. This change was meant to capture the regional market of video documentary production destined for television channels. *CESPA* also expanded its technical capability to other areas of multimedia communication, including audiocassettes, posters and photography. UNDP funding decreased as *CESPA* generated its own funds by producing institutional videos for NGOs and international cooperation agencies.

The production of "pedagogic packages" for training on technical issues remained as a key activity of *CESPA* over the years. Research at the community level, dialogue with peasants, assessment on cultural and traditional practices, as well as the input from specialised technical staff, make up the substance of the video productions. Post-production, however, is mostly done in Bamako at the *CESPA* centre, with little participation from rural communities. A rough editing is usually tested in rural areas before the training package is released.

As of 1999, 22 pedagogic packages had been completed, using various languages of Mali. The main topics include health, agriculture, environment, livestock and management. In addition *CESPA* produced 116 motivational videos and spots, 23 cultural programmes on local traditions, 20 institutional videos, as well as theatre sketches and newsmagazines for television.

BACKGROUND & CONTEXT

In Mali, 80 percent of the population lives in rural areas. Half of the country extends over the Sahara and the other half is mostly part of the Sahel. Regular rains benefit only six percent of the total territory in the most southern part of the country. The six million rural dwellers of Mali live mainly on agricultural and livestock production. This rural population is composed of at least ten major different ethnic groups, largely Muslim.

The whole country depends on seasonal rains; therefore it has always been very vulnerable to the changes in weather conditions. Natural disasters have haunted the country in the last decades of the past century: the long drought of the 1970s resulted in a mounting dependence on external financial support.

Though several governments since the 1960s had proclaimed that their priority would be rural development, they all failed to achieve any progress. Strong military regimes, as well as democratic governments, did not succeed in organising the rural population in the perspective of developing agriculture. As in other countries, governments in Mali fell short of mobilising community participation.

Only a few significant efforts made by the socialist government in the 1960s survived political changes: a handful of community radio stations and rural training centres. When *CESPA* was created, it took advantage of the experience of various institutions and communities in working within the framework of participatory communication.

ASPECTS OF SOCIAL CHANGE

CESPA has trained a new generation of rural development communicators. The core group of 16 staff members is—according to FAO reports—conversant in all stages of the process: research, concept development, scriptwriting, production, post-production and utilisation of the pedagogic packages at the community level. Another group of 248 (by the end of 1998), from various institutions working in rural development is now skilled in the use of the methodology for training peasants.

Several examples of social change induced by *CESPA* are quoted in the FAO case study report. For instance, the relationship between peasants and the rural banks that lent them funds was tense and characterised by a lack of mutual understanding and knowledge from both perspectives. A pedagogic package on credit is said to have diminished the gap by explaining the mechanism of banking procedures.

CESPA has become a reference of communication policy for rural development. It is said that no other institution in Mali knows so well the problems of rural development and the potential of local participation. Moreover, because of its philosophy of development and its methodology of intervention in rural areas *CESPA* is considered one-of-its-kind not only in Mali but in the West Africa subregion.

The language of development in Mali has changed under the influence of *CESPA* activities. The jargon of "communication for development" is not unusual in official speeches, institutional reports or seminars. Government institutions have created posts of "communication advisers." The concepts of participatory development have extended its roots within the development society of Mali.

Although it may not reflect on social change, the success of *CESPA* as a company that generates revenues to sustain itself is considered by FAO an important accomplishment. Since 1994 the revenue of *CESPA* grew steadily and UNDP funding decreased proportionally. NGOs and international cooperation agencies contracted services from *CESPA* to produce institutional and informational materials.

The methodology to produce training materials and "pedagogic packages" in *CESPA* remains similar to the one implemented in similar programmes in Latin America. The first stage is research at the community level, to define the general and specific topics that will be developed for training, and to absorb the community perception on each topic. Local knowledge is then contrasted with specialists in view of enriching both perspectives. The research team lends special attention to cultural patterns and values, as well as to the problems that are prevalent in the rural area where the training packages will be applied.

At the next stage, the pedagogic concept is developed, contrasting the information on local knowledge and practices, the technicians' experience and facts, and the prevailing cultural codes. Only then is a script developed. The video recording takes place in a rural setting, with the participation of selected peasants as "actors." The post-production process includes the development of supporting materials such as audiocassettes and printed manuals for both trainers and participants. These additions were incorporated by 1998.

Ideally, in the last stage of production, the rough editing of the video is presented to the technical staff for review, and also tested at the community level for reactions from peasants. Subsequently the final cut or editing is done and the video and pedagogic package is then available for training activities.

Training itself is a participatory process, with discussions and practical exercises being central components. The process starts with the agreement with community representatives on contents and logistics. The training is done at the village level and the trainers remain in the rural setting for several days, thus interacting with peasants even outside of the formal sessions. *CESPA* also trains development workers of cooperation agencies and NGOs interested in using the "pedagogic packages."

CONSTRAINTS

In 1993 as *CESPA* became an income generating initiative, its original orientation certainly changed in spite of the best intentions to continue providing support to rural communities. Only the continued technical assistance from FAO, while it lasted, kept *CESPA* closer to its original objectives.

The upgrading of video equipment, for example, took this tool out of the hands of those using it at the community level for training purposes. Clearly, the process became less important than the product, and the dependency on external contracts grew, leaving in the shadow community-based work. *CESPA* might have been very successful in becoming a self-sustained institution (though UNDP funding was still necessary), but it increasingly distanced itself from participatory development.

Though the production of "pedagogic packages" remained important, the process only involved community participation at very early stages of research and collection of information. The production and post-production processes are in the hands of professionals that often do not have enough contact with rural communities.

REFERENCES

The author visited Bamako by 1993, at the initial stages of *CESPA*.

"Le Centre de services de production audiovisuelle (*CESPA*)," a case study by N'golo Coulibaly. FAO, Rome 1999.

COMMUNITY AUDIO TOWERS

(1989) Philippines

BASIC FACTS

TITLE:	Community Audio Towers
COUNTRY:	Philippines
MAIN FOCUS:	Community development
PLACE:	Tacunan, Maragusan, Floryda (CATs), and Nagbukel, Pinagdanglayan Dolores, Concordia, Tulungatong Development and Support Communication (DSC projects)
BENEFICIARIES:	Around 4,000 in each community
FUNDING:	FAO/UNDP, UNICEF, Department of Agriculture
MEDIA:	Cone speakers mounted on towers

SNAPSHOT

Very early in the morning, just as the sun rises, the music from *Tacunan Audio Tower* filtrates with an echo through trees and plantations, providing company to peasants as they work over their crops.

From time to time an announcement can be heard between two songs: the teacher will not be at the school today, the lost *carabao* of Mr. Ostong has been found wandering near the main road, next Thursday is immunisation day at the health centre, station manager Jacinto "Jake" Sarco is calling for a meeting of all members of the Community Media Council tomorrow evening. ...

Six all-weather cone speakers, mounted on top of a mast, send the sounds through the air as far as 3 miles. A different person representing a social sector prepares each programme and airs it, thus becoming a voluntary broadcaster and earning additional respect from the *barangay* (community). They are all part of the Community Media Council (CMC) meeting every second Thursday of the month to discuss issues that are relevant to the community and prepare programming.

The CMC is meeting today, even if the station hasn't been airing its programmes for the last two months, since the Chinese amplifier broke down. The CMC is discussing the difficulties to get spare parts for the amplifier. The missing parts can't be tracked down in Davao City, not even in Manila. Nonetheless, the community has not just sat and waited.

During the months off-the-air, a new and higher mast has been built and placed on a better spot. Before, the station was housed in a small bamboo hut, now it has its own concrete building just beside the *barangay* hall. Plans to install a transmitter and thus become a radio station will not mean discarding the public address system: "Once the loudspeakers start talking, people turn into a captive audience," asserts Jake Sarco.

DESCRIPTION

In the late 1980s, FAO started the CATs (*Community Audio Towers*), and UNICEF, the ComPAS (Community Public Address System), in the late 1990s. Both are similar communication strategies based on community audio towers. Two microphones jacked into a Karaoke playback system connected to 20-watt (FAO) or 180-watt (UNICEF) amplifiers and four or six cone speakers mounted on small towers... that is the recipe for CATs and ComPAS. The difference between both development communication approaches is mainly in the process. The FAO project puts emphasis on community preparation through a diagnosis of the social and economic situation, and the establishment of a CMC, which democratically represents the various sectors of the *barangay*.

At the heart of both projects is the support for rural communities to use this *narrowcasting* technology for community communication and social development. The local communication system aims to raise and discuss local issues and mobilise community members on children's rights, health and nutrition, child protection, education, livelihood, agriculture, environment, religion, politics and social events that matter to them. Community leaders representing all sectors are trained in community broadcasting, interviewing, radio announcing, scriptwriting, radio jingles, drama and other radio production formats. Sectors that are represented at the Community Media Council may vary from one place to another, but generally include from its inception a very equilibrated representation from farmers, women, elderly people, youth, health workers, educators, local authorities, religious leaders and so on. It is important to note that women make up half of the representatives at the CMC, and are very active as broadcasters.

The *Tacunan Audio Towers* started its operations on August 16, 1992. Tacunan is a small *barangay* in Tugbok City, about a one hour drive from Davao City in Mindanao. Other sites followed: Maragusan (April 8, 1995) in Davao del Norte, and Floryda (February 18, 1998) in Kapalong. Maragusan became a radio station in November 1998, when a small 20-watt transmitter was installed with the help of the *Tambuli* project. Other sites feature Development Communication Support activities established by the FAO/UNDP PCARRD project, though not always centred around a *Community Audio Tower:* Nagbukel in Isabela, Pinagdanglayan Dolores in Quezon, Concordia in Guimaras, and Tulungatong in Zamboanga City.

So far, Tacunan has been the most successful experience, and according to the community, the station has been instrumental in all the development the *barangay* has lived through during the 1990s. The population has increasingly acquired a high level of consciousness concerning its collective needs and the potential solutions. Through very well-established programming, all the most relevant subjects are discussed week-by-week.

From six to seven in the evenings, as families gather at home after a long journey, *Tacunan Audio Tower* delivers some food for thought on topics of interest for the community: health (Monday), farming (Tuesday), women rights (Wednesday), *barangay* council (Thursday), cooperatives (Friday), community (Saturday), and religious programmes (Sunday). Programmes such as *Ayaw'g ingna Tigulang na Ko* (Don't Tell Them I'm Old), *Bahandi sa Kinabuhi* (Wealth of Life), *Agrikulturang Pangmasa* (People's Agriculture), *Ikaw, Ako usa ka batan-on* (You and Me, the Youth), and *Ang Kababayen-an Karon* (The Women of Today). By 1999 a new slot on children's rights was added with support from UNICEF.

BACKGROUND & CONTEXT

The Philippines has experienced a rapid growth of mass media over the last two decades due to the technology revolution, more liberal economic policies, the return of democracy, deregulation of telecommunications and decentralisation. The result is the growth of provincial media, mainly commercial radio and television. According to recent statistics, there are 328 AM and 317 FM radio stations covering 90 percent of the population through 25 million radio receivers. Even television is growing due to expanded rural electrification; about 128 stations are currently operating. None of these seems to have substantially modified the communication and information landscape in terms of real access to media by communities.

The very sharp characterisation of media by Louie N. Tabing, the coordinator of the *Tambuli* project, is as valid today as it was twenty years ago: "Profit, Propaganda, Power and Privilege" are the central motivations of mass media in the Philippines. The "PPPP" acronym still reigns over the vast majority of the population, except in those communities where small but important projects like *Tambuli* or CATs have been set. They are there only to make a difference.

The idea of community audio towers has been tried before to support social and economic development in poor and marginalised rural communities in third world countries. In Ethiopia, Thailand or Mozambique—just to mention a few cases during the 1980s—community audio towers have served the purpose of stimulating community organisation around issues of social development and the strengthening of cultural identity.

ASPECTS OF SOCIAL CHANGE

"Our condition has improved in seven years, since the *Community Audio Tower* was set up in Tacunan. We now have a road we didn't have before, we have electricity, we have water. ..." It might or might not be a direct result of the *Community Audio Tower*, but certainly the generalised perception is that the CAT brought a wealth of economic and social development to Tacunan. People do not even hesitate when been asked about the benefits of the communication system. It may seem a little thing compared to a radio station, but certainly those three or four villages in Tacunan or Maragusan have learned to value the impact of the rural communication tool that was put in their hands.

It is no surprise that Maragusan took a step forward and requested support to upgrade the *Community Audio Tower*—which in fact was set up with training and support from Tacunan—to a radio station. A transmitter makes the difference technology wise, but the contents and operational framework remain the same.

In 1993, one year after the Tacunan CAT started its operation, the first challenge in the problem tree was achieved: water. The next big leap forward was electricity in 1994. That was not all; according to the villagers the *Community Audio Tower* was instrumental in addressing agricultural problems, such as the control of banana pests and the drive against the rhinoceros beetle that affects coconut trees. The Maragusan CAT played an important role in the establishment of several agricultural ventures such as: the 3,000-hectare durian production project, and the tilapia hatchery which serves as income generating activity for DXLM broadcasters.

By 1994 the Tacunan community had drafted a five-year development plan with help from the Development Support Communication Project (FAO/UNDP). The plan was the output of a training workshop on Goal Oriented Project Planning.

The set-up of a *Community Audio Tower* involves a thorough process of training and analysis of community problems and solutions. This methodology enables the community to start their media activities with full knowledge about the causes of underdevelopment and the potential for resolving and overcoming problems. Before the cone speakers begin to air their messages, a group of trainees from the community participate in training that includes the development of a "problem tree," collectively drawn on a board and later translated into a plan that captures in detail the nature of the obstacles preventing the community from developing. In Tacunan, for example, the lack of water was identified as one of the main problems in the community.

Next to the problem tree, a "tree of life" will be updated every year, incorporating those objectives of development that have been met. The tree of life should blossom and grow as the community finds its way in social, cultural and economic development. These exercises are no doubt the basis of participation and the strength of the CATs experience.

CONSTRAINTS

The main obstacle is the limited reach of the sound. By 1999 Tacunan built a higher tower and placed it on a new spot to enhance its reach throughout the neighbouring communities. The Chinese 20-watt amplifier broke down and couldn't be repaired for several months.

REFERENCES

Field visits to Tacunan and Maragusan (Compostela Valley, Davao del Norte in Mindanao) and meetings with Jacinto Sarco manager of Tacunan CAT, with Mayor Gerome Lamparas Jr. and Loreta Gonzalez, President of the CMC of Maragusan, as well as the interviews with Frank E. Endaya, Project Manager in charge of development communication at the Department of Agriculture Regional Field Unit XI, and Louie N. Tabing, *Tambuli* project director, provided the basic information for this chapter.

The FAO Web site <http://www.fao.org/sd/CDdirect/CDan0004.htm> posts "A Farmer First Approach to Agricultural Communication: a Case Study from the Philippines" by Lydda Gaviria, among other interesting articles.

The DSC Newslink, a quarterly publication of the FAO/UNDP Development Support Communication Project (PHI/87/006) in Los Baños, Laguna, has printed several articles on the Tacunan experience.

UHAY, a quarterly publication of the Department of Agriculture, Region XI; and *Monitor*, published by Southern Mindanao Agriculture Resources Research and Development Consortium (SMARRDEC) have also printed several short pieces on Maragusan and Tacunan *Community Audio Towers*.

Information on UNICEF ComPAS project provided by Teresa Stuart, UNICEF Communication Officer in Manila.

KOTHMALE
COMMUNITY RADIO

....

BASIC FACTS

TITLE:	Kothmale Community Radio Internet Project (KCRIP)
COUNTRY:	Sri Lanka
FOCUS:	Community Development
PLACE:	Kothmale
BENEFICIARIES:	Population of about 350,000
PARTNERS:	University of Colombo
FUNDING:	UNESCO, Sri Lanka Broadcasting Corporation (SLBC)
MEDIA:	Radio & Internet

SNAPSHOT

As Sriyapali prepares to interview one of the stations' avid contributors, I take a look around the station and notice that it is Kothmale FM at its best.

In the staff room two local music teachers, Nilmany and Wijisinghe, are practising songs that they will record later in the day. They are both blind musicians who teach at a local school. Another six young girls from the nearest village are singing local folk songs. In the computer room Kosala is creating an animation piece for a Sri Lankan film company while on the other computer Buddhika—an enthusiastic regular who had never used a computer before he came to the centre—is chatting with someone in India while simultaneously designing his personal Web page. His e-mail inbox is filled with letters from newly made friends around-the-world.

Some studio equipment is being moved to the van: tonight there will be a live broadcast from the Wickramasinge College, where the students will perform a musical show.

The station is in its 11th year now and has obviously become an integral part of the community. Everyone in the area knows about Kothmale FM. I can travel 15 kilometres away, and when I ask people about Kothmale FM I always meet with a positive response. Many people will tell me that their sister or uncle or friend sang a song or spoke on a programme. They will tell me their favourite programme and announcer.

The interview begins in the studio. ... "My name is S.B.K. Wijarathna. My village is Dekekanawa Nawalapitya. I sell lottery tickets. I am 52 years old, and I am married with three daughters. ... I sent my first letter to the station 3 years ago; it was aired the next day. The feeling I had on that day was very joyful. Since then I write to this station, and I contribute with poems and historical stories and send facts and information ... I think this station is a very friendly broadcasting service; it gives opportunities to new singers and artists. Our listeners enjoy the songs very much."

S.B.K. goes on to talk about his own programme where he plays and discusses old film songs. "Athithayan gee mal dothak" is proving to be one of the most popular programmes to-date.—WRITTEN BY TANYA NOTLEY, AN AUSTRALIAN VOLUNTEER AT KOTHMALE COMMUNITY RADIO.

DESCRIPTION

Much poverty in Asia is concentrated in rural areas that have very limited access to information. New technologies can help alleviate poverty by providing access to development-related data; a combination of traditional community radio and the Internet helps optimise the information services in rural areas.

The Internet is increasingly used for broadcasting radio programmes. The *Kothmale Community Radio* Internet Project (KCRIP) in Sri Lanka, which aims at assessing the potential benefits of new communication technologies to remote areas, is implemented by UNESCO in collaboration with the Sri Lanka Broadcasting Corporation, the Ministry of Posts, Telecommunications and the Media, the Sri Lanka Telecommunication Regulatory Commission, and the University of Colombo.

Kothmale is located in the central part of Sri Lanka. It takes a three hour bus ride from Colombo to reach the location. *Kothmale Community Radio* serves an area of 25 kilometres radius, which includes a number of rural towns such as Gampola, Nawalapitiya and Thispane, with an estimated population of more than 350,000.

The project uses community radio as an interface between the Internet and rural communities. While UNESCO provided computer equipment and training, the Sri Lankan government, through its Telecommunication Regulatory Commission, provided the Internet connectivity to the community radio station through a dedicated 64 kilobyte line.

Three computer access points were established at different community centres. Due to a lack of landlines a microwave radio line has been established between Nawalapitiya and the Kothmale station and a Remote Access Server has been set up to provide a dial up connection to the Gampola centre and other future access points.

The telecommunication costs for dedicated Internet access at the community radio station and the other two access point are absorbed by the government for a two year period within which community radio will have to develop an income generating strategy to sustain the facility. This would mean that the community radio station would have to generate additional income of US$1,000 per month.

The project has incorporated computer classes and Web design with the assistance of Institute of Computer Technology (ICT), a volunteer worker from Australian Volunteers International (AVI) and radio staff at Kothmale FM. A Web design team has built the *Kothmale Community Radio* Web site in three languages; it will also include a live stream of the radio broadcasts.

There are three basic features of this project which combine new information technologies with the conventional radio medium:

- **Radio programme to "Radio Browse" the Internet:** Broadcasts a daily one-hour radio programme, in which community broadcasters interpret information from selective Internet Web sites. Listeners direct queries to the radio station to find specific information, which is returned in local language for those who do not understand English.
- **Community radio functions as a mini Internet Service Provider:** The community radio station has provided two free of charge Internet access points at Gampola and Nawalapitiya community libraries. Access points are also used as a direct link to the radio station to produce and air live programmes.
- **Community database development:** Kothmale develops its own computer database deriving information from the Internet that is often requested.

BACKGROUND & CONTEXT

Kothmale Community Radio began broadcasting in February 1989. At the time Mahaweli Authority (a governmental development body operating in the central region) had relocated more than 2,900 families for Sri Lankas' second largest damming project. Mahaweli Authority set up the station with the objective of giving information to people who had been relocated. Many people in the region lost their crops and farm land. The station was also used to provide information about self-employment and health.

By February 1991 the station was on-the-air only three days per week with three hours of transmission per day. In 1999 the station moved to its larger, current location in Mawathura and broadcast time extended to 8 hours per day. The morning broadcast was commercialised so the station would collect approximately 75 percent of its operational costs from commercial revenue. Financial management remained with the Sri Lanka Broadcasting Corporation.

By 1998 UNESCO provided US$50,000 to start the implementation of the Internet component. Thus the *Kothmale Community Radio Internet Project* (KCRIP) was born. KCRIP has aspired to provide extensive Internet access to remote and rural regions of Sri Lanka using only a few computers and a regional radio broadcast.

The station is located at the top of a mountain in the central region of Sri Lanka. The area is mostly rural with small farms, rice paddies and tea plantations scattered between dense rich green forest and small friendly villages.

ASPECTS OF SOCIAL CHANGE

Students of the access centres are designing their own Web sites, using the Internet for research and school projects, and obtaining information regarding educational grants and institutions.

Other members of the community have been able to directly access information regarding health, human rights, agriculture and other issues affecting their daily lives. Australian volunteer Tanya Notley, provides some examples:

> One man came here recently extremely upset and confused as a local doctor had diagnosed his son with Hirchsprung disease. He was able to get information and advice from experts in other countries. A local schoolteacher was able to interact with teachers around the world about short-wave radio teaching and apply this knowledge to a very remote school, which operates without electricity. A local farmer who hoped to expand his market by raising geese was delighted with the housing diagrams and feeding information he was able to gather from the Internet.

A campaign to increase blood donations, an exhibition for people interested in self-employment, a public health campaign aimed at preventing a cow disease epidemic, a fundraiser for local hospitals, and a campaign to donate books for the local library ... are some of the ventures supported through Kothmale radio.

Information on human rights has benefited from the convenient access to information on the Internet. Madhushini Nilmabandara and Nilma Samrakool do a weekly programme on human rights; the University of Colombo's Human Rights Centre funds their programme: "People were not aware of their human rights. So we give them information ... how to take action to protect it. Now we have set up human rights clubs in schools and do programmes with them (on radio)," she said. The local school students come to the station to produce programmes. They perform dramas about children's rights and women's rights and discuss issues related to war in Sri Lanka.

The project works in two ways. It allows for direct Internet access, mostly used by young people, and indirect access where listeners of Kothmale FM Radio are able to write in questions or provide topics for the radio station to broadcast. Trained volunteers research and gather information from the Internet and CD ROM's, and translate the information into Sinhala and Tamil. All but three of the weekly broadcasts are in the Sinhala language; the area has an ethnic breakdown of around 70 percent Sinhala. There are also large Tamil and Muslim communities. In January 1999, the station included Tamil broadcasts in its weekly programmes.

The questions are responded to within various radio programmes including: human rights, women's programmes, children's programmes, health programmes and international news programmes. Gradually all the data will be available for other community radio stations and citizens via the Web site. Furthermore, the station intends to broadcast online so to be utilised by other community radio stations throughout Sri Lanka.

A Friday evening programme is particularly popular. A local lawyer, hosts it and volunteers do the research during the week. His topics have included international cultural belief systems and practices, world leaders and social movements, law and change, scientific masters throughout history.

The staff and volunteers frequently visit the communities to do field recordings and live broadcasts. This direct communication is important, as many people are geographically remote. The station is able to bridge the communication gap by interacting with the community through live and recorded broadcasts. Music is a very important aspect of Sri Lankan culture; each day traditional songs are aired. Buddhist prayer is also broadcast every evening and on full moon Poya days.

Letters to the station average 50 per day (more on weekends). These letters include poetry, drama, history, songs and local event information. Members of the Kothmale FM listeners club deliver news summaries each day.

CONSTRAINTS

The initial Kothmale radio project, which started in 1989, seems to be the one still addressing the problems of the rural population. The Internet component that was added by 1998 is benefiting mainly those that either own a telephone line and can call in, or those that speak English and can browse the Web by themselves.

The domination of the Web by the English-language is a barrier to access, though at KCRIP they have enlisted bilingual speakers from the community to help programme producers. Doctors, lawyers and teachers get involved in the programme; they extract information from the Internet and interpret it for the listeners.

REFERENCES

This chapter was largely drafted on information provided through e-mail by Tanya Notley, Australian volunteer working on the Kothmale project.

"Villages Get Wired on Air," by Kalinga Seneviratne (Inter Press Service).

"Radio Brings a Revolution in Communication," by Anthony David, in *UNESCO Sources*, July–August 1999.

The Kothmale Web site is <www.kirana.lk>.

TEATRO TRONO

BASIC FACTS

TITLE: Teatro Trono y Comunidad de Productores de Arte (COMPA)

COUNTRY: Bolivia

MAIN FOCUS: Drugs, environment, gender issues

PLACE: El Alto, near La Paz

BENEFICIARIES: Street children in El Alto

PARTNERS: Cinemateca Boliviana

FUNDING: Caritas Nederland, Stichting Kinderpostzegels Netherlands (SKN), Terre des Hommes, Ashoka

MEDIA: Theatre

SNAPSHOT

Early in 1991, during a regular meeting of Teatro Trono, *street children are talking about creating a new project:*

"It's too difficult to have someone funding it!"

"And how much would it cost?"

"Well, we need a house for eight people where the whole group will live, and we need to eat as well!"

"We could steal!" says Ch'ila, a small Aymara boy, he's 13 years old, only looks like ten, "and then we deposit the money in a bank!"

His eyes shine while his hands describe in detail an improbable robbery, in some place in the city of La Paz. A vast list of other crazy and creative ideas follow, and are gradually transformed into what later becomes COMPA, the Community of Art Producers, made of street children and youth, that have joined Teatro Trono.

Why the name "Trono?" To confer a positive meaning to "tronar" (to be ruined), which is how kids nicknamed the Centre for Diagnosis and Therapy for Boys (CDTV) a government rehab shelter for street children. So now 'trono' will have a new meaning: to place children on a throne as the kings of imagination and fantasy. It is actually at that rehab centre that Teatro Trono *was born on Christmas of 1989.*

*With the amount of personal effort invested, stealing, like Ch'ila had
suggested several years earlier, became unnecessary. The persistent work of*
Teatro Trono *during the 1990s made possible the consolidation of COMPA,
the street children and youth cultural organisation which, other than the drama
group, now includes an art film club, a library, a magazine shop, a group of
puppeteers, and coordinates itinerant photo and art shows.*
—Excerpts from the book: "El Mañana es Hoy," by Iván Nogales Bazan,
Claudio Urey Miranda, Angel Urey Miranda and Juan Santos Cornejo.

DESCRIPTION

Teatro Trono is the "point of the lance"
of COMPA. It all started in 1989, as a result
of the experience of working with street
children initially within the framework of
a government shelter, but, soon gained independence and autonomy so as to continue
developing cultural activities for the children and youth of El Alto.

Most of the initial members of *Teatro Trono* were once street
children themselves. They were successful in building COMPA and
Teatro Trono, projects where children have a managing responsibility.

Over the years the group has developed an organisation structured
to respond to the activities that are offered to the public of El Alto:
theatre, library, film shows and art exhibits. Four drama groups are
currently active, one of them being a children's group that was
established at a boy's foster home.

Teatro Trono has a repertoire of 14 plays, all developed as collective
creations. Plays such as *A Dog's Life, The Legend of Coca Leaves,
On Donkeys and Flowers, Feeling Dreadful* have been performed not
only for audiences in popular neighbourhoods of El Alto, but also
during national cultural events and festivals—over 300 performances
for approximately 90,000 people. In addition, near 170 presentations
were performed for 25,000 people during international tours
through Europe and North America.

The topics that were developed during the first years had much
to do with the daily life of street children and their relation to the
community and the local institutions. A play such as *A Dog's Life*
exposed in a very unwavering manner the miserable life of street
children; another play *El meón*, ridiculed the bureaucracy in government institutions for street children.

Gradually the areas of interest widened to cover other important
issues. *Teatro Trono* is exploring some themes that are not sufficiently
discussed in marginalised urban areas of El Alto, such as children's
rights, national identity, drug trafficking, environmental awareness,
gender equity, leadership, etc. This is done in scenes but also through

other adapted media: dance, video and puppets. Although in-part some of these might have been donor-driven changes, it also shows that the members of *Teatro Trono* were evolving towards a more open perspective of their country and the world.

Currently, most of the work by *Teatro Trono* is on prevention. The life experience of the *Teatro Trono* initial founders has led them to work with children and youths before they step into the streets, thus supporting the initiatives of other social organisations that aim to strengthen family ties and promote children's rights.

Funding *Teatro Trono* activities has not been easy; during the first years the troupe performed in the streets and passed the hat to cover its basic needs. Ashoka and other organisations provided small seed funds, and recent three-year support from Caritas Nederland will provide *Teatro Trono* with a certain stability during the next few years.

The challenge is for *Teatro Trono* to remain as an independent group, to avoid bureaucratising and to continue functioning within a logical framework of self-management and collective decision-making.

BACKGROUND & CONTEXT

El Alto is the poorest city in Bolivia. It was an extension of the capital city only twenty years ago until it became a gigantic low-income neighbourhood and was declared a city in its own right. It has been growing steadily to turn into the second largest metropolis in the country, and may soon equal La Paz. With very limited resources, the majority of the population of 700,000 in El Alto lives marginally, health and education services are precarious, and cultural development is far from being a priority.

Children in particular, live under difficult circumstances. Because of unemployment and migration, there are more than 7,000 street children in the four main cities of Bolivia, including El Alto. Government-run shelters and rehabilitation centres are largely insufficient. Among the children that enter these centres, 25 percent are kept in custody for theft, 11 percent for vagrancy, and 18 percent for bad conduct. There are no entertainment options for children and youth, which make them easy targets of alcoholism, drugs and sexual promiscuity.

More than any other city of Bolivia, children and youth in El Alto suffer from the lack of educational and cultural alternatives. Some cultural groups and NGOs are struggling to provide these alternatives, creating options for adolescents to get involved in artistic activities such as poetry, sculpture, painting, theatre, music, dance, photography and video production. COMPA and *Teatro Trono*, are important examples of these alternatives.

The changes affecting the lives of those that participated from the beginning in the *Teatro Trono* experience are clear: they are off the streets now. "They moved from the street to the theatre scene, and the scene became the vehicle to become protagonists in the scene of real life," says founder Ivan Nogales. He adds: "We promote the protagonism of children and youth with the view of searching for leaders for the future. There is a vacuum of leadership among children and young people in this country, and we try to change this through theatre."

The influence of COMPA and *Teatro Trono* has expanded over other areas of the city of El Alto, and to other cities of Bolivia. Adolescent boys and girls now have access to alternative and informal educational activities that contribute to strengthen their self-esteem, their cultural identities and their gender perspectives, thus allowing them to work on new drama groups that generate their own resources and effectively participate in the local dynamics of the neighbourhood.

Teatro Trono has been providing a decent way of living to many children and youths that otherwise would not have had any opportunities in El Alto. In *Teatro Trono* are the foundations of COMPA, which over the years has developed an innovative process involving communication, education and culture, deeply rooted in the marginalised social areas of El Alto.

Performances of *Teatro Trono* have already reached more than 80,000 children in El Alto and La Paz, with messages on environmental issues; and 15,000 with messages on educational reforms. Plays on self-esteem, gender issues, cultural identity and youth leadership, have already had an impact on children and have prompted some groups to organise around cultural activities. Many street children and adolescents have been rescued from drugs and marginality and are now integrated in positive cultural activities of various types.

MEDIA & METHODS

The whole methodology of *Teatro Trono* is based on collective work and active participation. Though the individual growth of each participant is the most essential outcome, the main purpose is to strengthen the collective. The group is involved at all stages of development of initiatives, either relating to the creation of a new play or to the management of resources. A collective decision is needed in every instance in order to proceed.

Training is done along five "flexible" stages that aim to awaken the critical and creative talents of children and adolescents, through various drama techniques.

The process of creating a new play involves research at the community level, building the characters based on real people, the community "heroes" that can be easily identified by the audience. These are often characterised as people with strong will and determination to fight for their community and to stand for it in front of official authorities and decision-makers.

CONSTRAINTS

The total absence of external sources of funding during the initial years often put *Teatro Trono* in jeopardy. The troupe had to generate revenues from street performances, which had serious limits.

This had an impact on the young and recently incorporated actors, which for the most part were street adolescents who had no contact with their original families and had already adapted to live the "street culture" prevailing in El Alto. They were also emotionally unstable and the problems in their personal lives substantially affected their participation in *Teatro Trono* activities.

Ironically, the fact that COMPAS and *Teatro Trono* has more access now to external sources of funding, is having an impact on the very nature of its work. External funding has ties and conditions, such as prompting *Teatro Trono* to become a legal organisation, an institution within the law equipped with an administrative hierarchy and financial procedures. This is somehow resulting in *Teatro Trono* gradually abandoning street work and focusing more on other audiences, including those internationally. It may soon become a well-respected theatre group, but the risk is that it will be cut from its roots. Certain donor-driven topics, such as environment and gender, have become standard in *Teatro Trono* repertory.

REFERENCES

Information for this chapter was provided by Ivan Nogales through e-mail exchanges.

A book on *Teatro Trono* was written by its founders: *El mañana es hoy*, by Iván Nogales Bazan, Claudio Urey Miranda, Angel Urey Miranda, Juan Santos Cornejo. Editorial Plural, 1998. 358 pages.

Pata chueca by Stefan Gurtner. Editorial Los Amigos del libro, La Paz, Bolivia, 1998.

A short video documentary illustrates the work of *Teatro Trono*: *La Hoja Sagrada*, Directed by Iván Sanjines. Bolivia, 1993. 17 minutes.

Web site <www.compatrono.tripod.com>.

WAN SMOLBAG

BASIC FACTS

TITLE:	The Wan Smolbag Theatre for Development
COUNTRY:	Vanuatu, Solomon Islands
FOCUS:	Health, AIDS / STDs, environment, governance
PLACE:	Vanuatu, Solomon Islands
BENEFICIARIES:	General population of Melanesian Islands
PARTNERS:	
FUNDING:	British Development Cooperation (DFID), United Nations Fund for Population Activities (UNFPA), United Nations Office for Project Services (UNOPS), New Zealand Overseas Development Agency (NZODA), Australian Agency for International Development (AusAID), Foundation for the South Pacific (FSP), UNICEF, Save the Children
MEDIA:	Theatre, video, audio–cassettes

SNAPSHOT

Another rainy day at Wan Smolbag *house in Vila. It should be the dry season, but it feels like the sun hasn't shone for weeks! The rain has forced everyone inside the building and that makes things a bit cramped. There are ten extra actors from Tagabe as well as 11 full-time Smolbag actors for the 20-episode radio soap opera called "Sarah's Family" about reproductive health topics, produced with funding from Oxfam, New Zealand. The young part-time actors sit around reading their scripts and periodically disappear off into the radio studio at the back.*

The building is rather full today as another two of the Smolbag associate groups are in rehearsal before heading off for island tours. Wan Smolbag Kids is going to the island of Santo to perform plays around children's rights and reproductive health in schools and communities. Health Force Theatre, an older group from the Blacksands settlement, is also ready to go on tour to Tongoa. They are having a final run of Louisa's Choice, *a play about domestic violence. The play ends with the actors saying that it is "always wrong to beat your wife"; they then put down three cards reading "agree, disagree, don't know"; so the audience will choose the card they agree with. The discussion usually goes on for hours. An actor goes off to check the flights and comes back very upset: the plane can't land on Tongoa as the grass is too high. They will have to wait a few days and see if anyone cuts the grass.*

Later in the day a bus drives round to the side of the building and a group of women rush past the open double doors through the rain and on to the "Youth Drop in Centre" at the back. The women are brought from surrounding settlements to the centre to learn about family planning and reproductive health. Luckily the radio soap has finished early today, and a group of Wan Smolbag *actors is free to perform the STD sketches for the women. These sketches are like walking biological diagrams that show how STDs spread and what they do in the body. At the end of the session the women ask the nurses all kinds of questions, ranging from "how twins are made," to "why some STDs make men sore when they urinate." The nurses are relieved when it is time for tea and they can hand 'round fruit and sandwiches!*—WRITTEN BY FOUNDER JO DORRAS.

DESCRIPTION

In 1989, fifteen voluntary part-time actors organised an NGO to work with communities on social and environmental issues in Vanuatu. The group called itself *Wan Smolbag* (in Bislama, the language of Vanuatu), because they wanted to show people that a theatre group could go anywhere. With only "one small bag" to carry a few costumes, the troupe was ready to produce plays on health and environmental issues and travel to the most remote villages within the Pacific Islands.

Wan Smolbag has written and produced a large number of plays, drama sketches and participatory drama workshops about environmental, health, social and human rights. The troupe has developed plays with science messages and animated dramatic sketches with messages and information involving audience participation. They perform their pieces throughout Vanuatu and the Pacific Islands, using plays and participatory drama workshops to disseminate information and create debate at the grassroots level. The mainstay of the group's work is a set of short 20 to 50 minute theatre pieces on environmental, health, governance and population issues. Performing in remote villages gives the group the opportunity to stay the night and discuss issues in detail after the play.

The group has been core funded by the United Kingdom's DFID for six years and is well known in the informal education sector throughout the Pacific. Over the last four or five years *Wan Smolbag* has worked more and more with disadvantaged sections of society in Port Vila and the islands of Vanuatu. Many of the issues raised by people are in the areas of good governance: lack of services, ignorance of their rights, beatings in school, beatings by police, domestic violence, and women having no share in decision making.

Wan Smolbag Theatre has been working in the field of health education since 1989. Since that time the theatre has covered many different health topics. The main focus of its health work has been in the area of reproductive health, looking at the problems of teenage pregnancy, maternal health, STDs and HIV/AIDS. Plays are often aimed at a specific age group, and there are plays specifically for urban and rural audiences. About 50 plays have been produced since the beginning.

Wan Smolbag's first foray into good governance work was in 1993. The group was commissioned to produce and perform a play on Children's Rights for UNICEF at the then South Pacific Commission, to raise discussion on the Convention of the Rights of the Child, which the Commission was asking member countries to endorse.

While person-to-person live theatre is the most effective way of getting a message across, sometimes there is a demand for other media. In addition to the plays, books, radio programmes and videos using live actors and puppets have been produced to reach a wider segment of the public. Among the video productions: *George and Sheila* looks at the role of men and women in Melanesian society. *Pacific Star* is a comedy with music, but deals with development issues in a powerful way. *Things We Don't Talk About* (1996) is a film on disability. *Politics, Corruption and Voting*, is a film about corruption and politicians. *On the Reef* (1995) an amusing, poignant musical looks at marine life under threat. *Kasis Road* (1996) is a video on population and family planning. *It Couldn't Happen Here* (1998) shows where mosquitoes breed and how the Dengue virus spreads. *Wan Presen Blong Niufala Bebe* (1998) tells the story of Malaria through live actors and puppets. *Vot long Pati la!* (1999) is *Wan Smolbag*'s new video on good governance issues.

BACKGROUND & CONTEXT

Theatre is particularly popular because of the number of languages that are spoken in Melanesian countries. Vanuatu has over 90 languages; the Solomon Islands over 100 and Papua, New Guinea, had over 800. Nonetheless, Bislama, which started out as a communicative quick fix between monolingual English speakers and multilingual Melanesians, continues to serve important instrumental purposes in Vanuatu. The bulk of the programming on radio, the most democratic of the mass media in the country, is conducted in Bislama.

Wan Smolbag Theatre was started by Jo Dorras and Peter Walker as a health education initiative supported by the Vanuatu Health Department. With help from Community Aid Abroad and British Aid they set it up using community theatre to convey messages about health issues, and later expanded beyond Vanuatu to create a regional programme.

ASPECTS OF SOCIAL CHANGE

Wan Smolbag Theatre has been involved in exciting developments, which are a spin-off from its theatre work, and from the strong relationships they have built up with some communities.

In 1995 a series of workshops with children who were not at school resulted in *Wan Smolbag* Kids. The group members range in age from 11 or 12 to 16. They perform plays aimed at primary school children on dental hygiene, dengue fever and on how the body works. A core group of nine children became a semi-permanent attachment to *Wan Smolbag* Theatre and appear in plays and videos.

Wan Smolbag Theatre spent six months during 1997 working closely with the Blacksands and Tagabe Community. A community play, which intended to build stronger ties with the older people, resulted in the Blacksands Community Project. The eldest of the participants was in her sixties and the youngest about ten.

Wan Smolbag Theatre had been doing plays on reproductive health for ten years, targeting different audiences. The response has always been enthusiastic but the question remained: what if people have all the knowledge and overcome the shame, but the local clinic has orders not to give contraception to single people? Or if the nearest supply is a long way away? That is how the Kam Pussem Hed (Youth Drop-in Centre for Reproductive and Sexual Health Clinic) was created in February 1999, with funding from DFID, NZODA, AusAID, SPC and UNFPA.

Another spin-off initiative, the Turtle Monitor, is driven by a group of interested people who were chosen by their village to help with the *Wan Smolbag* turtle campaign. They watch for nesting turtles and advise people on turtle conservation. The network started in 1995 following a play on that very subject. This has led to most villages banning the eating of turtles and their eggs. What started out as a network of monitors in the island of Efate, has now expanded to five more islands.

The Electoral Commission of Vanuatu wanted to inform as many people as possible about their voting rights when a snap election was called in 1998. *Wan Smolbag* created a play with actors from many different islands and seven groups of five actors were sent out. About

90 percent of the villages in Vanuatu saw the performance. It was a short play so there was time to discuss issues after. Many people said that before the group came they had decided not to vote, but after seeing the play they realised how important voting was.

MEDIA & METHODS

"We are one acting as many. We are many acting as one."

In Vanuatu there are many people who do not read or write, many who have had only a couple of years of schooling. These people want information, but they have no way of getting it from books; the radio does not reach everyone either, as people do not always have radio sets and if they do, they cannot always afford batteries. People in the villages say the plays make things clear, they can understand the message.

Wan Smolbag Theatre has developed a model of popular theatre that explains to people at the grassroots level about environment, governance and reproductive health issues. The group has developed sketches, showing how diseases like gonorrhea are transmitted through sex. They have developed a lot of what they call "moving biological diagrams" in which actors run about dressed for example as sperm and eggs. The sketches are in very short sections, lasting no more than about 30 seconds. After each sketch the audience is invited to explain what they have just seen and to answer questions. The action stops and the performers address the public provoking a discussion. There is one play where the performance stops to ask the audience what should happen next. Depending on the questions, the process can take up to an hour.

Wan Smolbag in Port Vila has two full-time nurses to provide support. A reproductive health clinic has been set up attached to *Wan Smolbag* Theatre; it provides videos and other health education resources.

In the participatory drama workshops people aged 11 to 70 played drama games, engaged in role playing, worked on sketches and told stories, which formed the basis of the play they went on to perform.

CONSTRAINTS

Probably the most obvious obstacle faced by *Wan Smolbag* Theatre in its work on health issues, is that they provide information about sexually transmitted infections, but if the health professionals do not want to give out condoms to young people, the plays will have no further effect. Traditions can also be an obstacle, along with certain religious groups.

One of the challenges is to keep the work fresh and not to run the same plays for too long. The theatre group has found new and innovative ways of giving the same messages through different plays. The styles of the plays change to make the message seem new. *Wan Smolbag* keeps assessing the impact of their activities, trying to improve performances and content.

Yet another challenge is to find enough funding to keep *Wan Smolbag* going. Being a large employer of youth in a country where unemployment runs at 70 percent is a big responsibility. "We have managed so far, but some donors choose to fund big tendering organisations rather than in-country groups, which can make life very hard and make your blood boil too!" says Jo Darras.

REFERENCES

E-mail exchanges with Jo Darras and Peter Walker, founders of *Wan Smolbag* Theatre.

Wan Smolbag Theatre Web site <http://www.tellusconsultants.com/wansmolbag/>.

LA VOZ DE LA COMUNIDAD

1990 Guatemala

....

BASIC FACTS

TITLE:	La Voz de la Comunidad
COUNTRY:	Guatemala
FOCUS:	Community organisation
PLACE:	San José Buenavista, Guatemala City
BENEFICIARIES:	25,000 people in San José Buenavista, Santa Luisa el Milagro and La Trinidad.
PARTNERS:	Asociación Salud por el Pueblo, Guatemala (ASEP), Federación Guatemalteca de Escuelas Radiofónicas (FGER), ALER, AMARC, Red Cross
FUNDING:	ASEP, FGER, Proyecto de Desarrollo Santiago, Guatemala (PRODESA), Spanish Cooperation, World Association of Christian Communities (WACC)
MEDIA:	Radio

SNAPSHOT

San José Buena Vista hangs from a ravine at a mere one thousand metres west of the main square of Guatemala City. This short distance actually divides two worlds: on the main square sit the Cathedral and the Presidential palace—which recently became the Palace of Culture—while over the ravine are suspended, almost in the air, some of the poorest neighbourhoods of the capital city. Between the two places sits "El Gallito" (The Cocky), a dangerous barrio where not even the police dare to enter. Drug dealers and juvenile gangs control it.

From the top of the ravine only a cascade of metal rooftops can be seen. Hundreds of small houses have been built one on top of the other, like a fragile card castle. Cars can only get as far as the crest of the ravine; the rest of the route must be done on foot following a steep path that joins the La Barranca River, at the very bottom. Men and women climb laboriously carrying boxes and belongings.

A woman knocks on the wall of a two-story house. "What do you want?" Three metres above, the head of Don Juan Guzmán, the owner of "La Canasta" (The Basket) shop appears through a small window. "I need a soap bar and a set of batteries for the radio," answers the woman as she deposits inside the basket a 20 Quetzales note. The basket rises in the air attached to a string and comes down at once with the order.

Not far from there is *La Voz de la Comunidad*. The clear green of its walls makes the construction look like an emerald among the ensemble of houses in cement. Reynaldo Gálvez, the director, introduces two young announcers and Manuel "Meme" Alvarez Castro, one of the founding members. Meme is the living memory of the station, he remembers every difficult time that the people from the ravine had to live through, and how *La Voz de la Comunidad* provided support and guidance.

"Just a week ago five children drowned in the stream, their bodies only appeared 14 kilometres down the river. The station participated in the search through the night, orienting and mobilising the community, but it was too late already," says Meme. "When the Mitch storm hit us we saved many lives because we advised people to get out of their homes and run to the shelters. Several houses crumbled one over the next, and ended over the river," adds Reynaldo.

DESCRIPTION

La Voz de la Comunidad (The Voice of the Community) started on August 19, 1990, with a simple system of six cone speakers, a small amplifier and a couple of turntables. Some started calling it "The Voice of the Ravine" because of its location on the slopes of the La Barranca River, which runs near the centre of the capital city of Guatemala. ASEP, a local NGO, provided technical support, WACC and PRODESA, a Catholic institution in Guatemala, funded the equipment.

Over the next nine years the project developed in the heart of San José Buena Vista, until November 1999, when *La Voz de la Comunidad* became an FM radio station, thus extending its coverage over two other neighbourhoods in the ravine: Santa Luisa el Milagro and La Trinidad.

La Voz de la Comunidad airs its programming using the 108 FM frequency. According to the broadcasting legislation of Guatemala, the station is "illegal" or "pirate." In order to avoid sanctions it has kept a low profile during the past months. Ironically it is the only FM station that has decided on its own to limit its coverage by placing the antenna at the lowest point of its topography, instead of searching for the highest place available. Although it has a 20-watt transmitter, only 8 watts of power are in use.

The programming of *La Voz de la Comunidad* starts everyday at 5:30 a.m. and ends at 10:00 p.m. Most of the programme grid is filled with music, except for the children's segment ("Patojitos") and a youth programme "Entre cuates" ("Among Buddies").

Before the FM transmissions started, the programme grid was richer and included segments such as *News From the Barrio*, *Editorial*, *The Family is the Best Barrier Against Drugs*, *Learning Among Children*, and *Chatting With You* (interviews). All these were locally produced. Other programmes distributed by the International Red Cross on human rights, and by ALER and AMARC were also aired.

At the current stage, only a few months after the FM transmissions started, the station is fully engaged in promoting activities related to the internal organisation and training of staff. "We are in the process of accumulating strength," says Reynaldo Gálvez, who rejects the title of director. "I'm only accompanying the set of activities that the community has determined," he adds. In the near future new programmes with educational and cultural content will be produced in a more professional manner.

The new profile of *La Voz de la Comunidad* emphasises the participatory aspects: "A radio station that promotes community organisation as an alternative for the development of the community. A station where the microphones are always open for everyone, particularly for the poorest. A station that promotes the training of new community communicators."

Through its new programming *La Voz de la Comunidad* will provide the means to fulfill the need of education and democracy: "A radio station that strengthens community consciousness and national identity"; "A station that conveys to people new knowledge that will help to improve the living conditions of the poor"; "An instrument to guarantee the human right of freedom of speech"; "A radio station that guides the community and promotes a larger political participation in the civil society." These are quotes from the station "Profile, Plan 2000."

BACKGROUND & CONTEXT

Extreme poverty and wealth coexist in the Capital of Guatemala, only a few blocks away from each other. The topography of the city contributes to it: those that are better off live on the higher flat areas of the city while the poorest squash in settlements that grow on the ravines and river beds, with no electricity, water or telephone services.

No less than five thousand families live in San José Buena Vista, Santa Luisa el Milagro and La Trinidad, over the slopes of a ravine under the El Incienso Bridge, not far from the historical centre of the Capital. In the higher part of the ravine sits "El Gallito," a neighbourhood of narrow streets, better known for its violence and drug trafficking, than for the honest people that still live there. Hardworking construction builders, domestic servants and mechanics that can't afford anything better, live in improvised homes on the crumbly plots of San José Buena Vista, near the General Cemetery.

This is where the Health for the People Association (ASEP) has been working since 1997. This local NGO is helping to improve the life conditions of the population, through programmes of health, education, community organisation and communication.

In 1989 ASEP conducted a baseline survey to diagnose the social and economic situation in the community. One of the outputs was the need to undertake communication activities in the area. A previous experience had shown the effectiveness of using loudspeakers that were installed at the Social Centre of the community; which lead to establishing *La Voz de la Comunidad* as a permanent communication tool. Six cone speakers were installed on poles in strategic places.

ASPECTS OF SOCIAL CHANGE

La Voz de la Comunidad has transformed community life in the three settlements in the ravine. Its importance may not be easily noticed at first sight, as the regular programme grid consists mainly of music. However this communication tool has served the community well and contributed over the years to create a sense of unity among the settlers.

For instance, its role has been fundamental during the process of introducing pipe water in a few places within the settlements of the ravine. The whole community was mobilised through the speakers of *La Voz de la Comunidad* to participate in the project. Groups of volunteer workers were coordinated from the station, lists of people were established, and the name of each one was called through the loudspeakers to join the teams to work on the various tasks.

There have been moments of crisis for the community, where the station has taken action to coordinate and organise people in spite of its meagre resources. When Hurricane Mitch hit several countries of Central America in October 1998, the heavy rains also affected Guatemala City, in particular the ravine areas, causing landslides and collapsing houses which in turn carried other houses to the river bed in their descent. The mobilisation of people through *La Voz de la Comunidad* prevented higher human losses. Other nearby settlements that do not have a means of local communication registered more victims, as people were unable to promptly respond to the emergency.

From its inception *La Voz de la Comunidad* has adopted a participatory approach for the development of its activities. The decisions on the programming are collectively made by a local group of 17 young people that make up the "communication group" of the barrio, which holds meetings every Thursday.

A handful of social development organisations such as ASEP and the FGER accompany this process without directly intervening in the decisions that are made. FGER has included the station among its network of community radio stations, which groups around 12 stations in Guatemala, and regularly offers training.

La Voz de la Comunidad is in fact one of the stations that is part of FGER's Readjustment Project, which will extend over five years. The plan will be gradually implemented. It includes the strengthening of small community stations in five main areas: training, management, research, programming and technological update.

CONSTRAINTS

La Voz de la Comunidad is one of the 60 or more community radio stations that are considered "illegal" by the government. The current concentration of radio and television frequencies are in the hands of very few; the collusion between authorities and private businessmen to hoard the remaining frequencies contributed, in 1999, to the establishment of new legislation that gives the frequency to highest bidder. Community radio stations are thus divested of their frequencies since they can't possibly afford to pay sums in the range of US$20,000 to US$50,000.

No wonder that *La Voz de la Comunidad* operates virtually in secrecy. It constitutes a unique example of a station that although physically operating from a high slope has nevertheless opted to raise its antenna deep at the very bottom of the ravine. This, in order to prevent a potential government intervention with the argument that the station is interfering with the signal of commercial radio stations. *La Voz de la Comunidad* has thus voluntarily restricted its coverage to the five thousand families that live in the three settlements of the ravine. Only the award of its own license would improve the situation.

The fragility of its legal existence has been one of the main factors impeding a higher level of community involvement, and is evidenced by the limits of working with a staff of volunteers. At some stages, only three people held it together. This added to the technical problems, which on various occasions forced it to suspend transmissions for two or three weeks in a row. The fragility of the equipment is at greater risk because of the unreliable and deficient electricity supply.

Programming was also affected by the conversion to an FM station in late 1999. Locally produced programmes on social and cultural issues were removed, although the new design envisages new segments with improved technical quality.

REFERENCES

The information for this chapter was obtained during a field visit to *La Voz de la Comunidad* in August 2000; and based on conversations with Manuel Alvarez Castro (founder) and Reynaldo Gálvez (director).

La Voz de la Comunidad documents: Profile, Plan 2000 y Pilot Programming.

LABOR NEWS PRODUCTION

1990 Korea

....

BASIC FACTS

TITLE:	Labor News Production (LNP)
COUNTRY:	Korea
FOCUS:	Labour movement, democracy in media
PLACE:	Seoul
BENEFICIARIES:	Factory workers
PARTNERS:	Korean Confederation of Trade Unions (KCTU), JinboNet, Korean LaborNet, Nodong Net
FUNDING:	Labor News Production, Crocevia (Italy)
MEDIA:	Video

SNAPSHOT

I met once a labour activist in a restaurant. During the conversation people sitting with us asked him how he got the strength to continue the struggle despite the risks involved in being a labour activist in Korea. He replied very briefly that if he hadn't seen a Labor News video two years earlier he couldn't have gone through the difficulties he faced at the time. "That gave me a broader sense of activism, not just as propaganda, but as an emotional visual impetus." This man made me think that sometimes we underestimate the importance of our activities, and that we must be very cautious about our work, because it really affects people.

On another occasion, after screening in Seoul [the video] Fired workers *I saw an audience of four hundred totally shed tears while walking out of the theatre in complete silence. I then understood more than ever that video could really help people to comprehend the situation of other people. Without the video, they would have never thought about the lives of the workers fired during 1980s and 1990s, because the mainstream media totally ignored their struggle and their situation.*

There are also dreadful lessons. I never expected so many activists of the 1980s to be coopted so fast into the system, and some even became the vanguard of right wing politicians and practitioners for neo-liberalism.

On the other hand there are many newcomers in the progressive video movement who are former trainees of Labor News Production. *I never expected our small training programmes could make people think more seriously about their lives.*

The world must be analysed from the people's point of view, and though there are always things that can't be predicted it is important to think more systematically and act more rigorously without losing the belief in the progress of the world, without being trapped in the unreal imagination. Then we can change ourselves and can change the world.

That's one of the lessons from my twenty years of activism from student movement to labour movement and how I understand the term communication for social change.—RELATED BY MYOUNG JOON KIM, CHIEF PRODUCER OF *LABOR NEWS PRODUCTION* (LNP).

DESCRIPTION

Labor News Production's main goal is to strengthen the democratic and progressive labour movement in Korea and worldwide and to play an important role in making the situation of media in the country more democratic.

To fulfill its goal, this rather small organisation, with seven full-time staff, covers various areas, categorised as follows:

- **Production:** LNP has produced more than fifty video programmes including newsreels, educational video, historical documentaries, etc. The content and style varies depending on the partner organisation. LNP videos have not been broadcast on Korean television but have been distributed widely through trade unions, NGOs and student organisations, and often shown in international festivals.

- **Archive:** LNP records footage for specific productions, but also documents every important issue related to the labour movement. As a result the organisation has more than 3,000 hours of archives.

- **Training:** Since 1991, LNP has trained the workers and ordinary citizens both in video production and the critical reviewing and understanding of the mainstream media. Among the results of this activity are six videos made by collective video-groups composed of workers.

- **Organising and networking:** Various video groups are active producers, and LNP's mission is to support them to build their own solidarity network.

- **Solidarity:** LNP participates in different progressive communication networks: the Korean independent film and video makers, the Anticensorship forum, the Project for People's TV, the People's Coalition for Media Reform, the Human Rights Film Festival, the

Korean Progressive network, Korean LaborNet, and Videazimut. The organisation has been instrumental in preparing international conferences such as LaborMedia 97 and LaborMedia 99, considered by international activists as the most important conference on labour movement and media.

- **Research:** LNP has played a pioneering role introducing in Korea concepts such as public access, community radio, participatory communication, etc. Since 1997, it has established a research group as a separate branch, which publishes a bi-weekly Webzine on the progressive media movement called *Prism*.
- **Distribution & Festival:** The alternative distribution system in Korea being very weak, LNP uses different strategies to distribute its videos as widely as possible. The main distribution method is to use the network of affiliated trade unions of KCTU. Since 1997 another channel for video distribution has opened through the annual Seoul International Labor Video and Film Festival, which has become the best showcase for films and videos in the labour movement and a forum for video activists. The majority of the programmes screened during the festival are distributed nation-wide through agreements with each producer.

Labor News Production managed to survive through the political turmoil of Korea during the 1990s. Its activity contributed to the process of democratisation that has recently reached mass media.

About 80 percent of the annual budget of *Labor News Production* comes from its own activities, such as revenues from tape sales, production fees from coproduction projects with trade unions and NGOs, and training fees from the training programme. Only 5 percent is from individual supporters, and 15 percent is from rare public or international sources such as Crocevia (Italy).

BACKGROUND & CONTEXT

In Korea, as in most countries of the world, people are facing serious problems due to the globalisation strategies and to the current economic realities of inequality and profit-motivated exploitation of workers. The labour movement is called on to play an essential role for changing the situation, although many of the existing trade unions are not effectively playing this role.

Labor News Production believes that strengthening the democratic labour movement is essential for the process of making the whole society more democratic and guaranteeing decent living conditions for the working people, who are not only a majority but also the people who really contribute to development and progress. Thus,

Labor News Production wishes to be the driving force for using media in strengthening the progressive labour movement and also wants to make this movement internally participatory and democratic.

ASPECTS OF SOCIAL CHANGE

During the twelve years of activity of *Labor News Production*, important changes have taken place in video production, training, solidarity, distribution and advocacy, according to Myoung Joon Kim.

Video became an essential part of labour education and has played an important role in sharing information on the labour movement among working people, recording visual history of working people's lives and struggles. It sometimes represents hundreds of union members with a voice of their own, or targets wider audiences to articulate the perspectives of working people. A new audience for alternative video has grown. Inside the labor movement, *Labor News Production* has successfully introduced the significance of democratic communication. Subsequent to ten years of conducting training, there are now several workers' video collectives active in various regions, and many independent documentary video makers. *Labor News Production* has trained more than one thousand people. The solidarity movement led by organisations such as JinboNet, LaborNet, Association for Korean independent film and video makers, and *Labor News Production* has resulted in the establishment of the Human Rights Film Festival, and the International Labor Media Conference. *Labor News Production* is a member of the board or steering committee in every organisation mentioned above.

International video distribution of *Labor News Production* videos has expanded to Japan, USA, Australia, and other countries with alternative distribution circuits. Videos played an important role explaining to workers of other nations the situation of working people in Korea. *"From the crisis of the capital ... "* was broadcast by satellite by Indymedia during the Seattle demonstrations against international trade policies.

Labor News Production activities were partly liable for finally obtaining people's access to public broadcasting, cable and satellite TV. Alternative media became more attractive among activists in the social movement, as a result of LNP's struggles. Furthermore, government-funded institutions in the film and broadcasting sector have finally started research projects on the alternative media movement.

Last but not least, based on the activity of the Anticensorship Forum headed by Myoung Joon Kim, Labor News coordinator, several articles about censorship in video and film legislation were ultimately deleted.

Video is at the axis of media activities of *Labor News Production*, though other communication tools are used as well. LNP publishes a quarterly newsletter about its activities, and its research branch puts together a biweekly Webzine and e-mail newsletter. The LNP Web site has been accessible since 1998, and in May 2000 LNP started monthly Internet Webcasting of its programmes. Given the recent changes in public access to national broadcast, LNP plans to produce videos targeting the access structure, mainly aimed at the Korean Public Broadcasting System (KBS). This should be done without sacrificing content, according to Myoung Joon Kim.

Labor News Production is a participatory communication project. Internally all activities are decided with participation of every member. The video production methods also pursue a participatory process, which is one reason why most of the programmes are coproductions. LNP and workers learn from each other, and much of the production process is devoted to discussion. Often, the footage comes from cameras operated by the workers, as happened with *"One Step at a Time,"* a video portraying the struggle of hospital workers.

Labor News Production opted for a methodology of video production with the people not about the people. One of LNP's main activities is to help rank and file workers to make their own videos, which is an essential part of the participatory process encouraged within the labour movement.

CONSTRAINTS

The very nature of the activity of *Labor News Production* is meant to encounter difficulties and obstacles. Some of these constraints are internal, such as misconceptions, and sometimes, fear about democracy among trade union leadership and even NGOs.

Financial problems have often threatened *Labor News Production* activities, even though the organisation itself established the principle that most of the budget should come from its own revenues from the beginning. Very little funds turn up from other sources, as labour issues and grassroots training activities do not attract private or public funding. Recent changes in public institutions and policies will perhaps provide new sources of funding, though LNP foresees that it will not be among the real beneficiaries, in spite of the leading role that it has played in changing the policy. The political situation has generally improved since the early 1990s, when *Labor News Production* had to face repression too often. In spite of the changing political environment, the Labor Film Festival is nonetheless considered illegal in Korea because the Film Rating Commission does not rate the video productions that are screened. Though recently there has been no police prosecution, LNP still believes that government police continue investigating the organisation. If the political situation becomes more conservative, repression could happen again.

REFERENCES

This chapter is mostly based on e-mail exchanges with Myoung Joon Kim and his answers to a questionnaire on *Labor News Production*, May 2000.

The *Labor News Production* Web site <http://www.lnp89.org/english.html> and Webcasting <http://mayday.nodong.net>.

TAMBULI

(1990) Philippines

BASIC FACTS

TITLE:	Tambuli Radio Network
COUNTRY:	Philippines
MAIN FOCUS:	Community development
PLACE:	20 remote communities
BENEFICIARIES:	About 10,000 people for each station
PARTNERS:	20 community radio stations
FUNDING:	Tambuli, UNESCO, DANIDA
MEDIA:	Radio

SNAPSHOT

There is only one car on the island, and it's the ambulance. Riding on the back of a motorcycle I covered the distance that links Loreto to Tubajon on a thin dirt road and arrived in town after dark, just to catch the last half of the transmission hours of Radio Tubajon. Both Loreto and Tubajon are located in the most remote part of the small Dinagat Island, a bit lost in the north of Mindanao — the second largest landmass area among the seven thousand islands of the Philippines. This was only the last part of the trip that started before sunrise in a rented car that took me from Cagayan de Oro to Surigao City during the best part of the day, and continued on a speedboat to Loreto in about three hours.

Six local leaders of different religious confessions are around the table at the recording room of *Radio Tubajon*, DXTT-FM 95.8. Father Kiko Magnaye, a Catholic priest who is also director of the station, is sitting among them. They are discussing the contents and schedule for six months of *Langit Sa Yuta* ("Heaven on Earth") the religious programme that airs every Sunday from 7:30 p.m. to 8:00 p.m. It is amazing to witness this example of democracy.

As I meet them, the live transmission is done from the nearby control room, separated only by a large glass window. Inside the control room the technician is handling all the radio equipment and ... he is singing for the audience, aided by a karaoke device. He takes his job very seriously, and pleases his audience with new songs every once in a while. After all, it's already time for Harana ("Party"), the music radio segment that comes right after the religious programme on Sundays.

By 10:00 p.m. the lights will go off in town, and so will *Radio Tubajon*, until the next day. It's only on the air three to four hours every day, but the population depends on it very much. As silence and darkness regain the streets, many, as I do, go to sleep with the echo of words and music from the community radio station.

It happens in Tubajon, in Loreto, and at 18 other stations supported by the *Tambuli Radio Network*. The lives of an equal number of communities have dramatically changed since these small stations were introduced in the Philippines. It is a first for this Asian country and also a first in South East Asia, where mass media is mostly under government control.

DESCRIPTION

 Basco, Aborlan, Goa, Banga, Ibajay, St. Teresita, Barangay Imelda, Cabagan, Maragusan, Loreto, Tubajon, Inogbong, Mabuhay… and then Lobo, Cabayugan, Cuyo Island, Gonzaga, Sultan Sa Barongis, Ipil and Joló. Twenty *Tambuli* stations spread out in a country that is already spread over seven thousand islands. From Joló and Zamboanga in the very south, to the southeastern environmental frontier of Palawan to Batan in the extreme north of the country, these small community stations are making the difference. Maybe not for the seventy million Filipinos but certainly for the population of the twenty communities that never before had the opportunity of accessing a radio station that talks about their daily problems and works hand-in-hand with the community to find solutions.

Tambuli is the Tagalo voice for the *carabao* horn, used traditionally to call villagers for community meetings. It is also an acronym for "voice of the small community for the development of the under-privileged." A set of five objectives guides the project: [1] To provide local access to information, [2] To allow villagers to express themselves, [3] To link together as a community, [4] To strengthen the sense of identity, and [5] To transform the audience from mere receivers to participants and managers of a communication system. In short: the empowerment of people through communication so that they will strengthen their community organisations and seek better opportunities for development.

Clear criteria were defined since the beginning for the selection of potential communities to be integrated into the project. It was decided, for example, that *Tambuli* stations would only be supported in places that totally lacked access to communication, but had potential for social organisation, willingness to pool resources into the project and to interact with other communities.

The engine that makes a *Tambuli* station work is a multisectoral Community Media Council (CMC). The CMC decides on managerial and programming issues. Most of the members also have responsibility as broadcasters, each one contributes with a programme slot relevant to his or her sector: health, education, youth, agriculture, senior citizens, environment, fishermen, women and legislation among others. In the long run, the CMC should become the owner of the stations.

The programming grid varies from one place to another, as do the contents and the titles of programmes. For example, the programme slot on environment is called *Nature is Treasure* ("Ang Kinaiyahan Bahandi") in Tubajon, *We and the Environment* ("Kita Ug Ang Kinaiyahan") in Loreto, and *Caring for the Environment* ("Ang Pag-Amping Sa Kinaiyahan") in Maragusan. *Tambuli* stations also have a feature that is common to most community-based radio stations: useful messages on village meetings, marriages, death announcements, incoming mail, lost cattle, lost children, information on local legislative measures, farmers products, or agricultural services.

A few *Tambuli* stations have expanded activities to provide interest-free loans, with a system broadly based on the Grameen Bank experience: small loans for poor individuals or community groups to put up income generating projects. Even the broadcasters from the *Tambuli* stations can benefit from loans, as they are mostly volunteers.

From its inception the project had 1999 as the end date. Nevertheless, the need of more community radio stations, the numerous requests from other communities, has convinced Louie Tabing of the need for creating a permanent institution to support future projects as well as the existing network. A *Tambuli* Foundation has been created to take over the project from the year 2000.

BACKGROUND & CONTEXT

The Philippines has come a long way to reach the point where a democratic radio network such as *Tambuli* is made possible. No doubt *Tambuli* is the result of a process of struggle for democratisation that started during the Marcos dictatorship. And the man that has been the driving force of the *Tambuli* project acquired his experience and developed many of his ideas while working at Radio Veritas, a Catholic station that was instrumental in ousting Ferdinand Marcos in 1986.

Louie Tabing was very critical towards the situation of media in his country. He used to say that media is only motivated by "profit, propaganda, power and privilege." His "PPPP" approach became a solid platform in the struggle for a democratic media. Tabing contacted friends from international organisations to put together the *Tambuli* project, which started in 1990 with technical support from UNESCO and US$25,000 in funding from DANIDA.

The first station opened in Batanes, a place so remote and isolated that it didn't even get any signals from national radio and TV networks. Next, a full-blown project got support from the same organisations, with a US$900,000 budget for four years. By the end of 1994, five stations were operational and eight by 1996. The project gradually expanded until 1999, adding up to 20 stations. Each new *Tambuli* operation costs about US$90,000, with 60 percent spent on equipment and infrastructure.

Some of the *Tambuli* stations are actually upgraded *Community Audio Towers* (CATs), a project that was initially set up with support from FAO in the late 1980s and has been also supported by UNICEF in the late 1990s. CATs are a good example of community participation in a low-cost communication activity. *Tambuli* added onto some of the existing CATs, providing the transmitter and additional training. Louie Tabing had the vision of taking advantage of the experience already acquired by the community in managing a communication project.

ASPECTS OF SOCIAL CHANGE

The Municipal Mayor of Tubajon requests "permission" from the radio station to cut some trees and fix a bridge that had collapsed... Why? Because he fears that if he makes the decision without public support he can be later criticised as someone who is destroying the environment. In Maragusan the station has put pressure on local authorities to ban chainsaws and pesticides. The place has a great potential for eco-tourism with its numerous rivers and attractive falls, but has been menaced in the past by gold diggers, and recently by illegal logging and spraying of pesticides.

The environment is not the only concern on the agenda of *Tambuli* stations; social consciousness has developed on other issues that affect the community. In Camarines Sur, the Goa station convinced its listeners to give up gambling, something that law enforcement had not achieved. These examples are significant of how things have changed since the *Tambuli* stations started operations.

The cultural and political influence of the *Tambuli* stations is recognised by local authorities, which have established good working relationships with the CMC. Often local government authorities provided land and materials for building the station premises. The *Tambuli* radio broadcasters have become so popular in some areas that they were elected to serve as local authorities. The strict "code of conduct" has been an important factor in regulating the behaviour of broadcasters towards the community.

A whole set of principles, manuals and instructions have been developed to make the experience as sustainable and strong as possible. Far from just giving away some equipment *Tambuli* stressed the process of training, which includes technical topics but mainly the responsibility of communicating with the poor, a code of conduct for broadcasters, and a deep understanding of participatory development.

The code of conduct embraces issues such as: "Reporting the Truth," "Good Taste," "Fairness," "Innocence of the Accused," "Respect for Rights of Everybody," "Preference for the Positive & Constructive Approach," "Treatment of Hearsay, Gossip, Rumours," "Respect for Authorities," "Pinch Hitting," "Cooperativeness," "Care of Studio Equipment," "Conduct Outside the Radio Station," "Solicitation of Advertisement and Funds," among others.

Equipment is very basic: 20-watt transmitters, karaoke amplifiers, and cassette recorders … Some stations are already upgrading, on their own, with community and/or local government support.

CONSTRAINTS

The main constraint seems to be the lack of communication between the various stations. Most of them do not have access to telephone lines and are located in very remote areas of the country; the stations do not really operate as a network. They do not have the means to link with each other and the *Tambuli* project has difficulty conveying messages to each station when needed.

The lack of specific legislation recognising the rights of community radio stations has retarded the process of launching new stations. Difficulty in securing a license to operate a radio station has become even more critical now that the Philippine Congress is supposed to issue franchises for any community radio station to operate. A bill is being filed in Congress for an omnibus community media law that will exempt low-powered radio stations from obtaining a franchise from Congress.

REFERENCES

This chapter is mainly based on the field visits and conversations with Fr. Kiko Magnaye, Station Manager of *Radio Tubajon* (Dinagat Island), Pastor Domingo D. Reambonanza, Station Manager of *Radio Loreto* (Dinagat), Frank Endaya and the team of *Radio Maragusan* (Davao del Norte) and Louie Tabing, the driving force of the *Tambuli* network.

A great wealth of information can be found at the *Tambuli* Web site <http://www.tambuli.org.ph/>. Other than the "Newsletter," and a descriptive approach to the *Tambuli* experience, it also includes a detailed "Code of Conduct" for broadcasters, and even a "Production Manual." The "Newsletter" is also distributed in print along with other *Tambuli* publications, as few stations and few people in general have access to the Web.

"*Tambuli*: the Electronic *Carabao* Horn" by Colin Fraser and Sonia Restrepo-Estrada, in their book *Communicating for Development* (pages 190–218), is a very complete overview of the experience.

The FAO Web site <http://www.fao.org/sd/CDdirect/CDan0026.htm> posts "Rural Radio in the Philippines" by Fr. Francis B. Lucas, among other interesting articles.

POPULAR THEATRE

1991 Nigeria

BASIC FACTS

TITLE:	Network of Educational Theatre (NET)
COUNTRY:	Nigeria
MAIN FOCUS:	Health, Children's Rights
PLACE:	Oyo, Ondo, Osun and other Yoruba states
BENEFICIARIES:	Villages in 46 Local Governments
PARTNERS:	Local Governments Administration (LGA), Ministry of Health
FUNDING:	UNICEF
MEDIA:	Theatre

SNAPSHOT

The Ede LGA theatre group are consummate actors. The three men and a woman, clamber into the minibus while their two musicians don handsome green and white costumes before joining them. The music strikes up as the entourage weaves its way through the extravagant bush of Osun State. Imposing trees, heavy with foliage and fruit, conceal a background orchestra of insects, birds and animals. By the time the jolly crew reaches the community of Ogobi Ajibode, they are already in role.

The musicians alert the people to their arrival, leading them with their talking drums in traditional songs. Chairs are brought forth—the fancier, upholstered ones for the Oba (traditional ruler) and elders—and mats are unrolled for the small children.

Like the medieval morality plays, the characters are easily identifiable: there's Good and Evil and an attendant cast of local character-types. The costumes are appropriately zany and the laughter rolls in easily from a delighted audience.

Two hunters, Ola and Oye, are setting out to catch bush meat, chanting as they go. The two strike up a conversation about village developments, Ola is delighted with the prospect of a borehole for piped water; Oye is pleased enough, but not satisfied. He thinks roads and electricity are more important. They start to argue. Ola wonders how his friend could not be aware of the relationship between health and clean water. Anyone who has had guinea worm like him, would forever treat water with the respect due to it.

The attentive faces of the audience light up when a handsome young woman enters carrying a jug to fetch water. Ola alerts her to the dangers of her mission to the pond. Oye tries to ridicule his friend: who will the woman listen to?

Then there is a song demanding responses from the community, and now, the climax, a lad with guinea worm comes onto the set crying in agony.

Spontaneously, people approach the performers and slap Naira bills on their foreheads in a gesture of appreciation known as spraying. An elder addresses the assembly. He was a guinea worm victim. He pronounces the play to be absolutely true. The audience cheers.—STATES UNICEF's LYNN GELDOF

DESCRIPTION

 The success obtained by community theatre during the Extended Programme of Immunisation (EPI) led to the idea of sustaining and expanding the experience, by adding a strong component of training, by including health and children's rights topics, and by extending the theatre performances to other states.

By 1991 it was clear that the two or three existing community theatre groups would not be sufficient to perform in hundreds of new villages, so a thorough training programme was devised. The initial drama group, led by Nigerian director and scriptwriter Jimmy Solanke, was invited to organise the core group of trainers. A training manual and materials were developed to provide a methodology for ten intensive days of training that would cover everything from the history of theatre to modern drama techniques. The emphasis of the training was put on the actors.

The local government contributed food and accommodations during the training, which was always conducted at the LGA level. UNICEF agreed to pay the trainers and for script development. The training workshops included the preparation of simple props and costumes that would become property of the LGA drama group after the training, to support their performances at the community level. An important issue by the end of the training was the selection of a name for the newly formed drama group, a process that was done collectively in order to establish an artistic identity.

Jimmy Solanke developed twelve scripts based on "Facts for Life." Ten million copies of the popular UNICEF publication had already been distributed worldwide by 1991, in more than 150 languages. In Nigeria, the book had been published in four local languages (Hausa,

Ibo, Yoruba and Pidgin English); and nearly 500,000 copies were distributed, including those in English. The topics that were developed into scripts tackled health issues such as AIDS, immunisation, safe motherhood, basic education, guinea worm eradication, environment, food security, diarrhea, and malaria. Each script had plenty of humour, which came easily to Jimmy Solanke.

A new and totally different perspective was developed. In order to ensure sustainability of the programme, Local Governments were asked to provide transportation and seed funds for the newly trained groups to operate. LGA health services would accompany the theatre group during performances, for effective service delivery at the community level. As soon as new theatre groups came out of training, they would start performing; 46 groups were trained in an equal number of selected LGAs. Their mission was to perform in their own area, because of cost-efficiency, cultural pertinence and sustainability.

Financing the performances of the LGA drama groups touring at the community level was never a hindrance to the project. Most local government authorities were willing to provide the seed funds on the order of Naira 1,000 per performance, or US$25. Though initially some groups were not interested in such a small amount, soon they realised that by performing every night of the week the sum became interesting. And they also knew they could collect as much as Naira 200 per show from the *spraying* custom. That is, if the community enjoyed the performance.

It was made clear to the drama groups that the relationship with UNICEF was only temporary. Eventually they could offer their theatre services to any government or cooperation agency wanting to promote a programme in rural areas.

As time went on, other trainers for the Hausa-speaking northern region and for the Ibo region in eastern Nigeria, were involved in training more groups.

BACKGROUND & CONTEXT

During the late 1980s UNICEF took over the responsibility of supporting every country in the world in their attempts to achieve 80 percent immunisation for all children under one year of age. Massive media campaigns were put in place with the support of national networks, which generally provided free airtime for UNICEF supported messages.

In Nigeria no less than 15 radio and 13 television stations in ten states were involved. Monthly training sessions with journalists ensured that the right messages were delivered with quality. Weekly programmes were produced at each LGA, in an attempt to create competition for better immunisation results among the states.

But it was not enough to achieve the objective of 80 percent. "The limitations of mass broadcast and print media in a country such as Nigeria are fairly obvious. Electrification is confined to the cities and immediate suburbs or shanties. Even where electricity exists, television sets are too expensive for the vast majority. Television tends therefore to be the prerogative of the rich and the influential. With radio the reach is much wider though limited by the expense of batteries, a set of which cost the best part of a dollar," wrote Lynn Geldof.

Nevertheless, the top-down communication approach through mass media was insufficient. It was imperative to get down to the communities where not even radio is heard. That is how community theatre came into the picture.

The only strategy possible for reaching the poorest of the poor and the most isolated communities that were left out of the immunisation campaign in Nigeria was interpersonal communication, and one communication activity that could contribute to social mobilisation efforts at the grassroots level was the popular theatre. UNICEF identified one hundred villages in Oyo and Ondo States where immunisation coverage was at its lowest and then organised village performances by theatre groups, who would go along with the immunisation services to the villages. By 1991 this successful experience later led to the full blown project called the *Network of Educational Theatre* (NET), where training became the key element.

ASPECTS OF SOCIAL CHANGE

The beauty of popular theatre in Nigeria is that it can be built on existing ritual manifestations, taking advantage of local culture to communicate new messages of benefit for the community. Local culture not only contributed to strengthen message delivery, but also benefited from the process of digging into local traditions and reassessing the value of customary practices.

The important and immediate impact of the popular theatre activities resulted from marrying the dramatic performance with service delivery. For cultural reasons many women had until then avoided vaccinating their children, but eventually were convinced by Jimmy Solanke's play *The Postman Calls*. Right after the performance, nurses had to deal with hundreds of women and their children of all ages, lining up to get their immunisation shots or drops.

This had a double benefit: on one hand it created greater awareness among people in the villages; on the other hand, it ensured that the health staff from the local government would go out to the villages on a regular basis, which they were often reluctant to do.

One theatre group already made a difference. Moreover a continuous programme of training contributed to multiply and establish permanent drama groups in each of the selected Local Governments. The innovative aspects of the programme derived from the fact that each drama group was culturally relevant to the villages where performances would take place. Not only was the language the same, but other cultural codes which are very specific to each community were taken into account: the costumes, the songs and the local greeting.

Furthermore, the drama group would often arrive at the village a few hours before the performance in order to collect information and anecdotes about recent events in the village, to incorporate references into the play and thus ensure the involvement of the audience during the performance. The scripts were adapted to each concrete situation through improvisation, though carefully preserving the quality of the messages to be delivered as much as possible.

The whole project was designed to be: cost-effective, culturally relevant, directly related to service delivery, and sustainable. The idea was to deliver a medium as a tool for communities to use according to their needs.

The methodology of training and quickly making drama groups available for performances were the keys of a strategy that aimed to rapidly expand the coverage and the scale needed to reach thousands of deprived communities.

CONSTRAINTS

Apart from Jimmy Solanke, few trainers were interested in working at the community level, or if they did, their demands for compensation were far outside of UNICEF possibilities.

Some Local Governments did not fully commit to support the newly trained drama groups. They wouldn't provide transportation when needed, and wouldn't include seed funds for the drama groups in their annual budget, as was agreed with UNICEF.

Not all the groups took training with equal seriousness. The ten intensive days were sometimes shortened to eight because some groups were not willing to continue the training sessions over the weekend.

The very advantage of adapting the scripts to the concrete situations of the villages where performances were scheduled often became a dangerous practice, since some drama groups left out important messages and derived their performance into a sequence of funny situations with little or no content.

REFERENCES

Community Empowerment: Social Mobilisation in Nigeria by Lynn Geldof, UNICEF 1994. Pp. 132.

Popular Theatre by Alfonso Gumucio Dagron, UNICEF 1995. Pp. 176.

RADIO IZCANAL

BASIC FACTS

TITLE:	Radio Izcanal
COUNTRY:	El Salvador
MAIN FOCUS:	Health, human rights, education
PLACE:	Nueva Granada
BENEFICIARIES:	Population of Usulután Department in El Salvador
FUNDING:	Associación de radios y Programas participativos de El Salvador (ARPAS), Community Assistance Foundation, The Netherlands (CAF), Canada, Norway Ayuda Noruega, Cooperación de Canada
MEDIA:	Radio

SNAPSHOT

The dirt road to Nueva Granada disappears from time to time under a cloud of fine dust, as small trucks and motorcycles rush towards the village. No one in nearby towns wants to miss the II Festival of Arte, Cultura y Comunicación that *Radio Izcanal* has organised to celebrate both its eighth anniversary and the inauguration of its new building and digital equipment. The main square of Nueva Granada is full of people, moving from one corner to another to see the exhibition of trained dogs by the local police, or the exhibit of photographs and documents that trace the history of the station since its early days. The Mayor, the priest, guests from other Salvadoran institutions and even from abroad are already seated waiting for the official programme to start. A few speeches follow reminding the audience of the story of *Radio Izcanal*; then fun and free food for everyone. Young musicians and dancers from other provinces have come to pay their tribute to the radio station. The boys sing ancient songs in Nahua and the girls dance dressed in traditional Maya *huipiles*.

Izcanal or Ixcanal is a word derived from Nahua language, once important among the indigenous population of El Salvador. It names a common plant that grows large thorns as tiger claws. This is maybe why the founders of *Radio Izcanal* choose it as the symbol of the new community station. "*Ix* means leopard and also sacred place; and *canal* is where the energy is rooted into the earth," explains Basilio, one of the founders. "The radio has the force of a leopard, and it is rooted into our ancient traditions and culture," he adds.

A sample of the thorn plant has been placed beside the main door of the new building. Its sharp edges are a reminder that a lot of struggling and hard work were necessary before *Radio Izcanal* earned indisputable recognition. Even the Mayor, who is from ARENA, the rightist party that supported the military during the civil war, is an advocate for *Radio Izcanal*. He had to fight within his own political party for the existence of *Radio Izcanal*, too easily labeled as a "rebel" station.

Now is the time of reconciliation. People are holding on to democracy, as imperfect at it seems to be. Everybody wants to move beyond the bloody war that divided the country. *Radio Izcanal* is the expression of hope.

DESCRIPTION

Radio Izcanal was conceived and started in 1991 by a group of Salvadoran exiles, most of them peasants. They had returned home in early 1990. More exiles returned and joined the station when the Peace Accords were signed on January 16, 1992, after more than a decade of internal war. For eight years most of the exiles had been living at the San Antonio refugee camp in Honduras. It was there that they started planning the radio station. Meanwhile, they developed activities of popular theatre, puppets and other interpersonal communication tools. They did it to organise themselves around important topics such as health and education while strengthening their community.

The station started in a small community called Nuevo Guaicho, where the first group of former refugees were given land when they returned from Honduras on March 5, 1990. The influence of the station grew so fast that a few years ago the population of a nearby larger town, Nueva Granada, invited the community leaders of Nuevo Guaicho to move the station to the larger town. For several years they operated out of a small building over the main square of Nueva Granada, with simple nonprofessional equipment: a six-channel mixer, a couple of cassette players and recorders and a small volunteer staff.

On November 20th 1999, after the move to Nueva Granada, the station started operating in a new building, with a higher antenna, a bigger transmitter, a 24-track mixer, digital audio equipment and most interesting of all, computers that can handle most of the programming and recording.

Funding of *Radio Izcanal* has gone through a number of attempts. It started with very little means except for the direct support of the community, but as it expanded its influence, the needs of the station grew as well. Now, the station has various sources of funding and one of them is advertising. Being the only station located in that part of the country, *Radio Izcanal* is sought by small shops to air ads aimed at the local population. Educational messages are also important. The external support for *Radio Izcanal* has come from The Netherlands, Canada and Norway. CAF/SCO (The Netherlands) contributed the new equipment; Canada donated materials for the construction of the new building (the community had bought the land); and Ayuda Noruego (Norway) financed the training. All this was possible through the support of ARPAS.

Radio Izcanal is part of ARPAS, a leading organisation in El Salvador founded in February 1994. ARPAS is a network of twenty-four community stations, most of them transmitting on a common frequency (92.1 FM) which was purchased to prevent small community stations from disappearing under the heavy legislation imposed in recent years.

Ten new stations are soon to be added to the network, either under the 92.1 FM or 90.5 FM frequencies. At least six radio production centres are also associated with ARPAS, producing educational programmes often used by the radio stations of the network.

The mission of ARPAS is to "associate, coordinate and support participative radio stations allowing the expression of civil society, and especially the great majorities, thus contributing to the democratisation of speech and the construction of democracy in the country." The objective is to "have a presence all over the national territory with stations and participatory programmes of quality, which support the active participation in the development of the communities and the nation." ARPAS is member of the primary international networks, such as ALER, WACC and AMARC.

BACKGROUND & CONTEXT

During several decades the state of El Salvador existed in a similar political situation as Guatemala: civil war. The military in power violated human rights in their attempt to annihilate the popular guerrilla movement.

The community radio initiatives started during the war. One early attempt was Monseñor Romero's *La Voz Panamericana*, the AM station that the Bishop-martyr opened to the voices of the people in the late 1970s. That station was the only one to denounce publicly the murders, disappearances and torture by the military. At some point it was violently shut down, and Monseñor Oscar Arnulfo Romero was killed in his own parish.

During the 12 years of war, clandestine *Radio Venceremos* and *Radio Farabundo Martí*, both communication instruments of the guerrilla movement, fulfilled the role of alternative information tools, allowing the population in El Salvador and worldwide to learn about the war and human rights violations. They contributed in building international awareness and solidarity with the Salvadoran people.

The peace accords of Chapultepec did not take into consideration the topic of democratisation of media. The only reference to communication is the legalisation of the two guerrilla radio stations that were given frequencies and legal status. Ironically, *Radio Venceremos* turned its back on participatory communication and became a commercially driven station.

ASPECTS OF SOCIAL CHANGE

In the new democratic context of the 1990s, *Radio Izcanal* is a very good example of participatory communication and media that is totally "owned" by the community. One of the most interesting aspects of *Radio Izcanal* is that it grew from a very poor community station, owned by former refugees that were given only a piece of land to survive, to the main radio station in the Usulután department.

Radio Izcanal managed to represent not only the voices of those that had been victims of the war, those that had to flee and left everything behind, and those that lost their land and belongings because of their political beliefs. *Radio Izcanal* had the will, since its inception, to represent the voices of all rural people in Usulután, including small towns and urban areas such as Nueva Granada. People from the whole region quickly understood that *Radio Izcanal* was also their radio station.

Another interesting aspect is how *Radio Izcanal* constantly refers to the "ancient," to the Nahua and Mayan cultures. The language used by the station is permeated with references to the indigenous cultures, even though El Salvador, contrary to Guatemala and Honduras, has not been a country with a large Mayan population.

The fact is that by doing so, *Radio Izcanal* is contributing to restructure a cultural identity that was largely destroyed both by war and the modernisation of the country. One of the morning sections of programming is called *El Guiz*, in reference to a local bird known to be a symbol of good news. This section brings in a special guest from the community for an in-depth interview.

An outstanding thing that happened in the history of *Radio Izcanal* is that the Mayor of Nueva Granada, who belongs to the right-wing political party ARENA, has been a strong ally to the project since the beginning. He even fought inside his own party to preserve the right of *Radio Izcanal* to air. As a result the Mayor is well-respected among the population of Nueva Granada.

Young people from the community are being constantly incorporated in *Radio Izcanal* as staff, which gives the station a very refreshing sound and look. At least five founders, from the first generation, are still there, but they interact very easily with the youngest reporters and disc jockeys, such as Alexander Quinteros, who joined in 1994 when he was in his early twenties.

Communities in the Usulután department of El Salvador, have plenty of access to the radio station. Anyone can step in and request a message be sent through the station. Special slots are scheduled to take care of music dedications, anniversary congratulations, and any other community event.

By creating its audience not only among the former refugees but the general population of nearby villages, *Radio Izcanal* has ensured both that it is widely accepted by everyone and that the former refugees have been fully integrated within the community.

The most innovative aspect is no doubt the use of the same frequency to allow all the stations to air in their areas of influence. The topography prevents signal interference.

CONSTRAINTS

Community radio stations in El Salvador exist with similar restrictions and menaces as other stations in Central America and most of the world. Access to frequencies is becoming increasingly difficult due to the privatisation process and government legislation that puts frequencies in the hands of those who can pay for it.

Even after the Peace Accords were signed, the landscape of media in El Salvador remains as before—in the hands of the very few. Civil society does not participate in the public debate about development or policies. Legislation concerning the media is unfair, undemocratic and incoherent; it only guarantees the arbitrary means of conceding the benefits of official favouritism to private sectors.

If there were no institution such as ARPAS in El Salvador, it is clear that community and participatory radio stations would have had a hard time surviving in that context.

REFERENCES

The information for this chapter was based on direct observation and interviews with *Radio Izcanal* staff, during a field visit to El Salvador in November 1999.

Further details were obtained through ARPAS; in particular through Oscar Perez, its Executive Director.

ARPAS brochures provide a good insight into the network of community radio stations.

SOUL CITY

BASIC FACTS

TITLE:	Soul City
COUNTRY:	South Africa
MAIN FOCUS:	Health, women's rights
PLACE:	Johannesburg
BENEFICIARIES:	General population, several millions
PARTNERS:	National Network on Violence Against Women (NNVAW), South African Broadcast Corporation (SABC)
FUNDING:	European Union, UNICEF, Kagiso Trust, Japanese Government, British Petroleum (BP), Old Mutual, DFID.
MEDIA:	Multimedia: radio and TV shows, publications

SNAPSHOT

Matlakala comes back from work late, and Thabang is very angry. She tries to cheer him up by giving him a shirt she bought for him, but he throws it on the floor, verbally abusing her. He tells his children to go to their bedroom, and he slaps Matlakala hard across the side of her head, knocking her to the floor.

The next morning he acts as if nothing happened and apologises to Matlakala. ... Thabang is having a problem with his salary at school—he hasn't been paid for three months. He doesn't like the fact that Matlakala is supporting him. Nonceba [a friend] sees Matlakala's bruised face, and she asks her about it. Matlakala lies—she say that she fell.

The Serithi family goes out for dinner and have a good time. Thabang overhears Matlakala telling her father about the beatings, and he is furious, "I told you not to discuss our business with anyone!" The children are terrified, but Bheki [their son] stops him from beating Matlakala again. Thabang tells Bheki he will understand when he gets older and is the man of the house. Thembi tells Matlakala that Thabang used to beat up her mother too. Matlakala goes to her mother and tells her what Thembi told her. Matlakala's mother tries to tell her that she must endure because Thabang paid lobola [a dowry] for her, and it is a woman's duty to make the marriage work.

Matlakala gets a wake-up call when a woman is brought to the clinic. Her boyfriend has stabbed her. Later the woman dies. Matlakala goes to stay at her parent's house. She refuses to go home until Thabang's family and her family have a meeting about his violent behaviour. Thabang's father tells Thabang that he must discipline Matlakala—"according to tradition."

At the family meeting, Matlakala's father takes a strong stand as a man, against violence against women. The elder officiating emphasises that he has been around a long time, and nowhere in culture or tradition is violence against women condoned. A man who beats his wife is deemed a coward. Thabang apologises and the episode ends unclearly as to whether Matlakala will agree to return. —Excerpt from a TV Drama, Series 4

DESCRIPTION

 *Soul City* is a South African health promotion project that harnesses the power of mass media for social change. Garth Japhet, a doctor and part-time journalist, founded *Soul City* in an attempt to put the power of mass communications in the service of preventing the spread of HIV and promoting healthier lifestyles. *Soul City*'s programmes are "edutainment," (education plus entertainment) an enriched version of traditional TV, radio and print. They are popular; designed and produced to air in primetime, rather than in less-viewed educational time slots.

Though *Soul City* is first and foremost a television and radio series, the project pursues a dynamic, integrated and multimedia approach.

Television Drama
Soul City is one of the most popular programmes in South Africa, the winner of the Avanti award for excellence in educational broadcasting. About 2 million people watch the show every week. Each of the five series so far has focused at least some of their storylines on HIV/AIDS. Other health and social issues featured include mother and child health, diarrhea, smoking, rape and violence against women, disability, and alcoholism.

Radio Series
The messages and themes of the *Soul City* television drama are replayed through its radio series, entitled *Healing Hearts*. This consists of 60 15-minute episodes broadcast in nine languages on nine regional radio stations. The show was developed to appeal to more rural audiences who have less access to television.

Booklets / Newspapers
The *Soul City* campaign uses printed material to reinforce the broad messages conveyed by the electronic media and to supplement knowledge with more detailed information. The booklets are serialised in

two languages, published in ten newspapers nationally, and thereafter in a total of 2.25 million booklets that are distributed as inserts in these newspapers during the broadcast period. Clinics and community-based projects also receive copies for distribution.

Public Relations and Advertising

Public relations and advertising strategy have a dual role—to popularise the television and radio shows and to advocate for particular health issues. A variety of competitions on the radio and television and in newspapers and magazines encourage health and positive community-oriented behaviour.

Health Education Packages

To bolster the awareness and knowledge created by the television show, *Soul City* uses more traditional youth and adult health education materials in formal and informal settings. Materials include comics with information pages, audiotapes and workbooks.

"*Soul City* is increasingly focusing attention on media advocacy for healthy public policy, recognising that communication strategies for meaningful social change cannot focus attention solely on individuals. There are many structural and environmental barriers in the way of individuals making healthy choices. And the need to advocate for healthy public policy, that can help create a supportive environment for behaviour change, is vital," says Shereen Usdin, from *Soul City*.

BACKGROUND & CONTEXT

South Africa is starting to recover after decades of strategic discrimination and enforced inequality. Though it is regarded as a middle-income country, the majority of South Africans still live below the bread line and millions subsist in circumstances resembling the poorest countries in the world.

National health statistics reflect the inequities of society, with large portions of the population suffering from preventable deaths and diseases. Although there have been campaigns to spread knowledge, the backlog in resources and decades of poor education are difficult to eradicate.

Soul City was conceived just after Nelson Mandela's release in 1991. It was a period of intense political and social activity. The activist spirit of the day created a fertile environment for pursuing an innovative and educational use of the public airwaves. The programme's ultimate success has depended on the quality of the programming.

There have been very few health education programmes aimed at challenging social attitudes and changing unhealthy behaviour patterns; *Soul City* set out to do precisely this—in an imaginative and entertaining way that would be accessible to a broad range of people.

Dr. Japhet is quite clear-eyed about the impact of *Soul City*'s programme. By itself, the television and radio dramas do not dramatically change people's public health behaviours. Rather, the programme creates a more fertile and helpful environment in which other public health activities and initiatives can function and succeed. Independent evaluations have shown *Soul City*'s ability to increase knowledge, shift attitudes and move people to action.

Broad Reach

The evaluations of *Soul City* demonstrated the popularity and extensive reach of the series: 61 percent of all respondents were exposed to the *Soul City* media; 57 percent of TV viewers saw *Soul City* TV; 41 percent of radio listeners heard *Healing Hearts*; 37 percent of newspaper readers saw the booklets; 70 percent of young people, age 16-24 (*Soul City*'s targeted demographic) knew of the show. This kind of awareness was found equally in rural and urban areas.

A Conversation Stimulant

According to the evaluation, viewers and radio listeners talked about the show. Discussion took place at home between parents and children, at school between teachers and students, and among friends, particularly younger people.

Shifts in Knowledge and Attitudes

The second *Soul City* evaluation showed that 95 percent of those who had been exposed to *Soul City* media said they had learned something; 92 percent were aware of the AIDS epidemic, compared to 85 percent of those who had not been exposed to *Soul City* media.

While *Soul City* has had considerable success providing knowledge and changing attitudes around health and other social issues, it has had less impact thus far on actually changing behaviours. For example, despite the series' influence on smoking knowledge, no appreciable change in smoking habits was reported in surveys following the series.

MEDIA & METHODS

It is widely acknowledged that media is an efficient and cost-effective way of reaching large, dispersed and often illiterate audiences. The vast majority of South Africans, even in marginalised and remote areas, have access to at least one form of mainstream media—approximately 92 percent of South Africans have access to radio, 71 percent to television, and 17 percent read daily newspapers. The use of entertaining programmes to empower people with knowledge, however, is a relatively new concept in South Africa. *Soul City* has pioneered this "edutainment" approach, contextualising educational messages within a dramatic genre.

"I don't believe mass media is the silver bullet. It has to be part of an integrated strategy. It's a catalyst," asserts Dr. Garth Japhet. The strength of *Soul City* derives from a mix of strategies:

- **A multimedia approach:** Despite its reliance on television and radio, *Soul City* does integrate its health promotion with print and public relations activities.

- **A commitment to community-based research:** The messages and storylines of both the radio and television series are tested, refined and retested during each show's development. *Soul City* conducts extensive formative research to ensure the issues are dealt with in a way that is relevant and meaningful for audiences.

- **Leveraging the power of stories and brand:** *Soul City* is not obviously didactic, leaving the actual "teaching" to its educational support materials and to the other health promotion efforts. This leveraging is one of the most innovative aspects. The characters are featured in comic books, in school, and adult education materials.

- **Creating an environment for change:** The popularity of *Soul City* has brought the issues of AIDS, tuberculosis, smoking, and others into public conversation.

CONSTRAINTS

The media environment is changing in South Africa, providing a greater variety of viewing options. Many other programmes are competing with *Soul City*'s efforts to reach as broadly and deeply as possible. If *Soul City* doesn't keep the edge, it could lose audiences.

Soul City staff has developed significant and unique skills, but there are few people in the country who are trained or able to replace them.

The success of *Soul City* has led to significant growth in the last three years, and the organisation is just learning how to deal with the managerial and other challenges associated with this expansion.

REFERENCES

Soul City Web site <http://www.soulcity.org.za/>.

"*Soul City*—Using Multimedia for Social Change," in *Community Media News*, Usdin Shereen, Issue No. 5, October 1999.

"*Soul City*: A Case Story." The Rockefeller Foundation, 1998. Working paper for the Cape Town meeting on "Communication for Social Change."

ACTION HEALTH

(1992) Nigeria

···

BASIC FACTS

TITLE: Action Health Incorporated (AHI)

COUNTRY: Nigeria

MAIN FOCUS: Youth sexual and reproductive health

PLACE: Lagos

BENEFICIARIES: Suburban youth

PARTNERS: Communication for Change

FUNDING: MacArthur Foundation, Martha Stuart
                     Communications, UNICEF and
                     United Nations International Drug
                     Control Programme (UNDCP)

MEDIA: Video

SNAPSHOT

"Bola, what do you think about what we just said?" a voice echoed through my subconscious. It wasn't until Sandra, my friend in the video class, tapped me on the shoulder, that I realised I was too engrossed in my thoughts and didn't notice the question directed at me.

Barkley, our video production instructor, had just painted a vivid picture of the challenges we face as young people growing up and how the glamorisation of sex in the mass media, has influenced young people into taking risky choices about their sexuality. As he spoke, it seemed I was looking into a mirror and my life just stared back at me. When I was 13 years old, I thought only "mummies" made babies. How? I could not say. My busy parents were never around to talk with me about changes I experienced while growing up.

I can remember how terrifying my first menstruation was. In fact, I thought I was going to bleed to death. It happened when I was at school. Fortunately for me, my class teacher Mrs. Akinpelu, cleaned me up and reassured me that it was normal. When I got home, all mum said was that I shouldn't go close to a boy again, since I am now menstruating. "Why, shouldn't I?" She didn't tell me. I was "lucky." I got information from friends. Although I discovered later that not all I was told by my friends were true. They needed information as much as I did.

I live in a suburb Ifako. My friends and I learned most of what we know about sexuality in the "streets," so to speak. While hanging out with the girls, we talked about boys that had made sexual advances on us, and how the relationship turned out. You were teased if it was discovered that you were still a virgin. Losing your virginity was in vogue. My mum, who was the only one around most of the time, was not disposed to discussing sexuality. She was annoyed when I asked her about love and told her a guy was making sexual advances on me. She threatened to tell my father that I was becoming wayward. — COMMENTS BY YOMI IYIOLA-MARTINS AND NETU ILAVBARE, WHO WERE TRAINED IN VIDEO PRODUCTION BY *ACTION HEALTH*

DESCRIPTION

 The Participatory Video Communication (PVC) Unit was introduced in 1992 as an integral part of *Action Health*'s information, education and communication strategy. Communication for Change (C4C), a USA-based organisation, conducted a 16-day training workshop for seventeen members of the video team. Three project staff and four AHI members went through the basics of participatory video communication, particularly the technical skills for videotape production and playback facilitation techniques, as the initial group of ten adolescent peer educators trained.

The initial training had a multiplier effect as it began the training of trainers programme. These pioneering video members went on in 1993 to train 19 other adolescents to further strengthen and ensure continuity of the video project. The process of continuous training has ensured the continuity of the participatory video project through present times.

The PVC unit of *Action Health* has been crucial to the information and educational activities of AHI. The goals are:
- To establish a Teen Video Team (Teen Tee Vee) trained to produce videos on issues concerning reproductive health for educating other adolescents;
- To produce videotapes on AHI peer programmes that can be used for sharing experiences between groups across countries;
- To make videos targeted at sensitising adults, especially parents;
- To influence policy so as to reduce the resistance to accommodate the genuine needs of adolescents regarding reproductive health information and services;
- To use the entertain/educate approach to reach adolescents through playing back tapes.

The PVC Unit carries out certain specific activities. The first is video production, which encompasses the production of both dramas and musicals for reproductive health information and education. This involves a drama troupe made up of secondary school students and out-of-school young people. Their functions include writing scripts and acting in selected dramas. The drama troupe is used during outreach activities, performing in markets, halls and during road shows, using the participatory drama strategy to involve the audience in the shows. Members function in a volunteer capacity only and do not receive any remuneration except a transportation subsidy and an occasional honorarium. They join the troupe based on their interest and commitment, not for monetary gains.

So far, the PVC unit has 64 productions, in formats varying from documentary to drama and musical videos, covering many issues including: adolescent health problems, teenage pregnancy, drug abuse, the role of adolescents in overcoming communication barriers, teen sexuality, STDs/AIDS diseases, abortion, rape, pubertal problems, and family planning. In December 1998, the unit produced a musical video entitled *Be Wise and Other Songs*, a video for adolescent health in which young people wrote their own lyrics and sang their own songs.

Another function of the PVC Unit is video editing. This involves the training of new video project assistants on the techniques involved in editing videotapes produced by the drama troupe. Probably the most important function, particularly in terms of its education and information objectives is playing back tapes at the Youth Centre and at various schools and organisations. During the first half of 1999 alone, it was able to reach over 4,000 adolescents.

BACKGROUND & CONTEXT

The spread of AIDS/STDs in Africa has prompted NGOs to organise programmes aimed at promoting reproductive health. The *Action Health* Incorporated adolescent reproductive health programme was initiated to address the poor status of adolescent health in Nigeria where there are very limited channels that provide appropriate information to adolescents.

AHI action is predicated on the realisation that adolescents need to be aware of the various factors that influence the experience they have at this crucial stage of their lives. It believes that providing them with this knowledge will empower them to make informed decisions concerning their sexuality and life planning directions.

In pursuance of this goal, Participatory Video Communication (PVC) was introduced in 1992 as an integral part of AHI's information, education and communication strategy in collaboration with Communication for Change (C4C). While the PVC Unit administratively works as a subunit of the IEC Unit, it has carved a niche for itself, and could easily be said to make independent contributions to the functioning and overall efficiency of the organisation.

ASPECTS OF SOCIAL CHANGE

In Nigeria, as in many other countries, television, home video and films, have become a popular mode of communication, with enormous influence among adolescents who reside in urban areas. As a tool of information, education and communication, video is perhaps the most user-friendly and cost-effective medium for information dissemination to an audience.

Action Health video productions have been used to educate people both young and old on the reality of the problems encountered by adolescents on reproductive health issues. However, AHI considers that providing video production skills to more than 30 young people over the years has been its most important achievement with long-term impact. Training is empowering young people with skills that they can develop in the future to make their lives better and to use as a stepping-stone to success.

The PVC Unit also helped to discover and develop talents in acting and singing. These talents are mostly discovered from performances of the drama troupe. For example, the Unit's production of AHI's musical, *Be Wise and Other Songs*, gave the young people who were involved in the production the opportunity to expose their talents to a much larger audience and at a much faster rate than they probably could have achieved on their own. The Unit's approach is popular with adolescents and is easily reflected in the enthusiasm shown by youths desiring to participate in its activities.

It is evident that young people are becoming more and more dynamic in their mode of communication. This is the advantage of a participatory approach because the young people themselves make productions that will hold the interest of their peers and still get their message across to other stakeholders as well who can make a difference in issues that make an impact on their lives.

"The participatory video communication strategy is a good mirror of society. It uses 'real' people with whom the audience can relate their experience, thereby making the video more believable and effective for attitude change," wrote Yomi Iyiola-Martins and Netu Ilavbare, *Action Health* second generation trainees.

According to *Action Health*, video possesses several advantages over other media:

> The first advantage is its attractiveness: images are often remembered longer than verbal messages and moving images attract even more attention. Secondly, there is the "entertainment/educating" feature: video can educate while still carrying out the role of entertaining. Third, it is an influential medium: decision-makers and policy makers who are used to receiving information through these media often watch television, video and films. In the fourth place, videotapes can be played over and over again. A fifth advantage is its record-keeping and documentation potential. Finally, the activities are also participatory: during the video playback sessions everyone that is involved in the process has the opportunity to make individual contributions.

The method of continuously training other adolescents has ensured the stability of the participatory video communication project. *Action Health* has made a wise decision in the video project by allowing young people to run it, with minimal supervision from adults. Young people write the scripts, handle the production equipment and do the editing of tapes.

Moreover, in carrying out its function of making productions to pass information and education along, the project keeps a drama group made up of adolescents. These young people produce plays and musical videos, which are afterwards evaluated by a larger group of adolescents to see if the contents are appropriate for them.

The use of the strategy in facilitating discussion promotes sharing experiences among participants so that they can learn from one another. The audience is then able to assess their decisions or actions regarding their sexuality in this kind of forum.

CONSTRAINTS

Though *Action Health*'s Participatory Video Communication unit has contributed in making videos on sexuality education more accessible to young people, the challenges are still enormous. Participatory video can only positively affect the lives of small groups of youths, while the large majority is under the influence of the avalanche of pornographic material which is easily accessed by young people in Nigeria.

To compete in number and quality with foreign productions that misinform youths, *Action Health* would have to enter the grounds of professional video productions, which may be out of its reach and also beyond its current methodology. Currently, the PVC makes the best use of equipment that is quickly getting older. The Hi-8 analogue cameras and editing suite can no longer produce materials of high technical quality comparable to the output of modern digital equipment. In fact, *Action Health* has been renting professional video cameras for some high-quality productions.

REFERENCES

Information for this chapter provided by Nike O. Esiet, *Action Health* director.

The Mirror of Our Lives: Participatory Video Communication in Action Health *Incorporated* by Yomi Iyiola-Martins and Netu Ilavbare.

ECONEWS AFRICA

1992 Regional, Africa

••

BASIC FACTS

TITLE:	EcoNews Africa
COUNTRY:	Regional, Africa
MAIN FOCUS:	Information, networking and capacity building
PLACE:	Nairobi (Kenya)
BENEFICIARIES:	NGOs and CBOs in East Africa
PARTNERS:	Association for Progressive Communications (APC), Media Institute of South Africa (MISA), Zero, among others
FUNDING:	Humanistic Institute for Cooperation with Developing Countries, The Netherlands (HIVOS), Non Government Organisation Network (NGONET), Oxfam, Panos, IDRC, Swedish International Development Agency (SIDA), Both Ends, Netherlands Development Organisation (SNV), UNDP, Action Aid Kenya, Swedish Society for Nature Conservation (SSNC), TOCAIRE, Friedrich Ebert Foundation, among other
MEDIA:	Internet, e-mail, newsletters, multimedia

SNAPSHOT

EcoNews Africa *enables African CBOs and NGOs to be actively involved in decision-making on sustainable development by promoting timely strategic information flows at all levels.* —ECONEWS MISSION STATEMENT

Many of the NGOs and CBOs lack formal members. Those with members have only a few active ones, because of the diversity of their interests. The main recurrent problem is the lack of a longer term vision, because many of them organise and are established to address single issues of a short-term nature; for example, digging bore holes in order to resolve a water problem. These organisations therefore tend to be weak. The strongest CBOs and NGOs are those with unity of purpose. Their visions tend to go beyond that of meeting the basic needs to alleviating poverty or enhancing the ability of households to meet their own basic needs.

In spite of the increasing numbers of NGOs and CBOs, their survival rate is limited, as is their impact. Many of them also have limited analytical skills and lack the capacity to organise along systemic issues. Lack of access to information is a major constraint in this process. However, the move towards alliance building is having some impact.

CBOs tend to have more organising constraints than do NGOs. Their grassroot level organising is constrained by low literacy levels coupled with the strong regulation of rural communication channels and stringent legislation that inhibits freedom of association. The privatisation of education is likely to make the situation worse.

The nature of development support being pursued by many NGOs targets the "rich among the poor." The most impoverished are hardly reached because they are lacking in many respects.

In general, the NGOs that *EcoNews Africa* works with in advocacy are generally resource endowed. As such, the focus is oriented towards partnership building and pooling resources for greater impact.

DESCRIPTION

EcoNews Africa is an NGO initiative that analyses global environment and development issues from an African perspective and reports on local, national and regional activities that contribute to global solutions. It aims to enhance the dissemination of information from affected populations to the relevant policy makers in order to promote the involvement of civil society groups in decision-making on issues relating to sustainable development. ENA is a registered NGO in Kenya, operating at a subregional level and working with NGOs and CBOs in Kenya, Tanzania, Uganda, Djibouti, Eritrea, Ethiopia, Somalia and Sudan.

The overall objective of *EcoNews* is to "promote the involvement and active participation of civil society groups in governance at the subregional and global decision-making levels on policies that impact on national policy, in particular macro-economic and environmental governance."

Two aspects that hinder effective partnerships among NGOs and CBOs are the inequitable access to resources resulting in skewed responsibility sharing and these opportunistic partnerships yield inequitable commitment to meet even jointly defined objectives.

The organisation is involved in the following programmes:

The *Multilateral Development Initiatives* project is involved in research and documentation of external initiatives (in particular from multilateral and bilateral funding agencies) that undermine people-centred development; and it carries out advocacy, capacity building and networking activities towards this end.

The *Community Mobilisation and Combat Desertification* programme is involved in building the capacity of affected community groups in East Africa to input into the preparation of the national action programmes to be developed by governments within the UN Convention to Combat Desertification.

The *Community Media* programme is responsible for advocacy and providing technical support to communities for the establishment of an enabling regulatory environment and the setting up of appropriate and effective communications infrastructure.

The *Information and Networking* programme promotes the use of Internet Communications for advocacy and governance on issues relating to macro-economic policy and sustainable development; and facilitates prompt and timely access and exchange of critical information among affected community groups and policy-makers at the international level.

The *Environmental Learning with Communities and Schools* programme seeks to promote the acquisition of scientific and indigenous knowledge through informal learning systems, for better environmental management.

EcoNews is supported by: the HIVOS, NGONET, and many other international organisations. During the period of eighteen months (1997 to 1998) covered by the last available Annual Report, ENA's disbursements totalled slightly over US$900,000; the funds consisted of grants, gifts and subscriptions.

Web services are provided by Web Networks, the Association of Progressive Communication (APC) centre in Toronto, Canada.

BACKGROUND & CONTEXT

The organisation started in March 1992 when NGO representatives wanted to design effective information and communication structures to facilitate the flow of information about development. In June 1996 ENA was incorporated as an international not-for-profit voluntary organisation.

According to ENA's Wagaki Mwangi:

> Unless there is an obligation to enforce universal access they will result in an even more serious outflow of resources, knowledge and technology from developing to developed countries. Hitherto government controls that hindered knowledge outflow from communities

will collapse. But where there is an awareness in the development world about the value of knowledge, as a commodity for sale through patenting it, there is little of this awareness in developed countries. Disparities between the rich and the poor will increase.

Among the biggest problems are: the regulatory environment and government policy, as well as growing poverty within the community — especially with the reduction of the role of governments in providing education—threatens the sustainability of whatever they develop.

ASPECTS OF SOCIAL CHANGE

This is how the "vision" of *EcoNews Africa* has been worded:

> A society in which communities: are at the centre of decision-making on issues that affect them; control their local environment; and have choices and alternatives to enable them to act in their own, others, and future generations best interests.

Collaboration and networking with groups working on similar issues minimises chances of duplication of work, potential competition, squabbles and animosity arising from the scramble for financial resources, and increases goodwill. Still, there is the need to design better strategies, in particular with regard to information and knowledge sharing.

Each of the *EcoNews* programmes has built its own platform of information in an effort to share knowledge and also expand the influence of innovative proposals. The *Multilateral Development Initiatives Programme*, other than interacting with influential institutions such as the World Trade Organisation (WTO), World Bank, African Development Bank (ADB), Organisation for Economic Cooperation and Development (OECD) and the International Monetary Fund (IMF) on macro-economic policies, has also conducted research studies and issues a quarterly publication, *Development Watch*, to analyse multilateral development trends.

The *Desertification Programme* has assisted groups in Kenya, Tanzania and Uganda to work together and form the National NGO Coordinating Committees (NCCDs). In collaboration with the Environmental Liaison Centre International (ELCI), ENA has completed a guide in Kiswahili to assist local communities to understand the provisions of the UN Convention to Combat Desertification (UNCCD). It also produces and distributed a local newsletter, *Jangwa*, a publication concerned with the issues of governance within the context of arid land development. Its specificity makes it an effective civil society tool to monitor the UNCCD implementation.

The Community Media Programme has evolved into a separate institution, with its own financing, contributing to the networking of grassroots communication groups and supporting their skills development and organisation. It is a lead member of the Community Media Network of East and Southern Africa (COMNESA) and has focused on advocacy to promote an enabling regulatory environment for community media. It also produces for *EcoNews Africa* a newsletter, *Community Media News*.

MEDIA & METHODS

ENA's strategy is to facilitate the empowerment of CBOs and NGOs to undertake effective advocacy on strategic development policies at the national and international levels. To do so, the structural, organisational and cultural constraints are targeted. The programme's scope is research and information dissemination, advocacy, capacity-building and networking. The key activities are: building strategic alliances, strengthening information and communication capacities of the partners and the environment within which they operate, information and experience sharing, as well as research and policy analysis.

"The appropriate communication system is defined by the relevant communities through mobilisation initiatives. We simply offer technical support to adapt these communication technologies, not originally designed with such people in mind, to adapt them for their uses," says Wagaki Mwangi, *EcoNews* Executive Coordinator.

Methods used:

• Prompt access by NGOs and relevant government officials to information on global processes that affect national policy

• Growing involvement of indigenous NGOs in advocacy for their own benefit

• The recognition of the possibility of the use of the Internet by previously marginalised communities through the establishment of telecentres (promoted by the United Nations Economic Commission for Africa (UNECA) and IDRC among others) that is likely to benefit communities around Africa.

CONSTRAINTS

Advocacy-type groups are targeted and easily attract the ire of the government. NGOs focusing on infrastructural development and humanitarian work are less vulnerable to government intimidation. However, they require high running costs and a sound financial base. These factors, and the suspicion that exists between NGOs themselves, and between NGOs and donors, make NGO operations a big challenge.

There are few NGOs in the region involved in advocacy work that focuses on the inter-linkages in various sectors. Even fewer are those organisations carrying out these analyses in regard to how the global policies impact on their national policies.

REFERENCES

This chapter was written from information provided by Wagaki Mwangi, *EcoNews Africa* Executive Coordinator and L. Muthoni Wanyeki. A first draft of the case story was produced for the meeting on "Communication for Social Change" held in Cape Town in October 1998. Excerpts of the same case story were printed in "Communication for Social Change: A Position Paper and Conference Report," The Rockefeller Foundation, New York 1999.

The Annual Report 1997–1998 was also consulted during a visit to *EcoNews* office in Nairobi, as well as other bulletins and publications by the NGO that have been quoted in this chapter.

EcoNews Africa Web site carries additional information on activities, projects and partner organisations <http://www.web.net/~econews/>.

NALAMDANA

1993 India

BASIC FACTS

TITLE:	Nalamdana
COUNTRY:	India
FOCUS:	Maternal & Child Health, AIDS/HIV
PLACE:	Urban, peri-urban and rural Tamil Nadu
BENEFICIARIES:	Tamil population of Tamil Nadu
PARTNERS:	Society for Natal Effects on Health in Adult Life, India (SNEHA), Cancer Institute, Tamil Nadu State AIDS Control Society, India (TNSACS), Integrated Rural Development Trust (IRDT) and other regional NGOs
FUNDING:	Ford Foundation, Actionaid, UNICEF-Chennai, TNSACS, AVT Group of Companies
MEDIA:	Theatre, audio and video cassettes

SNAPSHOT

Every morning Lingesan opens "shop" in the Vysarpadi slum: he is the owner of a mobile ironing cart, a board on wheels that sports an iron box fuelled by pieces of charcoal. Every morning he collects pieces of clothing to be ironed from houses in the area. As he irons away the wrinkles of the neighbourhood's garments he often ponders the wrinkles in the lives around him. And as the day goes by he keeps his spirits up by composing songs in a style called "gana" that is unique to the urban slums of Chennai. He sings while he irons, sometimes to gatherings of people.

He heard one day about Nalamdana's *street performances from a friend. On his friend's urging he paid a visit to* Nalamdana *to offer his talents. He was surprised to learn that* Nalamdana *already used gana songs to communicate messages for social change to the people of the slums and villages.* Nalamdana *invited him to compose a song on HIV/AIDS. He had heard of AIDS but discussing it with staff at* Nalamdana *he gave thought for the first time to the perception of AIDS patients in society. He was moved and set about writing his song on care and protection of those infected.*

He was invited to record his song, and to his great surprise he was told he was going to sing it himself! Nalamdana *was recording 10 songs specially created on HIV/AIDS as part of their ongoing Information, Education, Communication (IEC) material development. Top playback singers from the popular tamil film music world had been persuaded to sing at concessional rates to create a popular, marketable tape with AIDS awareness messages.*

Lingesan recorded his song with only a tabla (rhythm instrument) to accompany him. Not used to studio recording, he was allowed to have the tabla in the same room—so that he could sing without the usual headphones, which he found uncomfortable to use. He sang nonstop in a single 'take.'

At the launch of the tape there were the galaxy of playback singers, music directors and special invitees on stage. Lingesan was a proud special invitee.

Lingesan continues to iron everyday, and as he does he continues to compose and sing and work with Nalamdana *in his spare time.*

—EXCERPT WRITTEN BY *NALAMDANA* STAFF

DESCRIPTION

Nalamdana

Nalamdana means, "are you well?" in Tamil and is also the name of an organisation started in 1993 by young people of various professional backgrounds with a common interest in theatre. *Nalamdana* believes that entertainment can be used to communicate information about socio-emotive sensitive issues. *Nalamdana's* mission is to provide health education and promote preventive behaviours through entertaining methods: street theatre, discussion groups, and songs with messages.

The logo represents the focus on health and the community based approach: a simple "kolam" or "rangoli," a pattern that symbolises the typical routine of every housewife in a traditional Tamil home—cleaning the house's front yard and decorating the front steps with the pattern drawn with rice-flour. This is the first sign of welcome a visitor sees on entering a Tamil home. It also signifies the basic need for cleanliness, health and hygiene of the entire family. Beyond this, it also represents the power of bringing people together with a common vision.

Nalamdana's efforts are focused on two areas: a) widespread communication of preventive health messages to help people make informed decisions about their health, and b) development of local leaders who can harness the cooperation of the critical mass needed for visible change.

The group is involved in:

- Researching, scripting and performing community drama to increase awareness of key health and social issues and positive behaviour change;

- Development of television dramas on social issues;
- Development of Information, Education and Communication (IEC) materials for awareness and behaviour change;
- Conducting workshops on awareness about STDs and HIV, especially for illiterate men and women;
- Facilitating fundraising for and the dissemination of *Nalamdana* Scholarship Funds;
- Building up resources by training college students in street theatre.

Nalamdana has used innovative communication methods to deliver key health messages on HIV/AIDS to semi-literate audiences in inner city slums and villages in Chennai. In order to effectively reach the target population, it has developed a unique style of street theatre that is shaped in the popular film styles of Tamil Nadu.

Street plays draw mixed audiences, ranging from 700 to 1000 people of different ages, sex and occupation. *Nalamdana* has developed three shows on HIV/AIDS in its repertoire, and has also performed shows on suicide prevention, cancer, literacy, hygiene and general health. Between November 1996 and May 1998, *Nalamdana* performed in more than 111 slums covering a total audience of 200,000 people. It is likely that half a million have attended *Nalamdana*'s performances altogether.

Nalamdana recruits many of its actors and actresses from the communities. During a street play local people are given the opportunity to demonstrate their talents on the makeshift stage. This draws the community closer into the effort because having actors from communities like their own allows delivery of the message in a style and manner that is specific to their micro-culture. It also gives *Nalamdana* the opportunity to develop its message strategies with a closer understanding of the more subtle beliefs and issues of the communities.

The audiotape is a new communication tool *Nalamdana* has introduced to reinforce other methods. Half of the 4,000 copies of the first tape had been already distributed a few months after its release. People from the community wrote the lyrics while *Nalamdana* staff and top artists from Tamil Nadu performed the songs.

BACKGROUND & CONTEXT

Today with a billion people, India, along with subsaharan Africa, are the only regions in the world where over 50 percent of the deaths are still caused by infectious and wholly preventable diseases. Among the highest statistics in the world, 53 percent of the children under the age of five suffer from malnutrition, 53 percent of the population lives in absolute poverty, and little more than half of India's population can read.

Chennai is the capital of Tamil Nadu. It has a population of 6.6 million, of whom nearly 30 percent reside in slums located along the city's polluted waterways and railway tracks. The influence of television and cinema has been so overwhelming in Tamil Nadu that four of its Chief Ministers had their roots in the film industry. Chennai is also the headquarters of at least four Tamil satellite channels that telecast Tamil programmes, 24 hours a day. Given this interest in film and related media, *Nalamdana* decided to use theatre to reach its target audience.

Uttara Bharath founded *Nalamdana* in 1993 with a seed grant from the Echoing Green Foundation in New York. R. Jeevanandham, an actor from Madurai, participated in an experimental performance of a street play for general health. The response was so overwhelming that Jeeva moved from Madurai to join Uttara and form *Nalamdana*. Since then *Nalamdana* has reached over half a million people through street theatre and many more through mass media.

ASPECTS OF SOCIAL CHANGE

An evaluation of *Nalamdana* theatrical activities showed that a significant increase in HIV/AIDS-related knowledge occurred as a result of watching the drama. Before the play, audiences had relatively high levels of accurate knowledge about HIV/AIDS, but lower knowledge levels of common HIV/AIDS misconceptions. The drama reduced these misconceptions and also increased the level of reported intentions to treat HIV-positive individuals more kindly.

Considerable misinformation existed with regard to HIV/AIDS knowledge. The pre-test sensitisation analysis showed that the pre-test may have accounted for no more than four percent of this inaccurate knowledge increase. Importantly, there were differences in baseline HIV/AIDS knowledge such that certain low-income areas had lower levels of HIV/AIDS knowledge. These lower knowledge areas had greater increases in knowledge and thus the drama served to reduce this knowledge gap. The knowledge gap that exists between lower and higher SES groups can thus be reduced with interventions, such as community-level drama that appeals to the audience and communicates information in a manner that is understandable.

Theatre can play a key role in reducing knowledge gaps associated with low levels of formal education. Drama can find wide applicability in many settings. Although sustained behaviour change resulting from this increased knowledge is harder to measure, accurate knowledge and awareness of where to go for further services like testing and counselling are the essential steps to behaviour change. The interactive street theatre performances facilitate this link.

The drama also changed self-reported attitudes concerning treatment of individuals with HIV. This self-reported attitude change is important given the stigmatising nature of HIV, particularly in low-income areas such as the ones studied here. It may be that theatre brings the audience members closer to taking a pro-action approach to problems since it decreases the amount of discomfort associated with discussing AIDS.

MEDIA & METHODS

Mass media channels can inform people about HIV/AIDS; however, given the stigmatising nature of HIV they may be less effective at persuading audiences to treat HIV-positive individuals kindly because they may not be as effective as personal contact in appealing to the emotional components. Moreover, mass media programming is not interactive and may not be adapted to local community needs.

Street drama has been a popular folk art in India for centuries. Traditionally, street theatre was used to dramatise mythological and religious stories. Later this technique was modified to address political and social issues. Abstract and symbolic styles evolved in different regions. *Nalamdana* has evolved a unique style of street theatre based on the popular Tamil cinema style to ensure maximum impact.

A strong argument can be made for street theatre as a medium to communicate information about health and sensitive social issues. Plays can be adapted to be culturally appropriate and context-sensitive. Theatre provides a public and non-intrusive forum for communication. In addition, plays are ideal to reach target groups and facilitate immediate feedback.

Community performances by *Nalamdana* have followed a formula of pre-play entertainment to gather the crowds, followed by a street play. The performance is followed by random interviews and counselling by the actors (who are specially trained in HIV/AIDS counselling). Information regarding the nearest counselling and testing centres for HIV is also provided. The drama productions are particularly effective when accompanied by interpersonal counselling.

CONSTRAINTS

Caste plays a very significant role in Tamilian culture and often the staff arrives at a remote village only to find it mired in caste conflicts. The results are sometimes directed violently towards *Nalamdana* staff, who need to be ready to improvise at any time to make the most of the situation and still get their messages across. In urban slums the problems are outbursts of violence related to alcoholism and local rivalry. Since *Nalamdana* primarily reaches out to illiterate slum and village audiences, the group decided to create simple, direct and contemporary scripts. The stories had to be credible everyday situations that the audiences could relate to easily. Their effectiveness is entirely dependent on the quality and skills of the actors involved. Where sensitive health issues are being promoted, the actors also need to be sensitised. Finding such skilled and committed actors can be challenging.

Another challenge faced by *Nalamdana* is sustaining funding for the intervention programmes for a period long enough to document and measure the amount of behaviour change resulting from the programme.

REFERENCES

Information provided through e-mail exchanges by founder Uttara Bharath with Nithya Balaji and Tara Thiagarajan.

An Evaluation of the Use of Drama to Communicate HIV/AIDS Information by Thomas W. Valente Ph.D. and Uttara Bharath, MHS. Johns Hopkins University.

Evaluating Drama That Imparts Information by Uttara Bharath, MHS., Nithya Balaji, B.Sc. and R. Jeevanandham, M.Com.

Also, *Nalamdana* Web site <http://www.nalamdana.org/>.

RADIO ZIBONELE

 1993 South Africa

BASIC FACTS

TITLE:	Radio Zibonele
COUNTRY:	South Africa
FOCUS:	Community development and health
PLACE:	Khayelitsha, Cape Town
BENEFICIARIES:	Approximately 120,000 listeners
PARTNERS:	Institute for the Advancement of Journalism, National Community Radio Forum, Deutsche Welle Radio Training Centre, National Progressive Primary Health Care Networks, South Africa (NPPHCN), Vuleka Production
FUNDING:	Open Society Foundation of South Africa, Vuleka Production
MEDIA:	Radio

SNAPSHOT

At the beginning the audience of *Radio Zibonele* thought something "magic" was happening: *After the first illegal broadcast, an old lady that was listening to the station recognised the voice of the presenter. She was mesmerised and amazed. Later she came to the station and asked how it was possible that the voice of her friend was coming through the radio. How have they managed to put the person inside?*

Radio Zibonele's competence in local affairs and its prestige has helped to solve local social problems many times: *On a Tuesday morning, when Vusi Tshose, the Station Manager, learned of a possible school strike because of overcrowding, he called the local Minister of Education and mediated a meeting with the different parties involved in the problem. They met on Wednesday and Thursday and announced the solution on-air on Friday, averting the strike.*

And again: *When rival taxi groups were in dispute, they were invited to come to the station, state their cases and ask the community how they wanted them to operate the services.*

The station has supported educational activities on environmental and cultural issues, promoting grassroots participation in actions that benefit the whole community: Radio Zibonele *organised a clean up campaign for the community of Khayelitsha in partnership with a donor and the local authorities, which provided trash bags, gloves, a truck and also drinks for the participants. Eight thousand young people showed up on a Saturday morning to pick up trash.*

Self-help is the underlying theme of the station. Vusi Tshose said it was up to the people to make Khayelitsha beautiful: *No one is going to come from heaven and develop it.* Radio Zibonele *wants to make sure that each particular person is safe and healthy, from the individual to the family; from the family to the community.*

As one volunteer presenter said: *If there's a shot, we hear it too. If the power goes out, it goes for us, too.*—Based on anecdotes reported by Gabriel Urgoiti.

DESCRIPTION

Radio Zibonele was established in 1993 in Khayelitsha, a homemade radio station that was set up under a hospital bed in an old container truck. The container truck served as a clinic for the Zibonele Community Health Centre. *Radio Zibonele* provided illegal broadcasts, which reached the community of Griffith Mxenge in Khayelitsha (i.e., approximately 20,000 people) initially every Tuesday morning for a period of about two hours. When *Radio Zibonele* went on the air, it did so with homemade equipment using a transmitter, power supply, amplifier, a mixing console, and a small ghetto blaster. The total funding to set up the initial radio station was R2,500.00. Additionally, R1,500.00 (US$1 = R6.9 dollars approximately) was needed to run the station for one year, with only one weekly broadcast.

On August 2, 1995, *Radio Zibonele* went on the air legally. At present the station employs nine staff members and has a pool of volunteers—between 40 to 70 people—from the broader community. The ages of the volunteers range from 10 to about 50 years. Many of the volunteers have no formal education, resulting from the legacy of the apartheid era that was fraught with inequities. To keep *Radio Zibonele* operational as a radio station, it was essential to provide aggressive ongoing training and capacity building interventions as a fundamental process.

The result was that a skilled group of broadcasters have been developed and now form a resource pool of skilled people who continue training on an ongoing basis. Training and capacity development is broad-based and gives attention to areas such as technical radio skills, general management, budgeting and financial management, administration, research, marketing, advertising and fundraising.

The granting of a license to *Radio Zibonele* required the station to transform, from a small illegal radio station, broadcasting primary health care programmes for two hours a week to the community of Griffith Mxenge, to a radio station that would reach the entire community of Khayelitsha. *Radio Zibonele* increased its broadcasting time to three days a week, five hours a day, for the first few months. There was a resounding demand from the listenership to increase the broadcasting time. *Radio Zibonele* rose to this challenge and began broadcasting five days a week for a period of nineteen hours a day. This was a marked increase.

One of the key objectives of *Radio Zibonele* was to become a self-sustainable community radio station. During 1994 and 1995, the station received financial support from the NPPHCN Media and Training Centre (MTC). In addition a grant was received from the Open Society Foundation for South Africa to purchase appropriate equipment and to soundproof the container truck in which the station was based, and where it is still located today.

As part of the strategy to increase *Radio Zibonele*'s chances of becoming self-sustainable, the NPPHCN's MTC provided a period of intensive training, capacity development and support.

Since 1996 the station has been financially self-sustainable through revenues from advertising, sponsorship of programmes, and donations. Today *Radio Zibonele* is a full fledged radio station, broadcasting a whole range of programmes, from community issues to sports; to music and women's programmes; local and national news; children's programmes; and messages based on Primary Health Care, thus contributing to keeping the community informed and healthy.

BACKGROUND & CONTEXT

Khayelitsha is a peri-urban township about 26 kilometres from Cape Town; 300,000 people live in the area, their home language is Xhosa. It exists as a result of the forced removals and displacement of people during the Apartheid years. Khayelitsha can be defined as a deprived community that has a high rate of unemployment and illiteracy. Public health conditions and public health services are poor. Community-based health workers programmes played a fundamental role in delivering Primary Health Care services during the Apartheid era. The Zibonele Community Health Centre was one such community-based programme established in partnership with the community of Griffith Mxenge, the Child Health Unit, the Community Health Department and the Student's Health and Welfare Organisation from the University of Cape Town (UCT).

In 1993 Khayelitsha was experiencing political violence and unrest. The possibility of reaching the community through radio was an appropriate alternative because of the high rate of illiteracy and because most of the people in the area owned or had access to a radio receiver.

Originally, the aim of the radio station was to reinforce face-to-face communication and education performed by the community health workers from the Zibonele Community Health Centre. In addition, it was also to establish a community radio station that would serve the broader community of Khayelitsha.

However, the Apartheid state had a monopoly on the airwaves, and it was not possible to access the airwaves legitimately. The decision of broadcasting illegally was reached on the basis that people have the right to access the the airwaves. At that stage community residents did not recognise the government as being a legitimate and true representative of their interests.

A significant gain was made when the IBA granted *Radio Zibonele* a temporary community radio license to enable it to function as a legitimate radio station. On August 2, 1995, the station went on the air, and legally broadcast on FM 98.2 for the whole community of Khayelitsha.

ASPECTS OF SOCIAL CHANGE

As one of the first community radio stations started in South Africa, *Radio Zibonele* played a significant role. The participants applied their experiences gained from *Radio Zibonele*'s rich history of community involvement through participatory processes, and lobbied and advocated for community radio throughout the country.

Radio Zibonele has shown that communities can become empowered and take responsibility for their own development, using radio as one such means. Community residents have access to *Radio Zibonele* and use the opportunity to express their opinion about the programming, as well as to actively participate in the development of radio programmes.

One of the achievements of *Radio Zibonele* was to demystify the medium. This was achieved through the processes of community involvement in the radio station. Anybody is capable of broadcasting, working behind a mixing console and producing programmes with some basic training and support.

This was successfully achieved at *Radio Zibonele* in spite of the fact that not all the volunteers were literate, nor were they exposed to formal education. The message was achieved in a powerful way (i.e., "you don't have to be an expert in radio technology or broadcasting; you need a strong will and a deep sense of commitment ...").

The philosophy behind *Radio Zibonele* is that of a community radio station. This means that the radio station is owned and managed by the community of Khayelitsha. In addition, the community of Khayelitsha programmes the station's broadcasting. *Radio Zibonele* is a nonprofit radio station, responding to the community's expressed needs and priorities, and, it is accountable to the recognised local community structures.

The annual general meeting representing the Khayelitsha community elects a board of Directors to monitor and oversee the operations of the station in accordance with the station's aims and objectives. A general council exists, and this comprises the membership of the station (i.e., members of the community).

There is no doubt that the core factor underpinning the success of *Radio Zibonele* as a community radio station has been the culture, philosophy and approach used to implement and promote all activities and processes through community involvement and community participation. The implementation of such an approach was a time-consuming process with slow incremental progress. The rewards and gains made from this approach resulted in the real empowerment of the people involved.

Since the beginning of 1993, at the inception of *Radio Zibonele*, the station had a participatory approach to programme development and programme production. The community health workers work-shopped the contents and format for each health programme with community residents. During the workshops the community health workers had to ensure that the content of the health programmes were adequate and relevant to the target population.

A range of methodological approaches was used to develop and produce programmes. Examples of these include health songs, role-plays based on common health issues and themes pertinent to the community, story telling, and poetry.

CONSTRAINTS & CHALLENGES

Radio Zibonele broadcast illegally for a period of one year. During this period several constraints were faced, including financial restrictions, violence in the area, and perhaps most importantly, the status of *Radio Zibonele* as an illegal community radio station. This was exacerbated by the constant fear of being persecuted through raids of the radio station by the security forces.

During March 1994, the Independent Broadcasting Authority (IBA) came into existence. Following its establishment, the IBA requested all existing illegal radio stations to stop broadcasting so that the process of licensing these stations could commence. In response to the IBA's request, *Radio Zibonele* agreed to stop broadcasting as of

April 27, 1994. This date coincided with the implementation of the first free and fair democratic elections ever to be held in South Africa. This period saw a heightened awareness of communities in terms of their role and involvement in forming the statutory processes in the country.

REFERENCES

This chapter is mainly based on *Brief Information Summary on Radio Zibonele* by Gabriel Urgoiti, July 2000, and e-mail exchanges with him and Vusi Tshose, station manager.

Community Radio Stations in South Africa: Six Case Studies, prepared by Bill Siemering, J. Fairbairn and N. Rangana, Open Society Institute for South Africa.

TELEVISIÓN SERRANA

1993 Cuba

··

BASIC FACTS

TITLE:	Televisión Serrana
COUNTRY:	Cuba
MAIN FOCUS:	Education, children, community development
PLACE:	Buey Arriba Municipality (Sierra Maestra)
BENEFICIARIES:	Children, general population
PARTNERS:	Asociación Nacional de Agricultores Pequeños (ANAP), Instituto Cubano de Radio y Televisión (ICRT),
FUNDING:	International Programme for the Development of Communication (IPDC)/UNESCO, UNICEF
MEDIA:	Video

SNAPSHOT

I will tell you how our Sierra Maestra is. Here we have very high mountains and clear rivers, we have plenty of fruits like mango and pineapple, and many animals such as cows, hens, ducks, mules, horses and birds of all kinds. … Most of people here are peasants, they wake up very early to work on their fields. … Thanks to them all of us get our food. …

One by one the voices of children add to the description of their environment. These are children of 8 to 12 years old, sending a *video carta* (video-letter) from the remote hills of the Sierra Maestra to the children of Guatemala.

As they talk the camera shows the surrounding mountains, the forests, animals and flowers, the village, the school, the peasants at work. … Children at play, children at work.

By the end of the video letter they also start asking questions. They want to know about how the children in Guatemala live, they would like to receive a reply:

"I want to know if you also have rivers, lakes and mountains," asks a small girl facing the camera.

"I want to know what kind of flowers do you grow, because I like flowers very much and often give some to my sister," adds a schoolboy.

"If you come and visit us, we will show you how we live in the Sierra Maestra," adds another.

Boys and girls face the camera very naturally as it is not their first time. They have learned to live with a video camera in their community every day. In the few years since the *Televisión Serrana* project started, the cameras have become familiar among the population and especially with the children, as most of the work is done with them and for them.

Video at *Televisión Serrana* is an educational tool, an instrument for strengthening cultural identity, and also a means of communicating with other communities in other parts of Cuba and the world.

DESCRIPTION

Televisión Serrana is a community video and television project that operates in the heart of famous Sierra Maestra in Cuba. TVS is located at the small community of San Pablo de Yao, in Buey Arriba territory comprising a population of 32,000 people, of which the 63 percent are in rural areas, mostly coffee growers.

In January 1993 several institutions got together to sponsor the project. UNESCO provided some funding and technical support, the Cuban government through the ICRT contributed staff and training, the actual "owner" of this experience being the Asociación Nacional de Agricultores Pequeños (ANAP), a nongovernmental organisation. Currently, UNICEF also supports *Televisión Serrana*.

A small team of videomakers with low cost equipment runs the project, which aims to "rescue the culture of peasant communities" in the region, and "to facilitate alternative communication for communities to reflect their daily lives and participate in the search for solutions to the problems that affect them." *Televisión Serrana* is involved in a process of "education for communication" which promotes the social and educational use of video, and the development of a cultural environment within the difficult to access mountainous zones, as a contribution to strengthening the capacity of the communities to act on their reality.

This is mainly done through the production of video documentaries and reportage, though other formats are not excluded. Culture and identity, education, public health, environment, gender issues, and children's rights are among the main topics of these productions.

In an attempt to encourage self-sustaining activities, *Televisión Serrana* offers a number of services to the population—mainly training workshops through the Centro de Estudios para la Comunicación Comunitaria (CECC), created in 1996. This institution provides training and advisory services and organises seminars for those willing to use video in their communities as a tool for participatory development and democratic communication. The building that houses *Televisión Serrana* has a meeting room, a library, and the capacity to lodge up to ten people.

Other services offered by TVS include transferring and copying videocassettes from/to Beta VHS and S-VHS.

Although the project aims to become a television station, as the name suggests, it has only operated until now as a video production and distribution unit. Other than having produced about three hundred documentaries and reportage, the project has tried to establish a presence at the community level. Often an electricity generator, monitors and VCRs are taken to small communities in Sierra Maestra to exhibit recent video productions.

One of the main features of the project is the production of *vídeo cartas* or video-letters, addressed by the children of the Sierra Maestra to other children of Cuba and the world. Children are the protagonists of these testimonial documentaries where they first tell about their daily life, the nature surrounding them, the school, their entertainment, their families, etc. And then they ask questions of the children who will "receive" or view the *video carta* in some other part of Cuba or the world. Some of these are specifically addressed to another group of children, for example "To the children of Guatemala." In that sense the communication tool has a built-in request for a reply.

BACKGROUND & CONTEXT

"Before the Cuban Revolution, in this region there was only silence," recalls Daniel Diez. Peasants were isolated from the rest of the island. A few doctors were only available at Bayamo, the provincial capital village, 80 kilometres away on a dirt road. Schools were also too far and too expensive for rural children who were excluded from receiving any education.

Things have changed since then. Cuban history features Sierra Maestra as the mountains where, in the late 1950s, Fidel Castro, Ché Guevara, Camilo Cienfuegos and other rebels planned their guerrilla actions against the dictatorship of Fulgencio Batista. Today, there is one doctor for every 800 rural people. Schools are free and have been developed in the most remote places of the Sierra Maestra, an area of 451 square kilometres has become a National Park. Two channels of national TV and one regional TV channel can be tuned in, though there are still blackout areas because of the topography of the zone.

"Television contributes to homogenisation of cultures." That concern was in the mind of Daniel Diez when he started *Televisión Serrana:* "In my country, television shows rural folks only as producers of staples, nothing is said about their dreams, their conflicts, their culture. ..." He adds: "We wanted to truthfully record the full reality of the daily lives of these men and women that live in the mountains and preserve this for our national culture, as well as improve their self-esteem."

UNESCO International Programme for the Development of Communication (IPDC) approved an initial project to purchase video cameras and editing equipment. The provincial government provided the land and the building, while the ICRT took in its hands the responsibility of training the staff. After the initial investment phase, the ANAP became the back-up organisation.

ASPECTS OF SOCIAL CHANGE

Televisión Serrana is important in many senses. First, it is a symbol for independent communication in a country where media is largely centralised by the government. It is only in recent years with the surfacing of NGOs and small private businesses that the shape of communication began to change. Secondly, it is a challenge for community participation in a very poor area of the island. Thirdly, it is indicative of the new generation of Cuban videomakers who value alternative media and community ownership of communication tools, something unthinkable a few years ago.

About 32,000 people are in the area of influence of *Televisión Serrana*, 10,000 live around the Buey Arriba Municipality and these are directly exposed to the activities of the project.

Besides the direct impact of the daily activities of *Televisión Serrana* over its main area of influence, there is also the impact of its documentaries when aired through national television, something that has happened several times. Many people in Cuba are now aware of the life conditions of the peasants from Buey Arriba and other neighbouring communities.

The production of *video cartas* has been an instrument for this recognition. Just the fact of being filmed is meaningful for the people of Sierra Maestra. For if a video crew comes to their community and stays with them, it increases their self esteem. And if their voices and the images of their daily life and their culture are sent to other communities in Cuba and the world, it means their identity is recognised and respected.

The tools of *Televisión Serrana* are very basic: VHS, Super VHS and Beta nonprofessional cameras and editing equipment. The staff includes three cameramen, three directors, two editors, two producers, two sound assistants, and three drivers who also have the responsibility of setting the lights when needed.

Scripts proposed by individual members of the staff are discussed within the group, which includes all those related to production. There is no direct participation of the community at this stage.

The most innovative feature of TVS are the video letters, a loose type of reportage that captures people's reality and dreams through their own words, thus the editing is somehow guided and structured by their reactions in front of the camera. These "video letters" are wholesome expressions of people that have not yet been contaminated by mass media.

Showing the video productions in small villages of Sierra Maestra is an important aspect of the communication process that *Televisión Serrana* has sparked. TVS uses mules to carry TV monitors and VCRs. Once the show is over, a discussion follows. If a video-letter was shown, the audience may want to respond with a video-letter of their own: their need to say, "we are here" is enormous.

New topics for production usually emerge from debates. During one of the after-show discussions the crew discovered an 82-year-old man that had been writing poems on Sierra Maestra for 20 years; he became the subject of a video production. Likewise, the contamination of River Yao by a coffee processing plant was first mentioned after a video show; a critical video documentary followed and pushed for the implementation of corrective measures.

CONSTRAINTS

There were many difficulties that *Televisión Serrana* had to face in the beginning. The foremost had to do with the lack of experience of filmmakers in development work. The team had to win the confidence of the local communities, so these communities would realise that the newcomers had good intentions. Training local youth in video production and editing was facilitated by the fact that the average education level in Cuba, even in rural areas, is very high (12 grades).

At the beginning authorities didn't understand the value of setting up a cultural video project. This indifference was coupled with the emergency situation of Cuba. Right after the end of the Cold War the country entered what is known as the "Periodo Especial," characterised by a lack of transportation and fuel, equipment and spare parts, restrictions in energy and even food. Only education and health, the Cuban priority social areas, did not suffer as much.

REFERENCES

Information for the chapter was gathered through interviews and e-mail exchanges with Daniel Diez Castrillo, Director and founder of *Televisión Serrana*.

Several documentary videos and video-letters were reviewed to get a better idea of the contents and quality of productions.

TVS publishes *El Colibrí*, an electronic bulletin on alternative media.

BUSH RADIO

BASIC FACTS

TITLE:	Bush Radio
COUNTRY:	South Africa
MAIN FOCUS:	Health, crime, education
PLACE:	Salt River, Cape Town
BENEFICIARIES:	General population in Cape Town
PARTNERS:	University of the Western Cape
FUNDING:	Nederlandse Institute voor Suidelijke Afrika (NIZA), Shell Oil
MEDIA:	Radio

SNAPSHOT

When Mr Shabalala, an 85-year-old senior, went missing, his family called the station. The call came in at 5:48 p.m., in the middle of our drive-time programme. Bush Radio's policy on missing persons states that priority is given to this very important issue. The broadcast alert continued every three minutes and was included in the station's main news. Mr. Shabalala was found aimlessly wandering, disoriented and confused, ten blocks from his home. The call came in at 6:20 p.m. It had taken 32 minutes to find Mr. Shabalala using the radio. We're getting better all the time.

Tracing Missing Persons, is vital to the community: Cape Town is considered the rape capital of the world. The girl child is particularly targeted. Everyone at Bush Radio is committed to bettering this situation. The station has an on-air policy that any programme can be pre-empted should a child or any person in the community go missing. The radio will also attempt to get the family's voice on-the-air to reinforce the appeal.

In Cape Town everybody knows about Bush Radio's story. We went up against the apartheid government and started just as a pirate station. People didn't even know that you could! But we went on-the-air illegally and blew everybody's mind. It would have been fine had we not advertised it for months ahead of time. So they busted us and kicked our ass real bad and took our equipment. We fought like hell and got it back. Because of our audacity, today we have 80 community stations in the country. Hopefully it will grow. I know that we only reach an estimated 150,000 listeners. Our output is only 250 watts, so we're not doing bad.

We actually are very proud of what we're doing. We may not be popular, but we will always remain necessary. We want to be good and successful, but only so successful as it is good for the people. We can't become too popular, because we would be a threat to certain political and commercial entrepreneurs. Up till now, nobody controls Bush Radio *but the community. That's why they call it the mother of community radio in Africa.*

—Emphasises Zane Ibrahim, the founder and director of *Bush Radio*.

DESCRIPTION

 *Bush Radio* has carefully tailored its programming through the years to serve the community and favour concrete social and policy changes:

- **Bush Radio Hello:** this is the station's newsletter. Issues that concern the organisation are discussed, and listeners are invited to voice their opinions.
- **Community Law:** this programme is run by 4th and 5th year law students; each week a different issue is dealt with, factual information, which is very seldom explained to the general population, is provided for the community.
- **Backchat:** representatives of various community organisations explain the role their organisation plays and how the community can have access.
- **Everyday People:** a magazine format is used for this programme that lasts for 3 hours each day. The emphasis is mainly on township developments. Local music is aired extensively interspersed with public service announcements.
- **TRC report:** since the start of the Truth and Reconciliation Commission hearings, the station has been hosting a member of the commission on a fortnightly basis. The producer is Bushman Beat Senzile Khoisan, the chief investigator of the TRC.
- **Africa on Time:** this programme, a coproduction sponsored by the University of the Western Cape, deals with the situation as it unfolds on the African continent.
- **Taxi Talk:** Shell Oil funds this programme aimed to stop violence and crime, and promote safety in transportation to the city centres. Role players are invited to the station to come and discuss their grievances.
- **Prison Radio:** *Bush Radio* supports the criminology department of the University of Cape Town in developing a training programme whereby young people convicted for various offences are trained to operate a radio station within the prison facility.

Everyone producing or presenting a programme on *Bush Radio* does so on a volunteer basis.

The majority of *Bush Radio*'s listeners reside in the "black" and mixed race township areas that are largely economically depressed. The age group ranges between 18 and 50, but representatives of children's groups and the aged have recently made strong demands to provide adequate programming.

Bush Radio shares the frequency with another radio station. The training of volunteers takes place during the times when *Bush Radio* is not on-the-air. This time is also used to produce public service announcements and conduct community-based projects: voter education clips were produced to prevent violence during the 1999 elections; community outreach broadcasts are organised in the townships; and the Tracing Missing Persons Project has helped to find missing children.

The Community Radio Literacy Project invites various stakeholders in the literary field to encourage listeners to read; authors and poets are invited to discuss their work.

Workshops on the various genres of music are organised by the Music Education Project to help people better understand the music to which they listen. A programme on health carries at least one message on FAS (Foetal Alcohol Syndrome). The station carries no alcohol advertising because of these kinds of hardships the communities face daily.

BACKGROUND & CONTEXT

During the apartheid regime, a group of people started producing cassette tapes with information on community issues that were totally neglected or ignored by the State media. The group called itself CASET (Cassette Education Trust). Members of CASET would record relevant information onto tapes, make duplicates and distribute them in the townships close to Cape Town. They informed inhabitants of the townships about the importance of learning to read and write, of hygiene, and the need to move away from considering crime as part of their everyday life.

The group's primary goal was to make the airwaves available to everyone in South Africa. To achieve this it was decided to have a small broadcast outlet located close to the community. The University of the Western Cape offered to host the station at the request of the founding members, who were students at the time. The University was formerly nicknamed "Bush College" because it was located miles away from the nearest settlement and surrounded by bush when it was first built in 1960.

After Nelson Mandela's release in 1991, South Africa lived through a period of intense political and social activity. *Bush Radio*, "The Mother of Community Radio in Africa," started formally in 1992 as a voluntary association, operated by individuals and community-based organisations that were invited to become members. Funds were sought from various international donors to help train the members.

This was the first time in the history of South Africa that "black" people had the opportunity to learn radio skills. Many requests for a license to broadcast were turned down; by the same time an Afrikaans group in the north was broadcasting without a license. It was decided that *Bush Radio* would begin to broadcast, even with no license, in April 1993. The action against *Bush Radio* was swift; the police broke down the doors and confiscated the equipment. After physically man-handling several people who were present, two members were charged with breaking the law.

Bush Radio was finally granted a license to broadcast on August 1, 1995. It was decided to hold off going on-the-air until August 9th, South Africa's Women's Day, as a symbol of appreciation for the role the women played during the struggle for liberation.

ASPECTS OF SOCIAL CHANGE

The station has accomplished important changes in the social environment:

- Pressuring the former government to open up the airwaves and the establishment of the National Community Radio Forum.
- Brokering many peace deals between warring factions in the townships. Brokering a peace between the gangs that control the taxi services in the region.
- Training of 500 people; journalists now working for newspapers in the country were trained at *Bush Radio*.
- Prison Radio convinced the authorities that the therapeutic effects the programmes had on the inmates were beneficial to their rehabilitation.

What makes *Bush Radio* unique is the fact that it is entirely member-driven. An eye is kept on the attempts by political groups who try to take over the station.

On a visit to *Bush Radio* in 1999, Noam Chomsky said: "*Bush Radio* is arguably the most dynamic radio station that I have worked with."

Since its inception, *Bush Radio* has done most of the training in the community radio sector. Every year in-service trainees in station management, music coordination, news and programming are trained at the station.

Bush Radio was expected by its membership to service a wide range of people speaking several different languages but finally decided to broadcast in only three of the country's eleven official languages, Xhosa, Afrikaans and English.

- **Open forum:** during the monthly open forums, the community is invited to give their input into the running of *Bush Radio*. All members of the community are eligible for membership, for training, and are entitled to vote on any issue that comes before the organisation.

- **The members:** anyone living in the area serviced by *Bush Radio* is entitled to membership. The majority of new members prefer to simply provide moral support while a handful show interest in participating as volunteers. The number of volunteers had to be kept down to a manageable 70 people. The community is regularly informed through the on-air newsletter programme, *Bush Radio Hello*. The finance committee, headed by a board member, regularly monitors the finances of *Bush Radio*.

CONSTRAINTS

Bush Radio has been required to share a frequency with another station since its opening in 1995. The other station shut down at the end of 1999 leaving *Bush Radio* with dead airtime on either side of the broadcast. It took four months to convince the authorities and finally be permitted to occupy the empty airtime.

The influx of religious stations coupled with the government's decision in 1999 to fund its own low power FM stations (39 to-date), could spell trouble for the already struggling community radio stations. The religious stations are receiving extensive support from right-wing Christian groups in the United States.

Bush Radio has, since 1994, received five 1-year temporary licenses. This makes it difficult to plan ahead and negotiate contracts with potential sponsors or advertisers.

Some very powerful commercial radio stations have copied features of the station's format. This has taken away from the success that *Bush Radio* has enjoyed on its way to becoming self-sustainable. The fact that *Bush Radio* has only 250 watts of output against the 2,000 watts allotted to the commercial stations makes competition very hard.

More than 31 percent of its advertising revenue is handed to the marketing agencies. This has also slowed the growth to some extent.

REFERENCES

This chapter was prepared with information from *Mission Statement* (draft, February 2000), and additional e-mail exchanges with Director Zane Ibrahim.

Bush Radio: *Cape Town South Africa*, by Francois Laureys, in Radio Nederlands Web site <http://www.rnw.nl/realradio/community/html/bush_radio061198.html>.

Bush Radio *History and Backgrounds*, by Adrian Louw, in Radio Nederlands Web site <http://www.rnw.nl/realradio/community/html/history_bush_radio.html>.

COMMUNITY MEDIA NETWORK

1995 Kenya

BASIC FACTS

TITLE: Kenya Community Media Network (KCOMNET)

COUNTRY: Kenya

FOCUS: Networking, communication and participation

PLACE: Thika, Eldoret, Ugunja, Kisii, Meru, Kiambu, Muranga, Kibwezi, Homabay and Nairobi.

BENEFICIARIES: A dozen grassroots organisations

PARTNERS: EcoNews Africa

FUNDING: Friedrich Ebert Sttiftung, Panos Institute, Ford Foundation, Conservation Development Fund (CDF-USA)

MEDIA: Training, print, radio

SNAPSHOT

Nkirote (the girl's name) is still in school and hoping to come home for holidays. Kimaita, Nkirote's father is very keen on his daughter becoming a "mwari" (a stage between a girl and a woman). He goes around the village telling his friends about the impending "ceremony" because he does not want his daughter to continue being a "mukenye" (an uncircumcised girl).

Come the holiday and Nkirote comes home oblivious of the plans her father has for her. Her mum has no say in this matter but obviously supports her husband. A neighbour, Mugambi is a teacher and currently spearheading a campaign where girls go through a mock ceremony (where they are not "cut") and are actually taken into seclusion and taught the importance and responsibilities of being a woman which results in a woman being respected by the community and vice versa.

Nkirote learns of her fate when people start visiting her home. Men are happy drinking "kathoroko" (local brew) and start singing circumcision songs as they are already in a festive mood. The women offer her words of encouragement and advise her not to fear for soon she will become one of them, a "grown up." Nkirote runs away and takes refuge at Mugambi's

house where she confides in him of the "ceremony." Mugambi leaves her
in his house and goes to Kimaita's house (Nkirote's father) where he
addresses the guests on the dangers of female circumcision and gives them
an alternative, which is the mock ceremony. He gives the example of
his own daughter who went through the same mock circumcision ceremony.
After a lot of arguments and explanations, the villagers agree that the
ceremony should actually go ahead but there should be no physical cutting.
They understand the dangers associated with "cutting" in this modern world.

They agree to go on with their celebrations, where Nkirote goes through
the mock ceremony. Nkirote's parents also agree and she undergoes the
ceremony, learn the values and get the education intended from this
ceremony. An added value is that she has not been harmed by the cut.
—WRITTEN BY JENIFER NJIRU OF THE MUTINDWA THEATRIX.

DESCRIPTION

KCOMNET favours development-oriented, horizontal communication structures, which are owned and run by communities, as opposed to top-down communication structures. Community media reinforces the values of solidarity and participation, which are important elements in the development process.

There is a clear potential for community media to promote people's participation in public affairs and discourse. Development involves the exploration of the natural environment by people. This must be done in a manner that takes care of earth and culture. People must be knowledgeable about their history, the needs of their community, and the constraints that limit the achievement of their aspirations.

Community media structures would fulfill the above by strengthening and empowering communities to become aware of new possibilities and options to address such needs and aspirations through the process of media interaction.

Over a dozen community groups have joined KCOMNET. These are a few:

- **Five Centuries** (Nairobi) is a group involved in civic education and using drama to convey knowledge on the Constitution.
- **Kairi Young Star** (Thika) is a group of entertainers from the Kikuyo community, who produce songs with social messages.
- **Eldo Theatre Group** (Eldoret) is the only theatre group performing in the Rift Valley and uses dance and songs to promote nutrition and AIDS prevention, among other topics.
- **Ugunja Resource Centre** (Ugunja) is a network of smaller groups involved in drama on STDs and AIDS and a library for youth.

- **Puppetry Family Health** (Homabay) addresses young people with issues of early pregnancy and STDs through string puppets.
- **Dreams of Africa** (Nairobi) is another theatre group using street children as actors.
- **Igonga Mirror Tech** (Kisii) group composes songs during performances to build stories that relate immediately to the audience.
- **Mutindwa Theatrix** (Meru) has tackled through drama the issue of female circumcision, educating audiences to perform a symbolic ceremony instead.
- **Mumbi Theatric** (Muranga) uses vernacular poetry, drama and songs to entertain and educate on health issues.
- **Mangelete Community Project** (Kibwezi) started as a women's communication resource centre and later became a pilot community radio project.
- **Talking Calabash** (Nairobi) is a music group using African instruments and composing songs on social issues.
- **Slums Information Resource Centre** (Nairobi) has a network of reporters and produces a community newsletter; they document their activity on video.

KCOMNET plans to increase group membership by the end of the year 2000 as well as to conduct training at the District level using member groups as focal points.

The network is also embarking on greater advocacy for setting up community radio and television in Kenya, as well as networking with other stakeholders to push for a comprehensive overhaul of the current legal regime governing the media in Kenya.

BACKGROUND & CONTEXT

A community-based medium is distinct from the mainstream media:
- It is not commercially motivated, and it is not state owned.
- It is participatory and action oriented, its main mission is community empowerment.
- It is free of outside interference from the state, as well as political and commercial sectors.
- It is funded by both the public and private sectors, as worked out by the communities involved.

Because community media enable marginalised communities to speak about issues that concern them at the local level, links are created between development, democracy and community media.

The *Kenya Community Media Network* (KCOMNET) was established in November 1996 during a subregional Community Media Workshop for Eastern and Southern Africa in Nairobi. The crucial role community media play in development was recognised, and participants from Kenya were in agreement that it was important to carry the process forward. Networking was identified as useful for harnessing and supporting efforts towards developing concrete programmes. Initially, the project was part of the larger institutional framework of *EcoNews Africa*, which provided legal cover, office space, communications expenses and a secretariat.

ASPECTS OF SOCIAL CHANGE

KCOMNET's main contribution is facilitating networking of small community-based groups that were dispersed over the various provinces of Kenya. These groups had little or no support and lived very much in isolation. The network has contributed to facilitate exchanges among groups, and the training provided has strengthened internal organisation, as well as enhanced technical skills to improve performances at the community level. Training includes modules that enhance skills in a member's area of specialisation, as well as providing new skills aimed towards para-commercialisation and other sustain-ability measures. Consequently modules have been covered in group dynamics, community participatory production techniques, entrepreneurship and marketing techniques, and introduction into social communication campaigns, etc.

The groups have also had to identify their problems and how they perceive them being solved. They have been instrumental in identify-ing their training needs and are conscious of the changing environment. They are more confident in articulating their issues. Some are now capable of handling the Provincial Administration and can carry out their activities without being harassed by the administrative police. Most are currently involved in social campaigns on the different issues affecting their various communities. In a nutshell, they now realise that they are a kind of "communication channel" that is available to majority or grassroots people.

It is also important to mention that the network is now a recognised institution, capable of influencing policy-makers on deci-sions concerning the communication policies of Kenya. It's within this lobbying that the position paper "A Regulatory Framework for Community Broadcasting in Kenya" was presented to the govern-ment Task Force on Media Law in 1996. Later a "Bill on Community Broadcasting" was presented to the Attorney General and to parliamentarians for approval.

KCOMNET has prioritised its work along two crucial areas:
a) Training and capacity building and b) lobbying for an overall regulatory framework for community broadcasting.

Training takes the form of workshops. KCOMNET core group members teach basic communication skills to members of the community communication groups. A needs assessment is taken and all the subjects identified are then used to help form a curriculum of courses already undertaken and those to be pursued. The workshops also help to formulate the course objectives.

The groups that are part of KCOMNET use a variety of methods and media to achieve their objectives: street theatre, songs, poetry, live music, puppets, radio listening groups and community newsletters are among the tools used more often.

The Network also organises an annual festival where all groups meet to exchange and share their experiences.

CONSTRAINTS

The concept of community media is not yet well understood by policy makers and communities of Kenya. KCOMNET believes that communities must be clearly defined especially given the political overtones that "tribes" have come to be associated with. In reality, there are different perceptions of community, and it is important to have a common understanding of the term "community," which usually refers to a geographical entity. A different notion of community relates to a group of people with common interests.

Volunteerism in community media and how long this should continue is an issue facing the Network. All the members of the KCOMNET core team including the coordinator are people who work for other organisations and therefore their availability to perform tasks at the agreed time is not always assured. The challenge is to have permanent staff to implement the Network's decisions at the national level.

Communication between the secretariat and the groups is not always prompt. This is because most groups do not have access to a telephone and have to rely on the postal services, which are not always efficient. Reporting back by some of the groups to the secretariat at times becomes problematic. Usually the process is slow and this hinders some activities being carried out on time and, as a result, these groups are unable to beat the deadline.

"Another challenge is to change the attitude of the society, so that community media can be given the place it deserves as opposed to treating the sector as just entertainers. This is especially relevant to community theatre where there is a tendency of treating the groups involved in theatre as clowns," says KCOMNET coordinator Grace Githaiga.

REFERENCES

Information for this chapter was obtained in a meeting with KCOMNET coordinator Grace Githaiga in Nairobi, in March 2000, and further e-mail exchanges.

Community Media News Bulletin, a newsletter that reached Issue No. 6 in December 1999, has been another source of valuable information.

Also, *EcoNews Africa* Web site <http://www.web.net/~econews/>.

RADIO CHAGUARURCO

1995   Ecuador

....

BASIC FACTS

TITLE:	Radio Chaguarurco
COUNTRY:	Ecuador
MAIN FOCUS:	Rural community development
PLACE:	Province of Azuay
BENEFICIARIES:	Rural dwellers of Santa Isabel and Pucará
PARTNERS:	ALER, Coordinadora de Radios Populares el Ecuador (CORAPE)
FUNDING:	Intermon, Caritas, Manos Unidas, community
MEDIA:	Radio

SNAPSHOT

Marcela Pesantez was there: *On January 1, 1995 we went on-the-air. It was the most beautiful thing. Beautiful. With lots of people listening. We were crazy. Greeting all the people. Thanking the ones who had been with us since the beginning, those who had taken courses with us, the correspondents. Making calls to Cuenca to see if the signal reached the city. We made calls to Machala to see if they were listening. There were some people who knew we were going to be on-the-air and they called us. It was crazy. We played lots of music and every few minutes going on-the-air,* "This is Radio Chaguarurco! We're on-the-air! Listen to us, at 1550 *kilohertz! Tell your neighbours to listen!" It was beautiful. After a while, we started to calm down. But it took at least three days until we were calm enough to start doing the real work of the radio station.*

Marcela Pesantez studied communication in Cuenca. When she finished, she went back to her hometown of Santa Isabel, not sure of what she would do, but wanting to help her own people break out of their precarious condition. When she heard about the project to start the radio station, she immediately volunteered to help. The fact that she had never studied radio did not stop her from immersing herself in the medium and becoming one of the project's trainers. "I think it was good that none of us knew anything about radio. It meant that we didn't have any preconceptions about how it had to be done, and that meant that we could do it in a different way."

It quickly became apparent that the *real* work of the radio station involved a lot more than simply producing radio programmes. After years of waiting, people's expectations were high. They were not going to be satisfied with a station that sounded like all the rest. They wanted to hear their own experiences and concerns told in their own voices and in their own language. "I think the famous phrase that described the radio stations, and what we wanted to do with it, was *now you're not alone*," explains Marcela Pesantez. "Now there's a communication medium where you can talk, say what you feel, and denounce that person who is giving you a hard time. *Now you're not alone*. That was the phrase that motivated people."

DESCRIPTION

In September 1992 the *Chaguarurco Foundation for Rural Development* was established with representatives from *campesino* organisations, from the Catholic parishes, and from the workers and volunteers of the radio station. From the beginning it was agreed that the parish or any single person would not own the radio station. It was to be owned by the grassroots organisations, by the people.

While the station did count on the support of international solidarity for major capital expenses (US$80,000 from Intermon), the Chaguarurco Foundation decided that the healthiest way for the station to operate was to pay its own way. The volunteer labour of the programmers is one way the community contributes. In addition, the studios in Pucará and Santa Isabel are in space provided free by the local church, and there is always someone around to offer their skills when the station needs to renovate a studio or paint the offices. However, volunteer labour cannot cover all the costs, and *Radio Chaguarurco* has to generate some US$2,000 per month to cover its operational expenses.

The station's financial situation is healthy. Chaguarurco not only manages to generate enough revenue to cover its fixed costs, it is also able to put aside a few thousand dollars a year to improve its equipment or cover unforeseen costs. Sources of revenue include advertising (20 percent of the revenue), community announcements (40 percent), production services, and remote broadcasts of cultural events.

Radio programmes are locally produced. Music, news and interspersed community announcements are the most popular segments.

The *radio dramas* — acted out by the station's own staff members — provide a valuable way of explaining complex issues in everyday language people can easily understand. Themes for the daily dramas are varied, covering health, environment, politics, culture and human rights.

Volunteers produce the weekly programme *El Mercado* (The Market), hosted simultaneously in Pucará and Santa Isabel. It looks at prices and trends, and has played an important role in controlling prices and speculation.

A recent change to the programming has been the inclusion of news from Latin America and the world that the station gets from ALRED, the radio service of the Latin American Association for Radio Education (via a satellite dish on the roof of the Pucará station) and the *Púlsar* news agency (via the Internet).

While Chaguarurco is located in the two towns, the townspeople are not the main audience. Of the estimated 65,000 people in the area, only 20 percent of them live in the dozen or so communities. The station's listening area is primarily mountainous, but also includes part of the coastal lowlands, where bananas and cocoa are produced and mining is an important activity. Most listeners dedicate themselves to agriculture.

According to a 1996 survey of 400 people, *Radio Chaguarurco* is number one in terms of audience in both the towns and the countryside. It is, however, most popular in the countryside, among adult listeners, and with people with less education. Of the respondents from the villages, 40 percent claim to listen to *Radio Chaguarurco* "everyday." In the countryside this figure rises to almost 50 percent.

The results of the survey showed that the radio station was being well received by its audience but they also showed where improvements could be made by adjusting the schedule, providing better training for the announcers, and putting more agricultural information in the station's programmes.

BACKGROUND & CONTEXT

Most community radio stations in Ecuador are licensed as commercial or cultural stations. Community radio was not recognised until 1996 when the government approved a law that made special provisions for community radio stations. However, it placed severe restrictions on them including prohibiting commercial activity, limiting transmission power to 500 watts, and requiring approval from the army for reasons of "national security." CORAPE, the national association representing community radio, brought a constitutional challenge to the law.

The idea of setting up *Radio Chaguarurco* started in 1990 with a series of workshops organised by *campesino* organisations and by the local churches in Santa Isabel and Pucará, in the province of Azuay in the southern part of Ecuador. The purpose was to organise the communities to gain access to basic services (drinking water and electricity) and to ensure that human rights were being respected.

The question of where to establish the radio station, in addition to technical and financial considerations, had a political dimension. The selected community, Santa Isabel or Pucará, would be more likely to have its concerns broadcast, its members interviewed, and therefore it would benefit most from the station. Decentralisation was one of the objectives of the project, and in the end it was clear that wherever the station was located, that community was going to benefit, possibly at the expense of the other.

Pucará did have one important advantage: while Santa Isabel was larger and a more important economic and communications centre, Pucará's altitude (3,100 metres above the sea level) and more central location meant that from a technical perspective it was a better place to locate the transmitter. The solution was to put a 5,000-watt transmitter in Pucará, the administrative centre in Santa Isabel, and studios in both communities linked via microwave.

ASPECTS OF SOCIAL CHANGE

This is how peasants themselves evaluate the changes brought by the radio station:

> Communication is easier now. The radio has a system of communiqués. Every day we can send all kinds of messages—the situation of patients in the hospital, deaths, lost animals, meetings. ... The radio is the telephone for those who don't have [one].

> The authorities, institutions and merchants are more democratic. Before it was easy to abuse a campesino, charge higher prices, or steal material intended for public works in the communities. Now when there is an abuse, everybody hears about it on the radio. The radio serves as a sort of guardian in the democratic game.

> The radio has served to let us share experiences and problems. People from communities tell about their experiences on the radio, and this helps the others see the process—solutions to everyday problems are shared.

> The radio is contributing to the valorisation of our culture, our music, our way of speaking. These programmes are generating renewed pride in our own culture.

Radio Chaguarurco's success is not just a result of being the choice of more people than any other radio station. It has worked alongside other development and democratic initiatives to make a number of important changes in community life. It has improved communication, helped bring about more democracy and less abuse, made a positive contribution by promoting the sharing of experiences and solutions to problems, and made people more aware and proud of their own culture.

Like other radio stations, *Radio Chaguarurco*'s programming incorporates news, interviews, music and cultural programmes. There are, however, a number of important characteristics that distinguish Chaguarurco from other stations. The most important of these is the priority the radio station gives to local voices, language and culture. Unlike radio stations in the city, with announcers who try to hide any regionalisms in their accents or their language, Chaguarurco's announcers celebrate their own way of speaking.

Another important distinction is the way the station actively seeks out the participation of people from the countryside, inviting them to visit the radio station, to tell their stories, sing, or just to greet their friends and family members over the air.

To produce the kind of radio that the community wanted required a different kind of relationship with the members of the community than an ordinary station might have, and a different kind of radio producer. Only four of the eight full-time staff and 20 volunteers at *Radio Chaguarurco* have ever formally studied journalism, the others learned their skills in Chaguarurco's own courses, but all of them work as journalists and programme producers, in addition to sharing the secretarial, sales, technical and administrative tasks. Five of the full-time staff are based at the station in Santa Isabel and the other three in Pucará.

The station never forgets its important role as a communication channel at the service of the communities, the telephone for those who don't have telephones.

CONSTRAINTS

The first problem *Radio Chaguarurco* faced was obtaining a broadcast license. In 1992, Ecuadoran law did not recognise community radio. Getting a commercial license involved a complex and long process that, even after years of waiting, was as likely as not to fail, unless one had better political contacts and more influence than the people of Santa Isabel and Pucará did. Fortunately, there had been a station in Santa Isabel a few years before. The man it had belonged to had died and since then the station had been off-the-air. However, the license was still valid and the former owner's son was willing to sell it. Buying a station still requires government permission, which involves a process almost as long and complicated as being assigned a new frequency, but it doesn't require the same political influence.

The need for continuous training and the time it could take was underestimated, resulting in the loss of volunteers and difficulties in replacing the staffers that left. "Some of the correspondents lost interest. Radio is lots of fun, but when you don't have a salary or a stable job, no matter how much you like radio; you have to think about finances. You grow up and you want to get married and have kids and all that stuff. So, little by little people started leaving."

Last but not least, successive changes of station managers during the initial years, affected the stability of the project.

REFERENCES

This chapter was entirely based on *Radio Chaguarurco: Now You're Not Alone*, by Bruce Girard, at <http://comunica.org/pubs/chaguarurco.htm> and e-mail exchanges with the author.

RADIO GUNE YI

1995 Senegal

....

BASIC FACTS

TITLE:	Radio Gune Yi
COUNTRY:	Senegal
MAIN FOCUS:	Rural children
PLACE:	Dakar and rural areas of Senegal
BENEFICIARIES:	Children of Senegal at large
PARTNERS:	Radio Television de Senegal (RTS)
FUNDING:	PLAN International
MEDIA:	Radio

SNAPSHOT

Rural children behind the microphone. Children talking to children on the radio. Children making information available to their parents. Children earning the confidence and respect of their community. New organisations emerging at the community level under the leadership of children. This is happening in rural Senegal since *Radio Gune Yi*, an unusual communication project, started its activities.

In villages where the radio recording activities are held, clubs are formed and attended by children who organise other initiatives, like the centres for collective listening. In certain communities, children have mobilised for setting up theatre troupes and door-to-door sensitisation activities.

In Goria, following a *Radio Gune Yi* recording on the problem of education for girls, the children organised themselves to sensitise their parents about putting their girls in school.

In the Louga region, a theatre troupe goes from village to village for paid performances. With the proceeds they buy tools to clean up their neighbourhoods.

"What they listen to on the radio makes them develop very diverse behaviours, the menu of choices is broader for them now. There are things which, in our time, were taken care of by adults, but which are now taken care of by the children themselves. There is information on illness, which I didn't know, like AIDS, and on the precautionary measures to take. All this is transmitted by children, which makes the broadcast a pleasure for them to listen to," remarked the vice president of the rural community of Mbodokhan.

Most of the initiatives are promoted by those who have participated in *Radio Gune Yi* recordings, and the admiration and respect that the other children have for them leads to their own participation in those initiatives. It was for this reason that in Mbodokhan, a youth of 18 years, who didn't participate in the activities, organised a theatre group which does skits on clean environment, AIDS, and the education of girls: "I followed the example of what I saw during a recording."

DESCRIPTION

Radio Gune Yi is a radio programme done by children for children. Its name identifies it because "Gune Yi" means "children" in Wolof, the language most widely spoken in Senegal. It is produced by PLAN International Senegal, and all the network stations of Radio Télévision du Senegal broadcast it.

The programme was established by PLAN International to promote the Rights of the Child, mainly in relation to freedom of expression and access to information. Since it started in December 1995, *Radio Gune Yi* has visited more than 100 villages. More than 1,000 children have participated directly in production, while several thousand children have attended the recordings. Hundreds of thousands of children listen to the programme regularly.

The main objectives of *Radio Gune Yi* can be summarised as follows:

- Promote the Rights of the Child, particularly the right of freedom of expression
- Permit youths to have access to information concerning their cultural heritage
- Encourage youths to participate actively in the development of their society
- Broadcast educational messages in the domains of health, the fight against AIDS, education of girls especially, and habitat
- Provide positive entertainment for Senegalese youth
- Encourage local decision-makers to take into account the aspirations of the youth of Senegal
- Introduce children to radio and offer them a unique creative experience
- Contribute reinforcement to the awareness promoted by PLAN

Once a year, in August, ten recording sites are selected. The selection is made based upon requests submitted by rural villages or urban towns which would like to receive *Radio Gune Yi*. On this basis, the *Radio Gune Yi* research person does a production research field mission during which the final selection of villages is made. He/she meets with the communities, explains the concept of the broadcast, organises focus groups with children and adults to identify subjects and themes.

During these visits to the villages, not only are the children involved, but the school or literacy programme directors, and the village authorities as well. This participative method allows a selection of themes directly concerning the communities and assures that the children in-part determine the broadcast.

The follow-up begins after a date has been confirmed for the recording—usually about ten days before the broadcast is scheduled. The village is reminded and the preselection of potential child-participants is assured for the broadcast. As a general rule, two sites relatively close to one another are chosen. Thirty children from the two sites are brought together for a four-day training.

After the recording and editing is done, the seven RTS stations broadcast the programme on different days and hours. The schedule of broadcasting allows *Radio Gune Yi* to enjoy as much national coverage as possible.

The contact persons are responsible for the follow-up and for encouraging activities in the listening centres, which are created in every community where a recording experience has taken place.

BACKGROUND & CONTEXT

The results of a study on communication and childhood in West Africa, conducted in 1995 by CECI (Canadian Centre for Study and Cooperation), and CIERRO (Ouagadougou Inter-State Centre for Rural Radio), showed that in general children are neglected. In Senegal, only 15 percent of radio and television programmes address children. Programmes for children and youths are very rare, and when they do exist and are broadcast regularly, they lack clear objectives and quality.

The Senegalese audio-visual environment offers very few time slots that concentrate on children. Radio Television du Senegal (RTS) broadcasts "Kaddu Xaleyi" (the word for children), a programme in which children are interviewed, but is conceived and presented by adults and recorded in-studio. Walfadjri broadcasts *Bébé Walf* a programme in which children dedicate songs by telephone.

Children make up more than half of the total population in Senegal. They do not have appropriate access to information and do not enjoy freedom of expression. According to the Convention on the Rights of the Child, the media should broadcast information and programmes presenting social and cultural utility for the child, encouraging the growth of his/her personality, the development of his/her capacities and mental and physical aptitudes.

ASPECTS OF SOCIAL CHANGE

The goals of *Radio Gune Yi's* programmes are to inform, educate and entertain the children. The various segments about history and tradition, mastering the language, the rights of the child, on socio-cultural themes, and on educational themes such as health, AIDS, education of the girl child, and on PLAN International's activities are conceived in such a way as to transmit important messages to the young public.

The results of surveys show that *Radio Gune Yi* fulfills its mandate to educate, inform and entertain the children. What is even better, it also does so for adults. The majority of listeners say that the programme entertains and informs them, and that they learn from it.

"We, the parents of students, were agreeably surprised to discover that our children had so much knowledge and so many ideas," says the president of the association of the parents of students at Mbodokhan. The adults realised that the children know lots of things that they learned at school and elsewhere, outside of the family. They know things tied to their traditions, which they demonstrate by telling fables, making reports on the history of their villages or their ancestors.

The parents were reluctant in the beginning, when they didn't know *Radio Gune Yi* or the content of the programming. After *Radio Gune Yi's* broadcast, they let their children try new experiences and generally had more confidence in them.

"My participation in *Radio Gune Yi* gave me more status with my comrades and friends. I became very popular after my participation in *Radio Gune Yi* because not many people talk on the radio. My parents even nicknamed me, 'Handsome!'" says a 13-year-old boy from Medina Gounass.

Children become more responsible. *Radio Gune Yi* allows them to question adults directly and to show their knowledge, which they couldn't always do. They enjoy a new respect from adults; and the entire community has gained new knowledge.

Says an elder from Mbodokhan: "Knowledge is like a lost needle. A child can find it as well as an adult."

MEDIA & METHODS

Radio Gune Yi is one of those communication projects where the *process* is as important as the product. The process of recording at the community level has an immediate impact, enhanced by the broadcasting of the programmes.

Radio Gune Yi is not only a radio programme; it is also a local event; a rare event, which has an impact on the child participants as well as on their parents, spectators and on decision-makers. Speaking on the radio during a recording session is clearly a unique experience for the children. It permits them the rare opportunity to express themselves in public, to learn by doing, to show others their capacities and competencies, and to be heard throughout the country. The performance evokes reactions and feelings.

The children's exposition, is a centre of interest and hope for the community. Children are seen as individuals who have knowledge and positive abilities, which should be promoted. They are viewed as members able to contribute to their community.

The programme mandate is to offer Senegalese youth a space for expression and exchange of ideas—to give the children a unique experience, to inform, educate and entertain—considering that children learn better by doing, and that messages transmitted by children are better received by children. They speak Wolof—a language understood by practically all Senegalese—and use children's words, which simplify the messages and make them more accessible.

CONSTRAINTS

The informality of the relationship between *Radio Gune Yi* and RTS and the absence of a formal contract is a potential threat to the programme; which remains dependent upon the goodwill of the two parties and has no guarantee of being sustained.

The research missions for the documentation are only done once a year over a foreseen period of one month. This has two negative effects: first, collecting information once a year makes it sometimes obsolete at recording time, several months later. On the other hand, visiting ten sites in five regions (a total of 50) in only one month is too heavy a programme to be carried out in-depth. The rule of one site per day could be introduced.

Another point concerning production is the paradox that although the programme is broadcast at Wolof, all the jingles and most of the theme songs are in French.

The role of the listening centres—which should be created systematically at the recording sites—is not well-defined. Also not defined is a coherent strategy for the setting up of listening centres and their activities. In certain regions the centres are set up at the recording sites to allow collective listening and to encourage activities for youths. In other regions, the centres are set up on sites where PLAN is active or where *Radio Gune Yi* has not yet come. Certain *Radio Gune Yi* contacts would like to create listening centres in villages that don't receive radio, and therefore, don't have access to *Radio Gune Yi*.

REFERENCES

This chapter is largely based on: *Radio Gune Yi: Evaluation Report* by Savina Ammassari and Jean Fréderic Bernard, Centre for Development Communication (CDC), March 1999; and also on e-mail exchanges with Mimi Brazeaum.

RADIO KWIZERA

1995 Tanzania

....

BASIC FACTS

TITLE:	Radio Kwizera
COUNTRY:	Tanzania
MAIN FOCUS:	Refugees, peace and reconciliation
PLACE:	Ngara, border town to Burundi and Rwanda
BENEFICIARIES:	250,000 refugees, local population of Ngara and Kibondo districts of Tanzania
PARTNERS:	United Nations High Commission for Refugees (UNHCR), Red Cross, Norwegian Peoples Aid (NPA), World Food Programme (WFP), Oxfam, Réseau pour le développement soutenible (REDESO), UNICEF and Atlas
FUNDING:	Jesuit Refugee Service (JRS)
MEDIA:	Radio

SNAPSHOT

From the air the sight reveals a curious geometric pattern on top of the hills; numerous parallel lines extend their design from one hill to the next as if a gigantic net had fallen from the sky over this isolated place on earth: Ngara is only 25 kilometres from the border of Rwanda and 35 kilometres from Burundi. It is not easy to get here: only humanitarian flights in a five-seater Cessna from Mission Aviation Fellowship (MAF) or UNHCR planes land once a week on the dirt airstrip near Ngara.

One of the newest cities in the world is growing here: Greater Lukole, a giant slum with no other urban setting nearby. A city where all houses are similar, there is no electricity or piped in water. There was nothing in these hills in 1994, but the next year thousands of people arrived on foot, and it suddenly became one of the largest cities in Tanzania. Still today, West Tanzania is one of the biggest refugee areas in the world.

As we approach, people are carrying wood from the field. "Soon there will be no more wood for cooking," says Hilaire Bucumi, guiding me through the camp. A teacher by training and a reporter at *Radio Kwizera*, he is also a refugee from Burundi. His house is one of the hundreds lining the top of the hills. He shares his fate with half a million people, mostly peasants, which were pushed across the border by ethnic violence. He has a special permit to leave the camp every day and work at *Radio Kwizera*.

He was a teacher in Burundi, he worked in several secondary schools in Musenyi, Jenda, Musema and finally in Kayanza, his own province. Then, violence exploded in 1993; he left for Rwanda with his wife and a baby of five days. When he came back home in April 1994 he found his house had been attacked, they were after him, his life was in danger. Not knowing where else to go, he managed to cross the Malagarazi River towards Tanzania. Not everyone in the family was that lucky: his mother and mother-in-law died around 1996, a sister-in-law was beaten to death, neighbours were killed. …
He learned about it only years later. He tells me about it with a poker-faced expression. He has lived through it with resignation; tears won't help now.

DESCRIPTION

In 1994 *Radio Mille Collines*—the infamous "hate radio" in Rwanda—incited the genocide against the Tutsi. One million were killed, and over the "thousand hills" of Rwanda remain the tombs of those that didn't make it to survival. Three months later Tutsi troops came from Uganda and took power in Kigali, prompting 600,000 Hutu refugees to flee across the border to Tanzania.

Radio Kwizera (97.9 FM) was born in 1995 as a response to hate radio. The name says it all: *kwizera* means "hope" in Kinyarwanda language. It is the first JRS radio project and was designed by Fr. Thomas Fitzpatrick. Initial funding for the equipment came from JRS and UNHCR. The station reaches a radius of 300 kilometres, including the Kagera and Kigoma regions in Tanzania, and some parts of Rwanda and Burundi. The annual budget of *Radio Kwizera* is funded by JRS; in 1999 it was US$154,000. In 2000 the budget increased to US$214,000.

Initially, JRS proposed establishing a network of information; other than the radio station it included public address systems, roadside billboards, a library, newsletters and posters. Eventually only *Radio Kwizera* remained. The objectives included improving the physical and mental well-being of the refugees, helping with reconciliation, assisting with camp management, being a pastoral tool for JRS, and keeping refugees informed of developments in their own country. Camp information committees were set up to serve as focal points there.

Following the mass repatriation of Rwandan refugees in December 1996, JRS decided that the station should continue to serve the remaining Burundian population. Over the years it has also developed an audience among the Tanzanian population. Three types of listeners are now under the scope of *Radio Kwizera*: the refugees, the rural villages in the western regions, and population in Burundi and Rwanda. The fact that these two small countries are also within the range of *Radio Kwizera* increases the station's commitment to contribute towards reconciliation and peace.

The station broadcasts from 9:00 a.m. to 10:00 p.m., a total of 91 hours per week, 30 hours in Kirundi and 48 in Kiswahili. Information and programmes amount to 49 hours, and entertainment and music to 42 hours. Not one programme is aired twice. The schedule includes educational broadcasting for primary schools; programmes on gender issues, mother and child health, environment, sanitation, agriculture and livestock management; news, current affairs, youth and children's programmes, religious segments, development initiatives, greetings and music; as well as a refugee-tracing programme that has contributed towards reuniting families. NGOs collaborate on various topics: education, health, women's issues (NPA), water and sanitation (Oxfam), food distribution (WFP), immunisation campaigns (UNICEF), and environment (REDESO). *Radio Kwizera* also re-broadcasts in English, French and Swahili from Radio France International (RFI) and Deutsche Welle; and airs tapes from RFI, UN Radio, Panos Institute (Bamako) and Africa Radio Service (Nairobi).

The station lists among its policy issues the concerns for the poor and powerless, women and youth, cultural creativity, interreligious dialogue, and staff development. It provides training to enhance broadcasting skills.

The languages of programming are Kirundi (for the refugees), and Kiswahili (for Tanzanians). The station also re-broadcasts programmes in English and French from Germany, France and United Nations Radio, but most of the programming is produced locally. Two production teams (Kiswahili and Kirundi) guarantee the production of news and programmes for the refugees and for the Tanzanian population.

In 1994, fearing retaliation from Tutsi troops, 600,000 Hutu refugees fled across the border of Rwanda to Tanzania, creating one of the biggest humanitarian challenges of the last decade of the century. This happened about three months after "the genocide" in Rwanda. A very complex history of ethnic rivalry and struggles for power detonated a war that the international community was not prepared to prevent.

The first refugee camps were created near Ngara, a small town near Lake Victoria less than 35 kilometres from the border where Rwanda and Burundi meet. In December 1996, the Rwandan Hutu refugees were practically pushed back to their country by the Tanzanian army, and UNHCR was sadly instrumental in the forced repatriation encouraged by the Tanzanian government. The changes in power in Burundi resulted in subsequent smaller waves of refugees. By March 2000, a dozen refugee camps lined the border of Burundi: Greater Lukole (114,503 refugees), Lugufu (50,386), Mtabila (55,630), Muyovosi (35,869), Myarugusu (53 384), Karago (45,244), Nduta (51,432), Kanembwa (17,684), and Mtendeli (48,269) are the most important. Around 80 percent of the refugees are women and children; only 20 percent are men, most are from Burundi (347,536) and the Congo (103,781).

The need for wood in such large settlements is so great that trees have largely disappeared around the camps. Refugees are not allowed by Tanzanian authorities to travel more than 4 kilometres from the camps.

ASPECTS OF SOCIAL CHANGE

Is it possible to measure the impact of a station promoting peace and reconciliation? The ultimate objectives of *Radio Kwizera* may not be easy to evaluate in the short run, but certainly there are other aspects of the station that have already shown it's great potential to change the lives of thousands of people.

The refugee-tracing programme, aired in coordination with the Tanzanian Red Cross (TRC), has had a deep impact among refugees and their families that were either left behind in Rwanda or Burundi, or escaped to other refugee camps along the border. Even the "greetings" segment differs dramatically from a normal radio station. In *Radio Kwizera* a greeting message may read: "I'm alive, I survived." Other NGOs collaborate in producing programmes: NPA (Norwegian People's Aid), Oxfam, WFP (World Food Programme), UNICEF and REDESO. NGOs have benefited from their relationship with *Radio Kwizera* and have improved coordination within their own work.

A central aspect of *Radio Kwizera*'s mandate as a community radio station involves providing the means by which the community may engage in dialogue with itself.

In 1998 an audience survey was carried out in Ngara and Lukole camps, to estimate listenership, develop new strategies, and ascertain the level of awareness about *Radio Kwizera*. The survey showed that broadcasting 13 hours a day gives the station a strong identity. The station has made the right choice to balance information, education and entertainment. For example, it has used soap operas to deal with important issues such as AIDS. The station remains popular among both the refugees and the local population.

The 1999 *Evaluation Report* on *Radio Kwizera* strongly recommended the Jesuit Refugee Service support similar projects and develop a "blueprint for setting up small, portable stations in other refugee situations" in the world.

MEDIA & METHODS

The *Radio Kwizera* compound at Ngara is well equipped with a 2.5-kilowatt transmitter, a 36 metres high antenna, parabolic receivers, computers and rooms that house three studios, a meeting room and enough space for reporters to work. A 50-watt booster in Kibondo started operation in July 1999 to serve the new refugee camps south of Ngara. The transmitter as well as the antenna and receiver are powered by four solar panels.

Among the twenty staff of *Radio Kwizera*, four are Burundian refugees who live in the camps and have special permits to join the station every morning. This is the only example of direct participation by the community. Everyone at the station is an announcer, a scriptwriter and a reporter. The station also has 60 people working as "stringers," providing news from the refugee camps.

CONSTRAINTS

In 1996 UNHCR contributed a bigger transmitter. This transmitter was at the centre of a dispute that was only settled recently. Basically, UNHCR only saw the station as a tool for repatriation, and by the end of 1996 the UN agency withdrew its support.

Because of poverty, very few radio sets are available in the refugee camps; only one in twelve families owns a transistor radio. "Free Play" wind-up radio sets were distributed in Karagwe but these haven't been very successful: plastic parts break easily, the charge lasts only 15 minutes and sets are too expensive. A WFP survey revealed that refugees prefer to save money to buy batteries, at 300 shillings (US$0.40) a pair. A small transistor radio will cost 14,000 shillings (US$18).

It has also been difficult to recruit experienced people to work in Ngara and a comprehensive training strategy needed to be implemented. Communication difficulties added to their problems. Standard telephone lines were only installed in Ngara in March of 2000, however, the ability to send and receive e-mail was made possible by using *Radio Kwizera*'s radio wave frequencies.

Because of the very sensitive political issues, the chief editor of the Kirundi programmes and news is a Tanzanian. Participation of the refugee population is still narrow; it will be moved forward step-by-step, preventing the spread of ideas that may contribute to igniting the ethnic rivalry among Hutus and Tutsis. The evaluation report of 1999 did not recommend handing over the station to the community. On one hand the refugees, though organised and motivated, may leave anytime if political conditions improve. On the other hand, the local Tanzanian population have no resources to run the station.

REFERENCES

This chapter was prepared with information retrieved during a field visit to *Radio Kwizera* in Ngara, and the Greater Lukole ("gathering") refugee camps A and B, in March 2000. Interviews were conducted with Fr. Hugues Deletraz, *Radio Kwizera* director, and of his staff, especially Hilaire Bucumi, Alex Modest, Januarius Rugaimukamu, Bonifas Mpagape, and Lioba Mbuva. Alice W. Munyua, the former project director, provided the initial information and motivation to visit Ngara.

A very important document, not available for distribution, is the July 1999 *Evaluation Report* by Barbara O'Shea, Grace Githaiga and Wycliffe Musungu.

Radio Kwizera can be reached by e-mail.

PÚLSAR

BASIC FACTS

TITLE:	Agencia Informativa Púlsar
COUNTRY:	Regional, Latin America
MAIN FOCUS:	Information dissemination
PLACE:	Quito (Ecuador)
BENEFICIARIES:	Community radio stations in Latin America
PARTNERS:	Centro de Educación Popular, Ecuador (CEDEP), AMARC, RedADA, Red Científica Peruana (RCP)
FUNDING:	CAF, UNESCO, SIDA, Friedrich Ebert Sttiftung
MEDIA:	Radio, e-mail, Internet

SNAPSHOT

We are still a long way from a world where all peoples are offered equitable access to information and to technological resources. New technologies can play an ambiguous role in the pursuit of this goal: they can make a notable contribution to the democratisation of information and communication or, if not mastered, can generate a widening abyss between the information rich and the information poor.

It is not enough to focus exclusively on the quantitative development of Latin America's communication infrastructure (more computers, more satellites, more bandwidth, more speed). We must also develop a strategy that will enable the consolidation of the social communication networks already present in the region.

By facilitating access to the Internet, Púlsar *will provide a modernising impulse for the news programming of the information poor radio broadcasters of the continent. In this way AMARC and CEDEP are contributing a grain of sand — or more to the point, a grain of silicon — to the democratisation of communication in Latin America.* —COMMENTS OF BRUCE GIRARD, FORMER *PÚLSAR* DIRECTOR.

The *Púlsar* project encompasses the following tasks:

1. Identifying appropriate sources of accurate and high quality news and information on the Internet.
2. On a daily basis, searching out international news and editing it in radio style for distribution to radio stations via the Internet. The service prioritises news from Latin America and the Caribbean. One third of *Púlsar's* news comes from other regions.
3. Providing training and support to community radio broadcasters wishing to receive the service.
4. Establishing a regional network of correspondents who feed news into a news pool available to all community radio broadcasters.
5. Supporting radio broadcasters who wish to make full use of the Internet. To this end the project will inform them of the availability and utility of data on themes such as human rights, agriculture, economy, etc.

DESCRIPTION

Púlsar
Agencia Informativa

AMARC, the organisation that groups hundreds of community radio stations worldwide, suggested as early as in 1986, during its second general assembly, that an independent radio news agency should be created to provide independent news for the increasing number of small stations in Latin America, Africa and Asia. The cost of such operation was considered very high at that time. The Internet was not yet well developed, software and computers were still expensive and not very powerful, and fax—the only possible way of conveying information immediately—was still very costly. Nonetheless, the idea of a news agency came back again at each AMARC conference, until, in 1995, at its general assembly in Senegal, AMARC realised that technology had sufficiently developed to allow the idea to become a reality.

Púlsar started in March 1996 with the purpose of providing community radio stations in Latin America with information useful to their listeners. *Púlsar's* number of subscribers grew from 48 in March 1996 to 1,860 in 1999. Mostly radio stations (441), but also NGOs (344), individuals (335) and universities (296) use the information for news, teaching and political analysis. About 40 percent of subscribers are outside Latin America.

At the start, *Púlsar* produced a daily bulletin with 12 to 15 news items. By the end of 1996, a monthly *Comunicado* to subscribers was added, and new specialised services were created during 1997 and 1998:

- *En Línea* and *Compendio*, news stories edited and distributed every day, including audio clips;

- *Ciberbrujas*, produced in collaboration with the Bolivian NGO RedADA, a weekly service featuring news and information about Latin American women;
- *Ñuqanchik*, daily news services in Quechua, main native language in the region, spoken by some eight million people.

The cost of operating *Púlsar* during one year rose from US$30,000 in 1996 to US$100,000 by 1997. Main funding came from Communication Assistance Foundation (CAF)—a Dutch NGO, UNESCO and SIDA. In March 1998, AMARC took over *Púlsar*.

From its inception *Púlsar* had the following objectives:

1. To improve the programming, establish the credibility and increase the impact of independent and community radio stations in Latin America.
2. To contribute towards modernising the technology of independent and community radio stations.
3. To ensure better information and knowledge of regional and global issues, and promote topics related to democratic development, regional integration, peace and human rights, and the right to communicate.
4. To promote pluralism and participation at the local, national and regional levels, giving priority to those sectors that are often excluded.

"*Púlsar* recognised from the beginning that to be a totally alternative service is not an option if you want to be used by the stations. Thus we tried to maintain a mix of those mainstream stories and alternative stories. The theory is that it makes a more 'complete' service and that many stations would not use an alternative-only service. *Púlsar* is accepted and is able to ensure a civil society impact on the agenda. Purely alternative agencies are discredited in the minds of many news directors," says Girard.

BACKGROUND & CONTEXT

Since the 1950s, community radio has grown very fast in Latin America. Early experiences were politically oriented as a reaction to state-owned or commercial radio networks that totally excluded the voices of the vast majority of people from their programming. More than any other medium radio speaks the language but also has the accent of the community in which it is located. The programming of community radio stations is relevant to local interests and usually makes important contributions to strengthening and protecting cultural identity and social values.

However, radio has not been spared from the *globalisation* trend. As much as television or newspapers, radio is largely influenced by international news agencies, most of them from the United States and Europe. National media conglomerates have been formed, gathering often a mixture of media companies—radio, newspapers and television—which largely dominate the flow of information.

Smaller radio stations have fought to survive, expand influence on the community and defend national and local interests. These radio stations are community projects, often supported by the Catholic Church, local NGOs, or even unions. "The same technology that makes possible globalisation also allows these citizen radio stations to work with civil society in an attempt to influence the global village," says former *Púlsar* director, Bruce Girard.

In 1995, the threat over community radio in Latin America was critical in the decision to search for alternatives:

- New liberal legislation resulted in hundreds of new commercial radio stations, which immediately began competing to capture a segment of the market;
- Several countries recognised the legal status of community radio and there were indications that more frequencies would be allocated;
- International cooperation, showed increasing interest in Africa. Latin America had to look for new sources of funding;
- The larger media companies established national networks that increased their control over the smaller stations.

ASPECTS OF SOCIAL CHANGE

Besides generating a volume of information previously out of reach for community radio stations, *Púlsar* facilitated their networking. Being able to have daily contact with hundreds of stations be it through e-mail via radio wave frequencies or via the Internet, whether to distribute news bulletins or to receive news from correspondents, helped build a powerful sense of identity among community radio stations.

Another important aspect is the encouragement that community radio stations received from *Púlsar* to modernise their equipment and take advantage of new technologies. For those stations that didn't have the means to purchase computers and services, *Púlsar* facilitated networking with NGOs—such as Red Científica Peruana (RCP) that had sponsored public Internet booths.

Quechua is primarily an oral language, spoken by eight million in the Andean region, but written only by a few intellectuals. The distribution through the Internet of programming in Quechua was another important breakthrough in a region where newscasts are mostly in Spanish and the Internet is dominated by English. Ñuqanchik is an alternative for promoting grassroots linguistic and cultural diversity.

When *Púlsar* started only a few radio stations were using electronic mail or the Internet, so the promotion of new technologies became one of the methods *Púlsar* used to ensure the expansion of the network. A disk entitled *Viaje Virtual* (*Virtual Voyage*) was specially designed and sent to 350 radio stations to explain the advantages of new technologies.

Training has also been a major concern of *Púlsar*. At the annual meeting of correspondents, training is always one of the main items on the agenda. There is also an electronic discussion list for discussion among the correspondents and the Quito office. *Púlsar* has developed a very comprehensive *Cartilla para Corresponsales*, very thorough guidelines for correspondents, covering the selection of news, editing, equipment needed, and a section about audio attachments.

The main goals of training were to: a) demystify new communication technologies and the Internet in terms of access (skills and cost); b) provide basic training with focus on e-mail; and c) take advantage of training to evaluate *Púlsar* services. The agency produced materials and manuals for the training sessions, including Web directories for reaching information.

CONSTRAINTS

Though *Púlsar* grew to 2,000 subscriptions (half from Latin America), few actually paid their dues. The original idea was to fund *Púlsar* through subscriptions: 500 subscribers at $25/month would give $150,000 per year. At some point *Púlsar* decided the service would be distributed without cost. "It is still difficult to bill internationally in Latin America. Between bank commissions and taxes you can lose all of a $25 payment from Argentina. The cost of billing, including the costs of the infrastructure, would force *Púlsar* to raise the subscription fee dramatically, putting it out of the reach of many stations. If we sell *Púlsar* to one station, dozens more will get it 'bounced' for free. The problem is that once the decision was made not to finance the agency with subscriptions, there was no serious pursuit of an alternative method. *Púlsar* went the convenient way of marketing itself to international aid organisations, rather than trying to invent something new," adds Girard.

REFERENCES

This chapter is mainly based on documents from *Púlsar* and exchanges with founder and former director, Bruce Girard.

The Web site <http://www.pulsar.org.ec/> was created in 1996 to promote the concept behind *Púlsar*.

Girard, Bruce, "Community Radio, Gateway to the Information Revolution." *Voices*, Vol. 3, No. 3, December 1999, Bangalore, India.

Girard, Bruce, "*Púlsar. Dos años de radio en Internet*," in *Chasqui*, la revista latino-americana de comunicación, #61, *Quito*, March 1998.

Girard, Bruce, "Pluralismo, radio e Internet" in Chasqui, la revista latinoamericana de comunicación, #59, *Quito*, September 1997.

Pinto, Lorencita, "Combinando la radio y el Internet," paper at ITU/FES regional symposium. Santiago de Chile, 25–28 August 1999.

MOUTSE COMMUNITY RADIO

1997 South Africa

··

BASIC FACTS

TITLE: Moutse Community Radio Station (MCRS)

COUNTRY: South Africa

MAIN FOCUS: Women empowerment, community development

PLACE: Moutse Mpumalanga Province

BENEFICIARIES: Rural women

PARTNERS: Rural Women's Movement (RWM), National Community Radio Forum

FUNDING: Open Society Foundation of South Africa, Community Assistance Foundation (The Netherlands), AusAID

MEDIA: Radio

SNAPSHOT

The women went to the presiding chiefs to seek approval for the radio venture. The chiefs said that it was a good idea to have a station but, despite the women's success at organising around issues of great importance to the quality of community life, the chiefs discouraged them, stating that if women were at the front of the radio project, it would fall down.

Two factors seemed to be at play. Firstly, in the chiefs' views it was seen as unsuitable for women to be engaging with technology—unlike water and electricity radio did not appear to have a direct relationship to the home. Secondly the chiefs were tiring of the women in the area being so well acknowledged for their successful campaigns and felt it was time for men to re-assert their leadership role in the impending new dispensation of South Africa.

After considering the practical implications the women returned to the chiefs and announced their determination to proceed with the project. Later, although some time had passed since the chiefs' comments, the women expressed the opinion that if men were at the front of the project everyone would fall in the beer!

After three years of hard work the Rural Women's Movements' dream of starting a radio station in Moutse came true. The station was switched on at 6 a.m. on November 8th, 1997. Hundreds of people turned out for the opening. The women wore traditional clothes and proudly displayed the names of their villages in ornate beadwork hung around their necks. Villagers arrived in 'sets,' milling about in a scene of rainbow coloured cloth surrounding the station building. Drums were beaten, songs were sung and speeches were made. The bones were thrown in the studio to diagnose and ensure its health.

Traditional and contemporary life were blended in a way which expressed the uniqueness of the Moutse community. Everyone had a turn on the microphone and then Ma Lydia Komape, MP for the area and founder of the Rural Women's Movement, the Mayor of Moutse Conrad Tjiane and Chief Piet Mathebe jointly cut the ribbon declaring Moutse Community Radio *a local resource.*—WRITTEN BY TRACEY NAUGHTON, AN INDEPENDENT CONSULTANT WORKING WITH *MOUTSE COMMUNITY RADIO.*

DESCRIPTION

Moutse Community Radio Station was founded by members of the Rural Women's Movement (RWM), a national organisation in South Africa, which lobbies around issues of concern to rural women. In the words of one movement member, Lahliwe Nkoana, "*Moutse Community Radio* Station (MCRS) was born of many years of our community struggle. During those years, the rural, mostly female community campaigned for rights to water, education, health care, electricity, democracy and an end to polygamy which discriminated against rural wives."

Powered by a 250-watt transmitter, its signal has the potential to reach 1.2 million people, well beyond the population of Moutse. Organisations from around the world have supported the development of the station. A national group, the Open Society Foundation of South Africa, however, funded its modest studio. The studio contains the bare necessities: a CD player, tape recorder, mini disc recorder, microphones and a mixing desk. The station is housed in an old building belonging to the Department of Agriculture, a more stable location than the room—owned by the ANC (African National Congress)—where members had been squatting.

The station operates with a board of trustees who set the overall vision and perspective, five management staff members who coordinate the training, administration, technical and programming departments, and twelve volunteer staff members who work as radio announcers. *Moutse Community Radio* is a member of the National Community Radio Forum, the national organising body in South Africa.

Various working committees contacted donors, obtained funds for equipment and sifted their way through the quagmire of impediments to mounting such a project in rural conditions. Initially, 45 women were trained in how to create and produce radio programmes.

Hardliners criticised the women for appointing a man as station manager, though the women supported the decision by saying that they also wanted men to be involved. For many years Sam Mashoeshoe, an "honorary woman," was a member of the Rural Women's Movement. He was present at the 1993 annual meeting when the decision was made to create a community radio station at one of its strongest branches, Moutse. He was subsequently appointed as manager of MCRS.

Many people external to the station saw the project through a feminist lens and over time the women of Moutse came to understand that they were being labeled in a way they did not really understand—in the context of their village life. They saw their achievements over the years as a logical extension of their roles as mothers and wives redoubled by the mitigating circumstances bought about by the absence of men who were forced to reside in the cities in order to work.

The on-air programmes cater to a wide range of listeners. The health programme regularly features medical practitioners for community phone-ins where they discuss an answer questions while the agriculture programme invites departmental representatives. The daily morning and afternoon drive programmes are entertaining yet informative and often include interviews on a broad spectrum of community issues. The station also catered to children, sports fans, jazz lovers, cultural music enthusiasts, cooks and dramatists. The community announcements of local events and the reading of funeral notices keep people living over a large area informed. Local, national and international news is read in a number of languages.

Cultural exchange remains an important goal: "We hope it will be heard by the white town nearby so that those people can hear our stories, our songs and our problems."

BACKGROUND & CONTEXT

With a population of nearly 900,000 people, Moutse, which is in the Province of Mpumalanga, was a politically active area during the apartheid regime, fighting hard against being incorporated into the Kwandebele homeland—one of the areas set up to enable the "separate development" policies of the regime.

For generations, several chiefs of the tribal authority have been presiding over these areas. The 48 villages in Moutse are spread over a large area and the transportation systems are poor and expensive. Lack of an adequate communications infrastructure has contributed to numerous conflicts.

During the years of struggle, the rural, mostly female community members campaigned for rights to water, education, health care, electricity, democracy and an end to polygamy.

Another legacy of apartheid is the existence of numerous migrant workers, men who were forced to live and work away from home in order to support their families, leaving the rural areas neglected as a consequence. A community radio project is seen as a tangible attempt to improve the situation.

Community activists were appointed as representatives during the 1995 local government elections, which radically changed the faces of the people governing the area. Community radio has been supported as an integral part of accomplishing the task of bringing together the villages. Ma Lydia Komape, says, "One project that has the potential to bring people together, inform and enable participation for the local citizens is the *Moutse Community Radio* Station."

The determination of the women who started the station was recalled during a group discussion: "When we started the station, as a group of women we knew how to organise; we did not know anything about radio, but we knew we could learn."

ASPECTS OF SOCIAL CHANGE

In terms of ownership, this is an example of community media. The radio station belongs to the Moutse community, men and women. However, at the time of station's license application hearing the station was operated primarily by women and one man. Therefore, the Independent Broadcasting Authority gave the radio station an opportunity to be a women's only group. Their station could apply for a license as "a community of interest" rather than "a geographical community."

Both definitions of community are permitted in South Africa's Broadcasting Act. The women saw that by being inclusive they had a better chance of guaranteeing the future of their community-based station; they opted to be defined as a geographical community.

Until 1994, there was strict state control of the media in South Africa. Media was used to re-enforce the divides of apartheid and functioned as a propaganda tool, effectively keeping the masses ill-informed at best and uninformed at worst.

For the first time in Moutse, a radio station made pertinent information available to a community where vast distances and lack of a transportation infrastructure make it extremely difficult to bring people together. Radio is able to disseminate information about health, including primary health care and information about HIV, TB, scabies and the importance of clean water and sanitation. The radio can be used to encourage parents to send their children to school and to engage people in local governance issues at a local, provincial and national level.

The MCRS is completely operated by volunteers including the board of directors, management, presenters (broadcasters) and administration support. A recent recruitment drive to incorporate new community members within the station was advertised over the airwaves and attracted a positively overwhelming 180 people, all for volunteer positions. Only 32 were retained for further training and evaluation.

The MCRS has a comprehensive Community Participation Manual detailing ways in which the community can interact with the station. Participation ranges from speaking as guests on programmes to attending the Community Consultative Forum, where both producers and listeners review schedules and content. Internally within the station both the weekly general meeting, which is compulsory for all station volunteers, and the management and heads of department meeting, enable all the volunteers to be informed about station issues and to be involved in important decisions.

CONSTRAINTS

MCRS has faced many growing problems and new obstacles in recent times. Technical problems such as the lack of electricity and telephone, as well as problems obtaining a license to operate legally delayed for three long years the launching of the station.

The state electricity supplier simply did not see the community radio station as a priority and delayed the installation of a cable up the Mapula Mountain for 18 months. The work was completed just in time for the switch-on date. Likewise, the station had to wait several months for a telephone landline.

Despite having a large sum of money to deposit, the local bank refused to open an account for the station until Tracey Naughton, the mlungu (white) consultant, suggested to the manager that the bank had policies that appeared to be racist.

The Independent Broadcast Authority was slow in granting radio licenses; the station had a credibility crisis while waiting for its authorisation. The community has recently faced the IBA again, this time requesting a four-year license.

During 1998–99, internal tensions grew as the few remaining women lost their grip on the project. According to Tracey Naughton, "the reality of MCRS today is quite different from the one envisaged by the women who started it and by the donors who funded it. The women made a deliberate choice to be a community resource for all and not a woman-only station. A project that had a well-defined starting point has experienced a gradual slippage from a clear development orientation of the project to a male-dominated culture of entertainment-focused, ego-boosting broadcasting."

As with many stations in South Africa the dynamic hits it's lowest ebb and then re-builds. This process, in which the Rural Women's Movement is paramount is now underway in Moutse.

REFERENCES

E-mail exchanges and papers by Tracey Naughton, consultant working with MCRS since 1992, and additional information by Nikki Marcel, director of MCRS.

The Local Village Speaks Up: Rural Women in South Africa Start Community Radio Station by Tracey Naughton, InteRadio, AMARC, Volume 9, Number 2, 1997.

Moutse Community Radio Station, Overview & Proposal Document for Donors, December 1999. CAF (The Netherlands), written and compiled by T. Naughton.

RADIO SAGARMATHA

BASIC FACTS

TITLE:	Radio Sagarmatha
COUNTRY:	Nepal
MAIN FOCUS:	Environment, health, community issues
PLACE:	Katmandu
BENEFICIARIES:	Rural and urban communities
PARTNERS:	Nepal Forum of Environmental Journalists (NEFEJ), Nepal Press Institute, Himal Association, Worldview Nepal
FUNDING:	International Programme for the Development of Communication (IPDC)/UNESCO, UNICEF, DANIDA, Panos, Canadian Centre for International Studies and Cooperation (CECI), Öko Himal, CAF and others
MEDIA:	Radio

SNAPSHOT

We know it as Everest, the highest mountain in the world, but Nepalese people call it Sagarmatha: "forehead of the ocean," a reference to a time long ago when Nepal was under the waters of the ocean. Who could tell it now, standing somewhere in the Kathmandu Valley at 1,300 meters of altitude.

Sagarmatha is also the name and symbol of the first community radio station in South Asia, the forehead of independent broadcasting in this country long ruled by a monarchical nonparty system. *Radio Sagarmatha*'s three-story building emerges in Patan, a city adjacent to Kathmandu, signalled by the long mast of the antenna. In 1999 they increased the height of their tower, which held that antenna, by 50 percent.

Not long ago, there was no building, no antenna, just a few enthusiastic journalists struggling for the right to communicate, playing hide-and-seek with the police. Upendra Aryal was the technical director when *Radio Sagarmatha* finally went on the air: "I thought it was a big fantasy to transform an outfit with a single mono Sony EV500 compact cassette recorder into a sophisticated FM station, the public radio station of Nepal. It was very difficult to even get a building for the proposed station. People were reluctant to allow the radio to transmit from their house, as it still had no license to run. Finally the station was in my house, and I was ready to rent out the land and the building for the next fifteen years. Even though we had successfully tested the signal from there, we had no license and officials from the Ministry of Communications were tracing us at that time. I had the transmitter hidden in my residence and at night kept it as if it were my pillow."

The dream of *Radio Sagarmatha* (RS) came true, and its example in Nepal has opened the way for newer community radio stations.

DESCRIPTION

Radio Sagarmatha is the first independent station in South Asia. It took five years to hit the air: "The story of *Radio Sagarmatha* is interwoven with the gradual loosening of government control over the airwaves in Nepal," wrote CECI's Ian Pringle. Even after 1990 the government was slow in relinquishing control of its monopoly over radio broadcasting. The Nepal Forum of Environmental Journalists (NEFEJ), was granted the first independent license in 1997, and this feat brought to life *Radio Sagarmatha*.

A seven-member autonomous board of directors constituted by NEFEJ as the broadcast license holder heads the station. Through NEFEJ by-laws, the board has representation from all four partner NGOs and meets monthly to review and plan activities, set policy, and provide broad direction for the station.

Since May 22, 1997 (Buddha's birthdate), *Radio Sagarmatha* has been broadcasting, through its 500-watt transmitter, a daily programme service on FM 102.4 in the Kathmandu Valley of Nepal. The station is noncommercial, community-based and dedicated to public interest broadcasting.

Radio Sagarmatha's programming is oriented towards the exploration and discussion of issues related to Nepali culture and environment. The primary language of broadcast is Nepali, and with the exception of traditional music from other regions of the world, the music is also Nepali. Community groups and NGOs are involved in programming.

The programme grid starts every day with one hour of music followed by national news and *Radio Talk*. Mornings also include a

BBC news service in English. The afternoons include social-oriented programming such as *Health Diagnosis, Clean Air Campaign, Folk Tales, Action & Ideas, Today's Concern, When Our Grandfathers Were Young, Public Platform* and *Community News*. And lots of music: *Musical Wave, Musical Dialogue, Our Music, Golden Oldies* and *Eastern Pop.* ... Saturday morning features a programme on human rights education.

Radio Sagarmatha's goal is to evolve as a self-sustaining "public radio" station: a source of high-quality, informative and cultural broadcasting and a conduit for the plurality of voices in the community. More specifically, the station aims:

- To facilitate democratisation and pluralism by increasing people's access to information, and by continuously advocating a freer and more responsible press;
- To set standards for public interest broadcasting in Nepal by programming to address the information needs of all sections of the listening audience, but especially marginalised groups such as women, children and the very poor;
- To produce a cadre of journalists sensitised in community and public interest broadcasting and provide them with a forum to sharpen their skills;
- To establish Sagarmatha as a national and regional resource centre for community-based and developmental media by building in-house capacity for regulatory and licensing consulting, training, programming and management.

International cooperation agencies provided equipment (UNESCO, Öko Himal, CAF), training (UNESCO, Panos, Radio Nederland), or technical assistance (DANIDA, CECI, International Non Governmental Organisations (INGO)). Local resources have been present from the outset of the campaign for *Radio Sagarmatha* through coproductions, production services and sponsorship.

BACKGROUND & CONTEXT

Much has changed in Nepal during the last decade of the past century. A civilisation which existed for a thousand years has gone through political changes that transformed its social landscape. Prior to 1995 radio broadcasting was the exclusive domain of Radio Nepal, the state broadcaster established in 1951. It reached about 60 percent of the country through its medium and short wave services. Established in 1984, Nepal Television (NTV) was the sole TV station until the late nineties when more than seventy cable and satellite operators came into being. Four commercial FM frequencies were granted by 1999, driven by advertising.

By 1990 Nepal had witnessed the culmination of a people's movement for democratic freedom that ended almost 40 years of monarchy. The new constitution of 1990 guaranteed the right to freedom of expression and opened the path for the first democratic elections of 1991. In 1992 a National Communications Policy was approved, followed by a National Broadcasting Act in 1993 and Broadcast Regulations in 1995.

From the outset, the Nepal Forum of Environmental Journalists, an NGO and an association of journalists, was the main organisational vehicle for *Radio Sagarmatha*. NEFEJ not only worked to establish a licensed radio station, it also works in a variety of different media focusing on environmental, developmental and human rights issues. Other three organisations joined later: Himal Association, Worldview Nepal and the Nepal Press Institute.

ASPECTS OF SOCIAL CHANGE

Radio Sagarmatha's programming has given thousands the opportunity to have their opinions heard in a public forum. On a daily basis, the station takes listeners into the streets and into locations of everyday life. The variety of voices gives the station a very different tone from other broadcasters in this part of the world, one of real life as lived by real people and ultimately programmed by real people. Interviewees and people profiled on the station come from a wide array of backgrounds and occupations.

One of the most successful programmes of *Radio Sagarmatha*, *Hamro Khaldo* (Our Valley), has tackled problems such as prostitution, AIDS, pollution, abortion, child labour and consumer safety. The topics are explored not only through investigative journalism, but also by interviewing a cross-section of characters from local society.

An important aspect of the station's community access exists in coproduction and collaboration with local groups. Weekly and monthly programmes by local NGOs, special interests, and arts and community groups are produced with technical assistance from the radio station.

Volunteers are playing an increasingly valuable role, and as awareness of the station has grown, so have the number of groups interested in and open to collaboration. New equipment, such as telephone interfaces for live phone-ins, along with expanded facilities, and the development of training programmes, offer many possibilities for audience and community participation in the near future.

Radio Sagarmatha has opened the path to new ventures in participatory communication. By the end of 1998, two new radio licenses were granted outside the Kathmandu Valley: Radio Madan Pokhara in the Palpa District and Lumbini Cooperative in the Rupandehi District.

Radio Sagarmatha identifies itself as a "public" rather than "community" radio, that is, a responsible spokesperson and facilitator, rather than a vehicle for open community participation. The mainstays of production have been through paid journalists, and programming that is centrally planned, organised and directed. RS has brought investigation, opinion and discussion onto the airwaves.

The station has worked to present listeners with a human package, a combination of issues and entertainment, social discussions and music, as well as to provide a vehicle for the variety of voices and opinions previously unheard on Nepal's radio channels. The station's difference from the state broadcaster and the growing number of Western-style commercial stations is most clearly visible in its programming content.

Public affairs journalism and broadcasting are at the heart of *Radio Sagarmatha*'s mission and vision for a more responsible press and a more pluralistic society, but with a long and powerful tradition of folk media and a rich musical heritage, cultural programming is also prominent in the station's daily broadcasts.

Immediate priorities for the station include the development of training programmes, building partnerships with local and international groups and providing much needed support to Nepal's emerging community radio sector.

CONSTRAINTS

Mass media in Nepal face formidable barriers. Low literacy levels and widespread poverty limit access to television, newspapers and even radio. The mountainous geography of the country is ill-suited for mass circulation of print media and coverage by electronic media. Only 15 percent of the population have access to electricity.

When *Radio Sagarmatha*'s license was finally granted, it came with a series of fourteen conditions and restrictions. Prominent among them: no commercial programming, no political commentary or news on political events, broadcasting was to be limited to two hours per day, weekly reports to the Ministry were required, news from Radio Nepal must be rebroadcast. Most of the restrictions were eventually lifted.

Annual license fees established by the government can be as high as US$1,500 for a 100-watt transmitter, thus limiting the possibilities for community radio stations to operate.

Men dominated operations and programming during the first years. Gradually women are playing a more visible and "audible" role as staff producers and volunteers.

REFERENCES

Most of the information for this chapter has been taken from *Radio Sagarmatha: A Case Study in Community Radio* (August 1999) written by Ian Pringle (CECI) and from the *Radio Sagarmatha* Web site <www.sagarmatha.org.np>.

A shorter version of the document appears in *Community Radio Handbook* (1999) published by UNESCO's IPDC.

Additional information obtained through interviews in Kuala Lumpur and e-mail exchanges with producer Madhu Acharya.

1998 Mexico

BASIC FACTS

TITLE:	Chiapas Media Project
COUNTRY:	Mexico in partnership with the U.S.A.
FOCUS:	Communication for democracy
PLACE:	Municipalities of Palenque, Ocosingo, Altamirano, Las Margaritas and San Andrés Larrainzar
BENEFICIARIES:	Chol, Tzeltal, Tzotzil, Tojolabal communities
PARTNERS:	La Neta, Instituto Latinoamericano de Comunicación Educativa (ILCE)
FUNDING:	The US-Mexico Fund for Culture, The Peace Development Fund, The Funding Exchange
MEDIA:	Video

SNAPSHOT

The aroma of locally grown organic coffee wafts through the air from a fresh pot on the kitchen stove at the *Chiapas Media Project* (CMP) office in San Cristobal de las Casas. In one room Feliciano logs videotapes for his new project about cultural restoration in the indigenous Tzeltal regions. In another room Moisés puts the final touches on his video, shot in his native language, about the autonomous education system that indigenous people have developed since 1994, when the Zapatista movement took hold. The entire office, which doubles as a home away from home for indigenous video makers from remote communities statewide, is bustling with activity.

Today, all five of the autonomous indigenous regions of the state have trained video makers working with the *Chiapas Media Project*, which has become: a forum for indigenous people to create their own media, promote their autonomy, and tell their own stories in their own words and images.

Feliciano has now produced three videos. *Women United*, his most recent production about a collectively run bakery, garden and store in the autonomous municipality of the "17th of November," was shot by two women from the nearby community of Lucio Cabañas. When asked about his video Feliciano says: "This video shows how women have organised the collective work in times of resistance. There are other communities that need to organise themselves, so we made this video for them to see how this is done. This video is for distribution in different regions. We have shown it, and the whole region now knows of the collective work of the women."

Others learn video to defend their communities from human rights abuses committed by the Mexican Army or paramilitary groups that terrorise remote communities.

Ruben, who has been trained in video as a human rights promoter says, "The only thing that we want is that we all know our rights and see that they are respected." Another human rights promoter chimes in: "What we are learning is very useful: how to use a video camera and how to record evidence that proves that we are the victims of the very things that the government accuses us of."—WRITTEN BY MEMBERS OF THE *CHIAPAS MEDIA PROJECT*.

DESCRIPTION

The *Chiapas Media Project* is a binational partnership (Mexico-U.S.A.) that provides video and computer equipment and training to marginalised indigenous communities in Chiapas, Mexico. Its mission is to nurture processes that, through video and computer technology, empower communities struggling for democracy, land reform and autonomy to develop alternative media so that their voices can be heard. The *Chiapas Media Project* began in 1997 with a series of consultations with indigenous community leaders throughout the state of Chiapas. At each of these meetings, the leadership explained the importance of information in their struggles for human rights, democracy, land reform and respect for indigenous rights.

The *Chiapas Media Project* works in the municipalities of Palenque, Ocosingo, Altamirano, Las Margaritas and San Andrés Larrainzar. The population is Chol, Tzeltal, Tzotzil and Tojolabal. Indigenous authorities assign young men and women to participate in the project as associates. With sufficient training, some will graduate to video-makers. In keeping with community traditions, members of the *Chiapas Media Project* apply their knowledge and creativity for the benefit of their communities.

Through video technology they can tell their own stories in their own words. Through computers they can distribute their stories via the Internet. This is a new kind of struggle that melds traditional values like dignity, democracy and autonomy with modern technologies that enable the voiceless to be heard. The demand for equipment and instruction continues to grow. The initial training involves basic camera usage, interviewing techniques, documentation of physical evidence, and shooting under difficult conditions.

Since the initial equipment delivery and training workshop in February of 1998, the *Chiapas Media Project* has delivered 40 video cameras to 37 communities. Three editing systems are up and functioning, including a portable non-linear system. Five portable projectors enable screenings throughout the region. Eight portable computers are used for computer training, and also serve the record keeping and correspondence needs of the communities. Potentially, the project can reach some 400 communities with a total population of approximately one million in Chiapas.

The use of video as a tool for preserving the local memory of struggles for democracy and justice has resulted in numerous productions. Among them, *Mujeres Unidas* (Women United) spotlights the indigenous women's collective work in the autonomous municipality of 17 de Noviembre; *El Curandero de las Comunidades Indigenas de Los Altos de Chiapas* (The Healer in the Indigenous Communities of the Highlands of Chiapas), is an intimate look at traditional Mayan healing practices; *La Familia Indigena* (The Indigenous Family) takes an intimate look at the role of men and women in the community of Ejido Morelia; *La Mala Cosecha* (The Bad Harvest) documents severe food shortages in 1998; *El Colectivo de la Caña de Azucar* (The Sugar Cane Collective) illustrates a central activity of the municipality of El Trabajo, where men, women and children combine efforts to produce sugar with hand-made tools, hard work and joy; *Consulta Nacional 21 de Marzo, Municipio Autónomo San Juan de la Libertad* (The National Consultation, March 21 in the Autonomous Municipality of San Juan de La Libertad) 5,000 Zapatistas left Chiapas to conduct a massive popular education campaign throughout Mexico on indigenous rights and the San Andrés Accords, the ensuing nine-day campaign led to the Consulta Nacional in which citizens were asked to vote on four basic questions regarding indigenous rights.

BACKGROUND & CONTEXT

The indigenous communities in Chiapas are involved in a life and death struggle for democracy, land distribution and respect for human rights. While they are struggling to break a cycle of poverty and injustice, mainstream media portray the difficult situation in Mexico's southern-most state from an outside perspective. Often with ignorance or malice, the mass media does not faithfully interpret indigenous peoples' struggles. Their stories often fit the prevailing political needs of the ruling elite, but do not accurately represent the lives of poor Indians. The result is widespread racism and a society of gross inequality, where indigenous peoples live on the edge of despair, without democracy, economic justice or respect for their historic culture. Without the ability to control their own truth, indigenous communities fight an uphill battle for lives of dignity. Information provides the framework for political, social and economic change. Information is power, and the redistribution of power is central to achieving a just and democratic society.

In 1997, a series of meetings between video/computer experts from the United States and Mexico, and indigenous leaders in Chiapas revealed the critical need for an indigenous voice in the national and international debate. Indigenous communities defined their needs and, working together with experienced technicians from Oaxaca, Mexico City and the United States, designed the CMP.

ASPECTS OF SOCIAL CHANGE

The *Chiapas Media Project* gives voice to the voiceless; its profound effect will influence the outcome of complex political and social struggles. The most powerful "weapon" in this struggle is the ability to make indigenous views known to the world. The CMP nurtures processes that, through video and computer technology, empower indigenous peoples. These tools can be used to strengthen tolerance and understanding, thus breaking down social, cultural and ideological barriers. The impact in the communities has been profound. In mastering video and computer technology, young people achieve a sense of empowerment. By demystifying technology they gain confidence and expand horizons. Most of the communities have been exposed to television, now they have the power to tell their own stories. In 1998 not one of the students had ever held a video camera or used a computer. Today they are producing videos and rapidly mastering useful aspects of computer technology.

In 1999, a young member of the CMP from the community of Nicolas Ruiz, documented an attack on the community by the State Police where several people were wounded. The wounded were interviewed and their wounds videotaped as evidence. This videotape is currently before a judge in Tuxtla Gutierrez, challenging the presence of the State Police in this community.

In February 1999 the community of Ejido Morelia organised their own video workshop in response to requests from surrounding communities. This was an important step in the process of self-sufficiency, which is key to the long-term success of the *Chiapas Media Project*. Students from Morelia ran the workshop, and eight people from four outlying communities learned basic camera techniques.

Many indigenous people began building an autonomous system of governance over their communities as a way to combat years of corruption, human rights abuses and neglect suffered at the hands of the Mexican government and Federal Army.

From its inception the *Chiapas Media Project* has been binational and multicultural. Indigenous leaders define their needs as well as the scope and pace of the project. Technicians from the United States and Mexico provide equipment and training to meet these needs and all of the equipment is owned by the communities. The development of this project would not have been possible without this collaboration. The board of directors includes an equal mix of United States and Mexican members and several indigenous community leaders from Chiapas who, for reasons of personal security, prefer not to be named in public documents. Their participation is central to the development of the project at every step.

Almost all of the introductory video courses and half of the introductory computer courses are given by indigenous youth in their native languages. As associates learn skills, they are empowered to become instructors, passing along their knowledge to the rest of their community. Eventually "associates" and "video-makers" that receive training through the project will serve as the next generation of instructors, and communities will achieve self-sufficiency. The lasting legacy will be a bridge of understanding and caring across cultures.

The *Chiapas Media Project* covers travel, material and food costs for these workshops. Increasingly, the instructors who come from outside of the communities act as consultants for new productions, handle advanced courses, and nurture the processes toward self-sufficiency.

CONSTRAINTS

Many of the students that are part of the *Chiapas Media Project* live in self-declared autonomous communities. These communities are establishing their own parallel and self-sufficient government structures; an important function of these is record-keeping. Four times during 1998 government forces invaded these communities and destroyed their files. By recording important community information on portable computers and diskettes, government forces are no longer able to destroy years of hard work in a single night.

All of the work of the CMP is done in the context of extremely difficult conditions. Low intensity warfare results in severe food shortages—as documented in Chiapas 1998: *La Mala Cosecha* (The Bad Harvest). Medical care is used as a weapon in this struggle and many Indians die of curable diseases. Army checkpoints had tripled by the end of 2000 making it difficult to travel without being stopped.

Nonetheless, the presence of video cameras offers a level of protection. In 1999 army troops tried to enter communities, but quickly departed when community members began to record their actions with video cameras.

Despite the exceptional enthusiasm and learning abilities, a series of technical, logistical and organisational problems often arise. If a piece of equipment doesn't work properly, the initial response is to put it away until the "experts" return to fix it.

REFERENCES

Information provided by Tom Hansen, Alexandra Halkin and Ana Hernandez, codirectors of *Chiapas Media Project*, through e-mail exchanges.

Chiapas Media Project Web site <http://www.chiapasmediaproject.org/index.html>.

GASALEKA & MAMELODI TELECENTRES

(**1998**) South Africa

··

BASIC FACTS

TITLE:	Gasaleka Telecentre, Mamelodi Community Information Services (MACIS)
COUNTRY:	South Africa
FOCUS:	Access to new technologies
PLACE:	Gasaleka and Mamelodi
BENEFICIARIES:	Rural and urban users
PARTNERS:	South Africa National Civic Organization (SANCO), Ellisras Technical College, IDRC
FUNDING:	Universal Service Agency
MEDIA:	Computers, Internet

SNAPSHOT

There are no roads to Gasaleka. The outside visitor spends two hours carefully and slowly driving on a path of swamped holes, stones and sand, surrounded by infinite extensions of palm trees, before reaching the first hut of the village near the borders of Botswana. This remote village of mud huts and red sand lanes accommodates the first telecentre established by the Universal Service Agency.

In spite of some infrastructure and economic problems, Gasaleka Telecentre *remains as one of the most active and vibrant in South Africa. The main reason for that vitality in the midst of daily adversity is Masilo Mokobane, the director of the project and a genuine telecentre champion. Mokobane is a telecentre visionary. From the first day, Mokobane has not only been fighting for the survival of the telecentre, but he has been enter-taining new ideas to better serve his community through the use of new com-munication technologies. He remembers the day the* Gasaleka Telecentre *was inaugurated. "It was a great day for us. Everybody came to celebrate it."*

The early success of the centre is partly explained by the computer train-ing offered. Another factor is that there is no other place in the area to make a phone call. However, according to Mokobane, "the business is going down due to the problems we have with the telephones. Sometimes the phones are not working. And the customers say the calls are very expensive." When I arrived in Gasaleka, the three telephones were not working due to days of heavy rain.

Mokobane is nevertheless optimistic about the future of the project. Hardships do not shadow his enthusiasm. He is full of new ideas, and he explains them with a wide smile. One of his most innovative plans is the publication of a community newsletter. The villages that integrate the Gasaleka community are not reached or covered by any news service. "We have many news in Gasaleka, but they are not reported to the community," says Mokobane. The telecentre will not only work as a reference resource centre offering access to information and communication technologies, but it will take on a new role as an organisation for the production and dissemination of local information. "The telecentre can become the memory, the history of this community," explains Mokobane.— WRITTEN BY RAUL ROMAN, WHO VISITED GASALEKA AND SEVEN OTHER SOUTH AFRICAN TELECENTRES IN 1999.

DESCRIPTION

Gasaleka, Botlokwa, Tembisa, Mankweng, Mohodi, Apel, Siyabonga and Mamelodi. … these are some of the places—villages or suburban areas—in the Gauteng Province and the Northern Province where telecentres have been established by the Universal Service Agency, a South African government institution.

The *Mamelodi Community Information Services* (MACIS) and the *Gasaleka Telecentre* are two good examples of the advantages and problems of countries such as South Africa aspiring to "universal access" in Information Technologies. Gasaleka is a remote rural area integrating 34 villages with a population of approximately 30,000 people, while Mamelodi is an urban setting; since 1998 this telecentre has been housed by the Mamelodi Heritage Forum, located next to the metro station, a shopping complex, a taxi rank, welfare services, and the Pretoria City Council.

The *Gasaleka Telecentre* was the first established by the Universal Service Agency in March 1998. It is owned by the local South Africa National Civic Organization (SANCO). The *Mamelodi Community Information Services* (MACIS) was "adopted" in April 1998 by the IDRC Acacia programme through the Universal Service Agency but it had been actually set up in July 1995 by the Council for Scientific and Industrial Research (CSIR).

The two telecentres have similar equipment: nine computers, telephone lines, e-mail service and/or Internet connectivity, photocopiers, scanners, printers and fax machines. Both offer computer training, which appears to be a factor for its success and acceptance. Students in Gasaleka receive a certificate from the Ellisras Technical College upon completion of the course. Alas, only one out of the ten first students found a job after taking the computer training. This may be the main reason why the number of students has decreased significantly in 2000.

The Mamelodi Telecentre is basically a reference centre. "We do not try to reinvent what is already existing in the community," says the manager, "we always refer people to outside community resources when necessary; many people come here just asking for directions or addresses." The mission of MACIS is to provide information on all aspects of life to community members to cope with normal day-to-day problems and to improve their quality of life.

"People are not aware of what is happening in the telecentre," says Gasaleka project director, Mokobane. He has employed seven agents that will inform the community about the telecentre and its services. It is a kind of proactive marketing. Mokobane is also aware of the value of assessing community needs. "It is very important to ask the community every time you offer a new service or start up a telecentre; there is nothing you can do if you don't consult the community. You need to have a regular consultation with the community, so that they know what's happening in the telecentre, and what services are you offering."

The villages that integrate the Gasaleka community are not reached or covered by any news service, due to the weak communications infrastructure of this isolated area. One of the most innovative plans of this telecentre is the publication of a community newsletter. The development of a newsletter would not only respond to the information needs of the community, but it would enhance the sustainability of the telecentre. The project will also reinforce the functions of the telecentre as a focal information point. The telecentre will not only work as a reference resource centre offering access to information and communication technologies, but it will take on a new role as an organisation for the production and dissemination of local information.

BACKGROUND & CONTEXT

Still today, South Africa is characterised by an alarming unbalance in resources available for different sectors of the society, even though the reforms after 1994 have generated a significant social metamorphosis. Statistics from 1996 show 89 percent of white households have a phone while only 11 percent of black households do. While state-of-the-art telecommunication networks are available in white urban areas, black rural areas have limited access to at best poor or non-existent services.

A handful of projects are aiming to introduce information technologies in education and development. The Technology Enhanced

Learning Initiative (TELI) is a Government plan that "focuses on the implementation of various key projects that introduce and use technologies effectively in South African education and training." SchoolNet, founded in 1997, is a national NGO, working to link schools and educate teachers and students in Internet technology skills. World Links for Development (WorLD) is a World Bank programme that "mobilises the equipment, training, educational resources and school-to-school partnerships required to bring students in developing countries online and into the global community."

Telkom has established a number of "Centres of Excellence," all based at South African universities. Cyberhost offers public Internet access and plans to launch one thousand coin operated Internet kiosks in public places across the country. The South African Department of Communications has launched a wide range of projects such as the Public Internet Terminals (PIT).

Another major project is the establishment of telecentres through the Universal Service Agency, which has set up around twenty telecentres in the Gauteng Province and in the Northern Province. Many other telecentres will be soon established. The Universal Service Agency was founded by the government in 1997 and is responsible for ensuring universal access to all telecommunication services.

ASPECTS OF SOCIAL CHANGE

It is too soon to expect social changes to be produced by the insertion of new telecommunication technologies in rural and urban areas of South Africa. Most of the Universal Service Agency telecentre projects have been functioning for less than two years, and their impact is mostly related to the potential of access, rather than changes in the community.

While the majority of the recently installed telecentres serve the better-off sectors of each community, a few are significant paradigms of an interest in promoting the vision of community ownership and participation. These are telecentres aiming to create, process and diffuse information for the development of their communities. The *Mamelodi Telecentre* through its project to become the Mamelodi Information Bureau and the publication of a community directory, and Gasaleka, chiefly through its intention to develop a community newsletter, can be included in this group.

The Directory of Services is an important output of the *Mamelodi Telecentre*. Its 22 pages contain useful information on the community, and it's updated every year.

The *Gasaleka Telecentre* has built good community networks; every organisation in the area supports and works with the telecentre.

According to one of the members of the centre's board of trustees, "the telecentre is well-known, although we need to engage the tribal authorities more. However, we don't have problems with any organisation." The aim of building networks is also to bridge the insecurities and perception of inaccessibility which surrounds the term "information" and to introduce information technology to disadvantaged communities.

MEDIA & METHODS

The *Mamelodi Telecentre* has tried to involve the community from the beginning. "We listen to the community to know what they want," says Esme Modisane, the project director. "We are very community rooted, we understand the dynamics and issues in the community; we have training in community work and facilitation, and we have good community networks." Yet, social exclusion is still a problem: "it is true that illiterate people do not come and use the telecentre." Business people visit the telecentre to use the Internet and communicate with clients via e-mail. They also use the computers to print documents and to do financial work.

The MACIS project manager was initially trained by the CSIR on information management, information facilitation and communication skills, interviewing techniques, the use and handling of computers, the Internet, data gathering, database development and maintenance, needs analysis and interpretation, and digital information kiosk management. Training should be an important component in all the other telecentres as well, but this is not always true.

CONSTRAINTS

In spite their equipment and trained staff, most of the telecentres set up by Universal Service Agency are essentially used for very basic access to telephony, fax and computers, as well as services connected to these technologies, such as typing. They can be identified as communication shops rather than multipurpose community telecentres. The managers of Gasaleka report that "nobody uses the e-mail" in the centre.

"The first obstacle to accomplishing the objectives of the telecentre is the fear towards technology, especially among adults so we have to do a very good job to direct them to technology. We have to make them realise that they can use the computers too. The second obstacle is that most people in the community are unemployed, and they cannot afford our services," considers Modisane.

Another main challenge is sustainability. Says Modisane: "that is a general rule: telecentres are not sustainable." The main sources of income are the phone calls, the faxes, the photocopiers, and the typing service. These revenues serve to cover the running costs of the centre, but there is no money left to pay the salary of the manager and the assistants.

Universal Service Agency did not do any kind of baseline studies to establish the telecentres. There was no planning stage, no baseline research, and no clear explanation and discussion of project objectives. Generally speaking, no tailor-made information is prepared to meet the needs of the community. Makoro, the manager of a Universal Service Agency telecentre in the township of Siyabonga, Johannesburg, metaphorically summarises the essence of the problem: "Universal Service Agency gave me a car, but they didn't give me a driver's license. Why do I want a car if I don't know how to drive it?"

There is also concern about electricity and telephone deficits, which is part of the reason why none of the telecentres in rural and isolated areas were connected to the Internet.

REFERENCES

Information for this chapter is largely based on *Towards a Training Framework for Telecentre Management: A Case Study in South Africa*, by Raul Roman, Cornell University, August 2000, also e-mail exchanges with the author.

GRAMEEN VILLAGE PHONE

(1998) Bangladesh

....

BASIC FACTS

TITLE:	Grameen Telecom's Village Phone Programme
COUNTRY:	Bangladesh
MAIN FOCUS:	Community development
PLACE:	Countrywide
BENEFICIARIES:	65,000 villagers (1999)
PARTNERS:	Grameen Bank, GrameenPhone
FUNDING:	International Finance Corporation, Asian Development Bank, Commonwealth Development Corporation
MEDIA:	Cellular phones

SNAPSHOT

In rural areas where isolation and poor infrastructural services are often the norm, telecommunications can play an extremely important role in enhancing rural social and economic development. The Village Phone is a unique undertaking that provides modern digital wireless telecommunication services to some of the poorest people in the world.

A Grameen Bank member (most often female) purchases a phone under the lease-financing programme of the Bank and provides telephone service to people in her village. Each Village Phone operator is responsible for extending the services to customers for both incoming and outgoing calls, collecting call charges, and ensuring proper maintenance of the telephone set. Repayment of the loan for the phone set is processed through the existing loan granting and collection procedures of the Grameen Bank.

The Village Phone programme contains many rural development "firsts":

- First rural development micro-credit facility in a developing country to target the creation of micro-enterprises based on information and communication technology (ICT) services.

- First rural development micro-credit facility in a developing country to assist in the creation of village telephone service businesses using digital, wireless telephony.
- First private sector rural telecommunication initiative that specifically targets poor village women for establishing a micro-enterprise (targeted, micro-level programme).
- First private sector telecommunication initiative with an explicit purpose of rural poverty reduction.

As a result of these factors, the Village Phone programme should be examined in-depth as an innovative model.

DESCRIPTION

 In Bangladesh, rural people's occupations are becoming increasingly diversified and many people live outside their villages. Fifty percent of rural households do not own any land; they seek off-farm and nonfarm income earning opportunities. Less than 8 percent of the Grameen Bank members surveyed for this report indicated that their main occupation is agriculture. Labour mobility has increased enormously in the recent past and millions now work outside their own village and abroad. Population mobility is a key indicator of demand for telephone services because when people move and relocate, they have a greater need to communicate with family and friends.

GrameenPhone is a commercial operation providing cellular services in both urban and rural areas of Bangladesh. A pilot programme of GrameenPhone, through the Grameen Bank and a wholly owned subsidiary, Grameen Telecom, is enabling members of the Bank's revolving credit system to retail cellular phone services in rural areas.

Already in 1999, the pilot project involves 950 Village Phones providing access to more than 65,000 people. Women access micro-credit to acquire a digital GSM cellular phone and subsequently resell phone calls and phone services within their villages. When the programme is complete, 40,000 Village Phone operators will be employed for a combined net income of US$24 million per annum.

The beauty of *Grameen Village Phone*, as well as of other initiatives by the Grameen Bank, is that the project is not only socially beneficial but also profitable. Few social development oriented organisations have been as successful in effecting such deep structural changes in society on such a large scale as the Grameen Bank.

Village Phone enables rural people to make calls from their villages and also to receive calls from outside. A Village Phone operator has a financial incentive to ensure that incoming calls are completed, and she/he is therefore willing to make the extra effort to find the person for whom the incoming call is destined.

According to Grameen Bank member phone users surveyed for the TeleCommons report (1999), 61 percent of the last phone calls completed were incoming calls received by villagers, and 58 percent of the last phone calls completed were connections with people (primarily family members) living outside of Bangladesh. Thus, the Village Phone provides an important link that enables relatives who have left the village to stay in touch with family at home. And almost 42 percent of Grameen Bank member phone users indicate that their main reasons for using the phone involve discussions of financial matters (primarily discussions about remittances) with family members. Only 7 percent of calls were made for business and trading reasons.

The TeleCommons data reveals that the Village Phone plays a key role in facilitating family relationships and the flow of remittances to family members in the village when a family member has left the village for work in another country or Dhaka City.

For example, 54 percent of Grameen Bank member phone users indicated that they were willing to spend between 100 to 300 Taka (US$2 to US$6) for a three minute phone call involving a financial matter with a family member overseas, and 27 percent said they were willing to spend between 300 to 600 Taka (US$6 to US$12.25) for this kind of call. Given an average reported monthly income of 5,000 Taka (US$102) for respondents' households, these figures represent significant proportions of monthly household income ranging from two percent to 12 percent.

BACKGROUND & CONTEXT

Bangladesh is, like many other countries in the developing world, an example of telecommunication systems that do not work. On the other hand, thanks to the *Grameen Village Phone* project it may soon become an outstanding example of telecommunications that work for social change and rural development.

A summary of indicators provides a picture of the telecommunications sector: The telephone density of 0.26 lines per 100 people is one of the world's lowest; the waiting time for a connection is more than 10 years; the installation charge of US$450 for a new line is one of the highest in the world; on average, only 2 of 10 calls are successfully completed.

The Village Phone initiative was developed by combining the Grameen Bank's expertise in micro-enterprise and micro-credit with the latest digital wireless technology. Grameen Telecom (GTC) is a nonprofit organisation—part of the Grameen Bank, focusing exclusively on the deployment of the Village Phone programme in rural

Bangladesh. GTC owns 35 percent of the shares of GrameenPhone (GP), a private sector urban cellular telephone operation from which GTC buys airtime in bulk and passes on most of the savings to the Village Phone (VP) operator, making use of Grameen Bank's extensive network (1,140 branches spread over 39,346 villages) and its loan system to collect revenue from the operators.

An estimate of the percent of cellular vs. landline telephone subscribers in Bangladesh is over 20 percent: 500,000 landlines vs. 100,000. GrameenPhone plans to double the number of subscribers each year. This is an unprecedented situation where a cellular network is poised to dominate the national telecom industry. Personal voice communication beyond hearing distance is simply not possible today from 90 percent of the 68,000 villages of Bangladesh. The Village Phone programme provides an opportunity for universal access: a person may not own a telephone but he/she should have access to a telephone within a ten-minute walk.

ASPECTS OF SOCIAL CHANGE

This is what the *Grameen Village Phone* is achieving:
- The Village Phone programme appears to be the best available technical solution under current regulatory and commercial circumstances.
- The Village Phone programme is a technical and organisational solution to rural telecommunications access.
- The marriage of Grameen Bank's revolving loan system and network of branches with the cellular phone loan programme is unique and working very well.
- Grameen Telecom staff is committed and provides excellent service to users.
- There are significant positive social and economic impacts, including relatively large consumer surplus and immeasurable quality of life benefits.
- The Village Phone programme raises, perhaps for the first time, the important issue of gender when considering goals of universal telecommunication access.

Social calls to family and friends frequently involve transfer of information about market prices, market trends and currency exchange rates, making the Village Phone an important tool for enabling household enterprises to take advantage of market information, to increase profits and reduce productive expenses.

Grameen Telecom first gathers information on villages that have cellular coverage emanating from GrameenPhone's existing network of cellular towers. The current coverage expands through fibre optic cable along the Bangladesh Railway network. GTC officers then visit the Grameen Bank branches and prepare a list of villages where network coverage is satisfactory to provide Village Phone service.

The Grameen Bank has a special set of criteria for the selection of the operators: they must have a very good record of repayment of loans; they should be literate or at least have children who can read and write; their residence should be near the centre of the village; they should have a good business, and the spare time to function as operators. Initially, this may be a side business and eventually switch over to telecom business on a full-time basis.

After the initial selection the Unit Officer ensures signal availability in the house where the operator intends to use the phone. Experience has demonstrated that a weak signal can be improved by use of a high gain antenna mounted on a four- to five-metre bamboo pole. The high gain antenna effectively makes the cellular phone a "fixed-mobile" phone, although the antenna and pole can be moved within a village, if needed. GTC then buys from GrameenPhone a cellular phone user subscription on behalf of the operator, provides the connection to the member, and supplies the necessary hardware and the training to operate the phone.

The basic Village Phone package (Nokia transceiver, battery, fast charger, sign board, calculator, stopwatch, user guide in Bangla, and price list for calling different locations) costs approximately US$310. The Village Phone operator pays for the phone through weekly loan payment installments of US$4.50. These payments are made through the local Grameen Bank branch. On average, the Village Phone operator earns a net profit of 2,000 Taka per month (or US$40).

Widespread access to electricity in rural Bangladesh enables the phone operator to recharge batteries or power the phone directly from an electrical outlet. Solar power sources are provided in non-electrified villages.

CONSTRAINTS

The Government's card phones installed in towns may represent a competition for the *Grameen Village Phone*. Because tariffs for card phone use are lower than tariffs for Village Phone use, and because rural phone users are very price sensitive, the Village Phone initiative may see a drop in demand for outgoing calls if card phones and prepaid calling cards are more accessible in towns.

GSM cell phone technology is a high-cost solution for universal access in rural areas. Limited cellular coverage of rural areas may only be viable under the current set of cumbersome regulatory practices. GSM cell phone technology also places much higher tariffs on rural phone users than would be the case for wireless local loop (WLL) technologies. Cellular phone technology is currently not a viable option for inexpensive email/Internet/data connectivity.

REFERENCES

This chapter is based on Grameen Telecom's *Village Phone Programme in Rural Bangladesh: a Multi-Media Case Study*, by Don Richardson, Ricardo Ramírez, Moinul Haq. TeleCommons Development Group (TDG), March 2000.

KIRITIMATI RADIO

(1998) Republic of Kiribati

BASIC FACTS

TITLE:	Kiritimati Radio
COUNTRY:	Republic of Kiribati
MAIN FOCUS:	Education in water and sanitation, information, entertainment
PLACE:	Christmas Island (Kiritimati)
BENEFICIARIES:	Population of around 4,000 in Kiritimati
PARTNERS:	Telecom Services Kiribati Limited (TSKL)
FUNDING:	KWASP (AusAID), Linnix (Government)
MEDIA:	Radio

SNAPSHOT

Everybody wanted to help. The first task was clearing the scrub, pushing over trees and bushes, clearing and levelling the site for the building and its 100 foot guyed tower on which we had to mount our FM transmission antenna. On our third day on the island we were digging into the coral for building slab, the tower base and guy anchor points, and on day four, we poured the slab and tower foundations.

Our next building task was timber frame construction; two young men, who seemed to be quick learners and could work with reasonable accuracy, assisted us. After completing the frames we went back on-site to assemble and erect the tower. This task lasted for two days, and once again everyone involved did the work with much enthusiasm. We continued on-site to erect the building frames, to put on the iron roof and do the cladding of the exterior of the building, the internal insulation and cladding. Working 10 to 11 hours each day, the building work on-site took about two weeks to complete. The end result was most impressive.

Because the radio station was sited on the edge of London town, everybody coming into town would see the station as it was being constructed. School children showed interest by calling out and waving as they went past. Many locals driving into town, would sound their car horns as they went past, and some called in to have a look. The new radio station was "a real buzz" around town.

We actually "fired up" the radio station for the first time one month after arriving on the island and it happened to be on a Friday. We decided to carry out reception tests on Sunday by travelling right around the island, to measure the strength of our FM radio signal. To do this we prepared a 30 minute test tape which we then set up to operate continuously (a repeating loop). And so we had a repeat of the same programme (a mixture of local and Western music) for 36 continuous hours. We would think, 'how boring,' but not so for the locals. Local people kept telling us how much they enjoyed listening to Kiritimati Radio *over the weekend. We would say, "didn't you find it boring having the same music repeated every half hour" —but the reply was usually, "no we just loved hearing our own radio station."—* WRITTEN BY RON EHRKE, A CONSULTANT AND RADIO SPECIALIST.

DESCRIPTION

There was no radio station on Christmas Island before *Kiritimati Radio* (93.5 FM) transmissions started, six hours every day, seven days per week, in late November 1998.

Right after the radio station was constructed and equipped, a seven day period of intense training followed for four local people who had been selected to become radio announcers and programme presenters. The trainees were taught a range of skills necessary to operate a radio studio; such as voice production, interviewing, music production using cassette and compact disc, all blended together to produce composite programmes, through a studio on-air mixing console. An amazing fact of this part of the project was that most of the trainees had never seen a radio studio before but within a few days, were competently operating the equipment.

Kiritimati Radio's programming, which airs through a 500-watt transmitter, includes mostly music, announcements and news. In the evenings, from 7:30 to 8:00 p.m., programmes with social and educational content are aired: *Education* (Monday), *Radio Quiz* or *Interview* (Tuesday), *Water and Sanitation* (Wednesday and Saturday), *Health* (Thursday), *Magazine* (Friday) and a religious programme (Sunday). Groups or institutions that support *Kiritimati Radio* and want to take advantage of its outreach possibilities produce most of these programmes.

- On a weekly basis, different church groups are participating with on-air religious services.
- A wildlife unit of the Ministry hosts a weekly programme involving primary schools in promoting environmental issues regarding birds and corals.

- The Water Project (KWASP) does weekly awareness programmes on water and sanitation safety issues. KWASP prepares the messages that are mainly on water and sanitation, as well as some on the progress of the project. Overseas technical consultants are sometimes invited to discuss issues on-air.
- The programming includes bringing community groups—singing groups for example—into the studio, to record them and then replay the tape at a later time. The station also has a portable cassette recorder which the announcers can take "on location" to record interviews and meetings.

There are no funds available from local sources. The community, as well as private businesses, are charged whenever they lodge their announcements. Announcements could be on-air every session— each morning, afternoon or lunch, and evening programme.

Funding for the building, the equipment, the training and for technical support was provided by the water project (KWASP). Nonetheless, considering that by 2002 the project will end, the government was invited to take over *Kiritimati Radio* and is currently funding two salaries of announcer/presenters.

Telecom Services Kiribati Limited (TSKL), the Government authority which manages communication systems on the island, and is also the licensing authority, was very supportive of the efforts to establish the radio station. Since TSKL is the organisation that has and will continue to provide local technical support in the event of breakdowns, technicians from TSKL participated in some basic "first-line" maintenance training.

BACKGROUND & CONTEXT

Kiribati comprises 3 groups of islands—Gilberts, Phoenix and Line islands; formerly under British rule; it became a republic in 1979. The people of Kiribati are Gilbertese of Micronesian decent; their local language is known as Gilbertese.

Christmas Island is the largest island and has the largest population (about 4,000) in the Line group although there are people living on the other islands. Captain Cook discovered the island on Christmas Eve 1777 and so he named it. Nonetheless, the local name for Christmas Island is Kiritimati and all the locals refer to it as Kiritimati. The island is the largest coral atoll in the world, and it is virtually flat. The British had military bases in the 1950s and 1960s while they conducted atomic tests. There is still some evidence of their presence in the form of military hardware dumps and deserted airfields.

The island is a long distance from the next nearest country with radio services. Hawaii has a number of radio stations, mostly for local consumption, but 3000 kilometres is too far to transmit to Christmas Island except under rare atmospheric conditions.

The establishment of a radio station in Kiritimati was only a small part in a larger water project, known as Kiribati Water Supply & Sanitation Project" (KWASP), funded through Australia's International Aid Agency (AusAID). The addition of the community FM radio station into the project was an initiative inspired by the KWASP contractor's project director from the Overseas Projects Corporation of Victoria (OPCV). A requirement of the project is to educate the local people in health and hygiene throughout the five-year life cycle of the project. Since there were no media on the island (no newspaper and no radio), the project director came up with the idea of adding a small radio station into the project as the "vehicle" for the educative role in the project.

Ron Ehrke, a consultant and radio specialist, was called in to put the radio project together: "As my designs and plans began to unfold, these plans were passed on to the local government representatives for information and comment but I never received any advice to make changes or include anything extra, based on local input."

ASPECTS OF SOCIAL CHANGE

The presence of a community radio station, even if it is not highly participatory, has an immediate impact on the population; especially on an island like Kiritimati, where no other media existed before. Small stations such as *Kiritimati Radio* usually start airing music for most of the day: this already has had an impact on cultural identity and community pride. The next step, closely associated with music programming, is to make announcements and dedications, which contribute to the strengthening of the local social networks. When the station grows in experience and skills, local production of health- or education-related programmes start. These programmes help by disseminating information on important issues that affect the community.

In Kiritimati, for the first time, the local population has access to primary health messages, stool specimen tests by the microbiologist, well-water results, songs on environmental practices, home gardening for better diet, recipes on cooking vegetables, and general cleanliness. *Kiritimati Radio* is a useful tool for the education and social awareness of the community of Christmas Island.

"This radio station has instilled a lot of soul and fun into the island life now," says an observer who has visited the island many times.

Christmas Island radio announcers speak in the local language, Gilbertese. One very interesting aspect is that they are all women. Three local women manage and operate the radio station. One of them is an older person who had had a number of years of radio experience in Tarawa before moving to Christmas Island.

Linnix Government representatives selected the women from a small field of applicants. All three had to resign from their paying jobs in order to train for their new career in radio. The women began as volunteers with no guarantee that they would be selected after their training was complete. Fortunately all three women were quite outstanding and after only eight days of intensive operational training, they were able to run on-air programmes. After a few months of operation, Linnix decided to pay them.

Only a handful of radio receivers were available on the island, because of the nonexistence of a radio station prior to *Kiritimati Radio*. In order to counter this problem, portable units running on solar or dynamo power (wind-up radios) were bought in bulk and then sold locally at US$26.

CONSTRAINTS

All radio stations, even low-powered community stations need to have a license to operate, approved by appropriate government authorities. This might be normal in every country with a radio history, but not in Kiribati. Moreover, the government authority had agreed that no license was required. However, the proposed site was in close proximity to the Telecom authority's building, which included sensitive satellite equipment. When basic radio building site preparations were about to start, the local Telecom Manager said that the station had to have a license to operate, but they would not approve a license for a radio station to be built on that particular site—Telecom was concerned about possible interference with its sensitive equipment. All parties agreed to a new site, one on the edge of London town, all in a matter of four weeks—a very quick resolution to the problem and perhaps indicative of how things can happen in a place like Kiritimati.

In the near future *Kiritimati Radio* may not become a communication experience with a strong component of community participation in decisions concerning content, management and ownership. Access is guaranteed, but not full participation in decision-making.

By the end of 1999 the Ministry of Line and the Phoenix group of islands took over the station; two announcers are paid under the Government Recurrent Budget while a third announcer, the account clerk and the night watchman are paid from the proceeds from *Kiritimati Radio.* The Senior Radio Announcer is responsible for the content and format for the programmes, but she must consult the Ministry on any new additional programming to go on-the-air.

REFERENCES

This chapter is entirely based on information, e-mails and papers written by Ron Ehrke.

Ron Ehrke. "Radio comes to Christmas Island." *Pacific Magazine*, March/April 1999, Volume 24, No. 2, issue 134.

MANENO MENGI

(1998) Tanzania

BASIC FACTS

TITLE:	Maneno Mengi
COUNTRY:	Tanzania
MAIN FOCUS:	Community development
PLACE:	Mtwara, Lindi, Hangai, Zanzibar and others
BENEFICIARIES:	Rural and urban communities, fisherfolks
PARTNERS:	Rural Integrated Project support, Tanzania (RIPS), TV Zanzibar, Historic Cities Support Programme (HCSP)
FUNDING:	Finnish Cooperation, SIDA, Aga Khan Trust for Culture (AKTC)
MEDIA:	Video

SNAPSHOT

Consider this scene at the Kilwa fish market, in the Mtwara Region of southeastern Tanzania: the image shows a group of fishermen accusing the district executive director of not sharing the collected tax with the marine environment fund and the village. "This is the truth. Money is collected, but the way they use the money is bad, as you can see. First he does not know himself what he collects, and then we don't know what we should get. That is how they grow big stomachs, while we are becoming very thin."

The discussion goes on as if the camera was not there; people have gotten used to having the camera inside the circle, as another participant. Nobody looks at the camera; nobody modifies the wording or the attitude to please the camera. This is one of the participatory video sessions organised by *Maneno Mengi* and it is only one step in a long process of using the video tools to help a community better understand a social or economic development initiative.

The final product, "Utuambie Wananchi" is a video "digest," a short report on how the interactive process developed over a period of several months. But this is neither an end result nor the main objective, only a way of sharing with others the process in an encapsulated form. Several months after being released, the video became "a popular account of how villagers fight against corruption."

The real objective of *Maneno Mengi*'s work is in the interactive participatory process. The fisherfolks Association for the Protection of the Marine Environment in Mtwara and Lindi Regions, also known as "Shirikisho," requested the support from *Maneno Mengi* to follow-up on the fish market, which had continuously failed to deliver revenue. Initially, it was decided that 5 percent of the turnover of the market should be collected and shared between the village (20 percent), the district (30 percent) and the Marine Environment Fund (50 percent) in order to finance local development activities. It didn't happen until through the process of participatory video the problem was analysed by all stakeholders.

The evaluation of the performance of the Kilwa fish market was done in front of the camera, in the very fish market. People knew that the camera was an ally, since they had been working with Maneno since 1994 on another issue that also was solved through video evaluation: the struggle to stop dynamite fishing.

DESCRIPTION

Meaning "many words" in Swahili, *Maneno Mengi* is a small video company that was formed in 1998, after the members had been working with media for communities in Tanzania since 1994. With compact digital cameras and portable editing equipment, this collective consisting of four communicators of different nationalities (Swedish, German, English and Tanzanian), has put into practice one of the most interesting projects of participatory video.

The group members started to develop participatory media when involved with the Rural Integrated Project Support (RIPS) programme funded by Finland in Southern Tanzania. By then, important issues such as dynamite fishing were put aside as "too difficult" to deal with. Several "quick fixes" were tried with no success. It wasn't until the issue of community participation was brought into the discussion that they were successful: the only way to deal with the problem in a definite way was by addressing the issues from the community level. Video was then used for the first time as an enabling tool for participation.

The process started by analysing the situation: 28 species of fish had been decreasing, several fishermen lost their hands by accidental explosions, coral reefs were damaged, corruption of authorities prevented them from finding solutions. The video segments included "formulating the claim, linking communities, participatory appraisal, participatory evaluation and mediation." Villagers reviewed rough edits of footage, which were instrumental in revealing the issues when meeting with the ministers, donors and policy makers. The outcome of this process included the intervention of the Navy to stop dynamite fishing, a savings and loan programme, construction of fish markets, strengthening the community organisation (Shirikisho) and a national debate. Dynamite fishing eventually disappeared by 1997.

The above shows the kind of interventions used by *Maneno Mengi*: using video as a tool for self-assessment and evaluations, for strengthening local organisations and for providing a loud voice to previously unheard people. "We define participatory video as a scriptless production process, directed by a group of grassroots people, moving forward in iterative cycles of shooting-reviewing. This process aims at creating video narratives that communicate what those who participate in the process really want to communicate, in a way they think is appropriate."

Between 1996–98 Maneno was actively supporting a process of involving villages in the design and management of a proposed forest reserve. Village Natural Resource Committees were formed to enable the dialogue with district officers on decentralising the management of the Hangai forest to the villages. A "digest" reflecting the process was edited: *Misitu wa Hangai* (The Hangai Forest).

Video was also instrumental during the 1997 campaign to prevent the worsening of cholera outbreaks in Mtwara and Lindi regions. It contributed to building a situation analysis and to support participatory planning. In the end, villages made their own plans of action to prevent cholera. The video "digest" *Tukomeza Kipindupindu* (Let's Get Rid of Cholera) was produced along with a radio play.

Other interventions included stopping foreign land owners from evicting villagers from Naumbu ward (Our Village Is Being Sold); sharing knowledge about the implications of the Land Bill for villagers in Newala (Conflicts Over Land?); and interventions also contributed to giving a voice to the tenants of Stonetown in Zanzibar, while promoting the preservation of this old city (*Baraza*, a TV series). Only in this last activity were the video products the main output of the process.

BACKGROUND & CONTEXT

At the origin of *Maneno Mengi* is the Interactive Communication component, one of the three focus areas of the Rural Integrated Project Support programme (RIPS). The objectives aimed to promote regional rural media to provide villagers access to information and to give villagers a voice. Maneno was registered as an independent group in 1998 in order to be able to offer media services all over East Africa. RIPS is now one of their partners in a growing network of rural media centres.

In the context of Tanzania using video technology for the purpose stated above was an important breakthrough, considering that most of what was done in terms of community participation and media in the past related mainly to the use of radio. Though radio is, without a doubt, the most powerful medium in East Africa, it has scarcely been used to give a voice to rural communities. The main social use of radio was as a vehicle to convey messages with social content. Its use as a communication tool in the hands of the community is still far away, though the very RIPS programme was successful in establishing a village radio network (Radio Kijijini) where 12 village groups would record on their own cassette recorders messages that were later aired by the local radio station, part of Radio Tanzania.

Video technology seemed to be an interesting alternative in a context where access to radio is very limited for communities. Within the framework of RIPS, video was viewed as a tool for: a) Negotiating partnerships and mechanisms for local natural resource management; b) Linking participatory research with national policy debate; and c) Participatory learning to improve social service provision.

ASPECTS OF SOCIAL CHANGE

Maneno Mengi has the advantage of being able to extend the experience of participatory communication and at the same time to develop a serious reflection on its accumulated experience. The entire process of working with various communities has been documented and is considered a sole body of work that goes in one direction.

Social change has been happening in most of the projects where *Maneno Mengi* has become involved. The results of their interventions on issues—such as the dynamite fishing and the fish market in Mtwara, the forest in Hangai, or the renovation of Stonetown in Zanzibar—wouldn't have been possible without the changes that occurred inside the empowered communities in terms of: increasing local participation, getting better organised, applying democratic principles to decision-making, and overall, having a clear understanding of the problems. The two strategies, media for claims making and media for mediation, have been successful in the search for solutions.

Video has supported the process and has been used by the community as a learning tool of immense educational value. The video camera acts as a microscope sometimes, and as a collective mirror at other times. It can focus on details or allow the community to self-analyse and self-evaluate. The fact that the community has become in each case so familiar with the video equipment proves that the tool has been accepted and adopted; the next step is the transfer of ownership.

"Access to video," writes Lars Johansson in *Participatory Video and PRA*, "has expanded the process both vertically, through policy dialogue, and horizontally, through mobilising political support for locally articulated causes and claims. ... Through letting grassroots groups and individuals speak for themselves, participatory video fuels political struggles over democratic rights and power."

MEDIA & METHODS

The process of interactive use of video is the key element of *Maneno Mengi*'s work. The final video product, a "digest" in the words of the producers, is only a report on the process, often aimed at showing to other communities and also donors and policymakers, the role of video as a facilitating tool for development.

Digital low-cost video technology has made the difference. If not equipped as it is, *Maneno Mengi* could not have gone this far in terms of the participatory and interactive processes. The small digital cameras not only guarantee a high quality of images, but also the possibility of easily transferring the technology into the hands of the community. At some point, it is no longer important to know who holds the camera, as the community is involved in the whole process.

But the impressive leap forward is achieved through the use of new editing technology. Up until very recently, editing equipment was chained to editing rooms because of the size and number of the various editing machines needed (monitors, mixers, recorders); but the technology used by *Maneno Mengi* totally frees editing from being dependent on room, transportation, and even, electricity. The whole editing suite is held in an Apple PowerBook G3 laptop computer, loaded with the Final Cut software and enough memory. In terms of quality there is no difference between these and standard professional formats, but the cost has gone down by twenty-fold.

CONSTRAINTS

In spite of this awesome low-cost technology, the process of transferring ownership to the community is not simple, considering that the media utilised is so new and that "ownership" is not just a matter of hardware and property. Maneno acknowledges that the process can take months or even years: "1) A few minutes to learn how to press the buttons; 2) A few days to learn how to get framing, focus and exposure right; 3) A few weeks learning how to tell stories in moving pictures; and 4) A few months or even years to get into helping other people tell their stories."

REFERENCES

Information for this chapter was gathered during a visit to *Maneno Mengi* headquarters in Zanzibar, Tanzania, in March 2000. The author met with Lars Johansson, Verena Knippel, Dominick de Waal and Farida Nyamachumbe, partners in *Maneno Mengi*.

The following *Maneno Mengi* edited productions or "digests" were reviewed: *The Hangai Forest* (1999), *Bahari Yetu Hatutaki* (1994), *Utuambie Wananchi* (1998) and *Baraza* (1999).

The December 1999/January 2000 issue of *Forest, Trees and People* newsletter carries four key articles on the work of *Maneno Mengi* by the members of the collective.

Additional information can also be found at the *Maneno Mengi* Web site <http://www.zanzibar.org/maneno/> which includes these papers: a) *Travel Report* by Kamal Singh (July 1998), b) *Communicative Aspects of Participatory Video Projects: An exploratory study* by Bernhard Huber, and c) *Stonetown Baraza: Participatory TV and Community-Based Rehabilitation in Zanzibar* by Verena Knippel and Lars Johansson.

NUTZIJ

1998 Guatemala

BASIC FACTS

TITLE: NUTZIJ—Centro de Mujeres
Comunicadoras Mayas

COUNTRY: Guatemala

MAIN FOCUS: Women development and empowerment

PLACE: Sololá

BENEFICIARIES: Mayan women

PARTNERS: Red de Desarrollo Sostenible
(RDS)/UNDP, Asociación para el Desarrollo
Integral, Guatemala (APDESI), Autoridad
para el Manejo Sustentable de la Cuenca del
Lago Atitlan y su Entorno, Guatemala
(AMSCLAE)

FUNDING: Padma Guidi, UNDP, FAO/Ministry of
Agriculture (MAGA), Friedrich Ebert
Stiftung (FES)

MEDIA: Video and Internet

SNAPSHOT

The camera sweeps around, loose and free, showing smiling faces,
feet, objects and animals. It lowers as a small child approaches it until
one of his eyes covers the lense and becomes the whole image, he
celebrates his feat; then the camera goes up again sweeping textiles of
magnificent colours.

Two young Mayan women are filming each other and everyone
around. The small video cameras do not seem to bother the Aguilar
Reynoso family, Maya Kaqchikel who live in a village near Cantel,
Quetzaltenango. Emiliana Aguilar, the daughter, holds one camera; she
and her sister Elena were trained to produce videos, and they do it as
naturally as they dress or speak their mother-tongue.

A panoramic view of clothes drying under the sun, a close-up of
hands that are peeling potatoes, a small dog rushes between legs. The
choice of what to film may seem erratic to someone used to television,

but it isn't: in only 12 minutes, the life of the Aguilar Reynoso family passes on the screen through vibrant testimonies about culture and life in good times and hard times.

"Things have changed," says an old man, "we used to take care of the sick with natural products; but now there are chemical drugs that cost 1,000 quetzales. We can't afford to buy them so we continue using our traditional medicine." A woman shows some leaves and explains the properties of each one. "But of course, if you don't have faith, you can't pretend to be cured," she adds convincing.

The camera moves toward a group of women washing clothes with small children on their back. "The father of my first child was killed by the military, I never saw him again," says one, remembering the repression in the 1980s. Many fled, leaving everything behind. Some survived.

The video continues to flow like a clear stream, regardless of the do's-and-don'ts and the sacred rules of documentary filmmaking. Who made those rules anyway?

Music emerges from a guitar, prompting members of the family to sing and dance. Life goes on, these are better times. Several children play hopscotch, using a stick to draw the cells; then, jumping on one foot, they land in "heaven."

DESCRIPTION

 *Nutzij* ("My Word," in Maya Kaqchikel), also known as the Centro de Mujeres Comunicadoras Mayas (CMCM) is a communication access centre in central Guatemala. Located at Sololá over Lake Atitlán, it is run by a collective of young Mayan women, mostly teachers at the Nueva Esperanza school in Xajaxac. *Nutzij* offers hands-on training and employment for indigenous women in visual media communication, mainly concentrating on video and the Internet. The centre aims to provide access to media-awareness and production skills for local communication in rural areas, as well as use of the Internet for marketing and international communication.

The centre initially provided services of technical education and employment opportunities through access to information, communication technology, and video production, as well as workshops on media awareness and participatory communication. Through the use of the Internet they're aiming to provide useful information for development groups involved in cooperatives, farming, fishing, health, education, etc. One of the tasks that *Nutzij* is developing is browsing the Web for information that can be of use for the local population.

The centre started its activities by the end of 1997 with a private donation of US$50,000 worth of video equipment, which included four Video 8 cameras, editing equipment and three personal computers.

The activities of *Nutzij* are essentially divided in two: video production and training, and Internet access and training.

The video component is made of three main areas:

- Workshops on "interactive autodiagnosis," which helps development projects, organisations and communities include a participatory process in their planning and implementation
- Video productions done by women members of *Nutzij*
- Training of women as video producers or rural communicators (*comunicadoras populares*)

During 1999 *Nutzij* developed new partnerships; for example with AMSCLAE, an organisation that requested support for training a team of young Mayan women in video production and environmental issues.

The Internet component includes training on the basics of computer use and Web search functions, as well as research on issues that can be of benefit to the community, such as environment, farming, education, women empowerment, etc.

The strategy of opening telecentres at the community level started in the village of Chaquijya, in partnership with APDESI. This pilot experience will certainly provide valuable information to set up the other planned telecentres.

Funding has been of constant difficulty for *Nutzij*, primarily because all activities, including training and access to video equipment and the Internet are provided free-of-charge to the indigenous populations. By 1999 the centre devised a strategy to raise funds through the establishment of workshops for foreign communication students who would pay for their participation in video coproductions with Mayan women. Other than providing an income to sustain the other activities, this experience is important in terms of facilitating cultural exchanges while maintaining a spirit of respect and solidarity. In 1999, five students from Europe and the United States participated.

BACKGROUND & CONTEXT

The situation of education in Guatemala is dreadful. Succesive ladino and military governments have bluntly ignored the education needs of the Mayan population, which constitutes the vast majority of the country. As a result, the illiteracy rates are very high (45 percent), particularly among Mayan women; and Guatemala ranks the second worst in the Americas, Haiti being the last. The attempts of forcing the Mayan population to learn to read and write in Spanish has proved a failure, but governments blindly persist in spite of UNESCO recommendations that early education should always take place in the mother-tongue, before gradually introducing a second language.

Mayan communities in Guatemala speak twenty different languages; in the central part of the country, in villages surrounding Lake

Atitlan, three are most important: Tzutujil, Quiché and Kaqchikel. Because of attachment to language and tradition, these Mayan communities have a strong cultural identity, which has survived not only the Spaniards conquest and colonisation, but also nearly 40 years of civil war and massacres where the Mayan population, women and children included, was specifically targeted.

In that context, the ability of the Mayan—even the illiterate—to adopt audio-visual tools and place them at the service of their culture and their social struggle opens extraordinary opportunities—moreover when these tools are integrated with the Internet and modern communication technologies.

Nutzij debuted by the end of 1997 when Padma Guidi—who had been working with women in India, Czechoslovakia and on Indian reservations in the United States—trained a group of Mayan women in video production skills. Four of these women organised in the Asociación de Mujeres Comunicadoras Mayas. Padma Guidi provided funding, donated her own video equipment, subsidised the initial activities and remained as their technical adviser.

ASPECTS OF SOCIAL CHANGE

Video is cheap and easy to use and distribute. It has been successfully utilised by development projects, sometimes as a tool for self-reflection, analysis and evaluation, and other times to support organising within groups. It is particularly adapted to rural Guatemala where TV sets are found in many homes lacking basic services, and where local cable television operators are happy to broadcast locally made programmes.

Women who never dreamed of a life beyond carrying water and having babies, who never learned to read and write, are able to manipulate small video cameras, make personal choices about values and representation, document important community events and contribute to revitalising their culture while interacting with other cultures. "People here have been continually misinformed or uninformed about everything from economics to health care. Seeing is believing, and videos made by the indigenous community can bring information in people's own languages and in images they can recognise and relate to," says Padma Guidi.

Another contribution of *Nutzij* is making video tools available to communities, organisations and development projects for auto diagnosis, which has enormous implications in generating community participation for development purposes. This type of approach was conducted in collaboration with FAO and MAGA (Ministry of Agriculture).

MEDIA & METHODS

Nutzij values the role of visual communication especially in a culture where from one generation to the next the oral transmission of human values and history is the most important system of communication.

The *Nutzij* strategy takes advantage of the full potential of video and Internet tools, and combines both adequately according to the needs of training and service delivery. The video component wisely combines training with the use of cameras for production, research and auto diagnosis. Consequently video is conceived as a tool for production of messages ready to be disseminated, and as a process for stimulating dialogue within communities, projects and organisations.

Though at its initial stages, the Internet component is as participatory as the video component. Management of the existing telecentre is in the hands of local people who receive support from *Nutzij*.

CONSTRAINTS

The access to the Internet is certainly a challenge among the Mayan population, especially women, who speak little Spanish (and read none) and even less English. Knowing that 90 percent of the Web is in English is not very encouraging for a project that intends to use the Internet to link the indigenous population with the outside world. Nonetheless, the women associated in *Nutzij* are making enormous efforts to trace Web pages in Spanish, that bring the information needed a step closer to the community. Only the development of new Web sites, with contents adapted to the needs of the local population, may change this.

Because of the style of life in rural areas of central Guatemala, Mayan women are not easily available for training or group activities. The curriculum and schedule of training at *Nutzij* had to adapt to this reality.

Rural areas of Guatemala are not yet well served in terms of telephony and electricity, which limits certain activities of *Nutzij*, in particular, those involving the use of the Internet. Telephone land lines are unreliable when they exist, making Internet access a tortuous operation.

Funding has been a major difficulty for *Nutzij*. From the beginning the activities and equipment of the communication centre had been funded through sources personally related to Padma Guidi.

REFERENCES

Information provided by Padma Guidi (technical adviser) and Fermina Chiyal Jiatz (president), during a visit to *Nutzij* centre in Sololá, in May 2000.

The video productions from *Nutzij* were reviewed by the author. Among other documentaries: *La educación como una luz*, *La mujer guatemalteca y su mundo natural*, *Abriendo voces*, and *Un día en la vida*.

Annual Newsletter 1999, Centro de Mujeres Comunicadoras Mayas.

Web site <www.rds.org.gt/cmcm>.

RADIO MAMPITA & MAGNEVA

(1998) Madagascar

BASIC FACTS

TITLE: Radios Associatives Mampita and Magneva

COUNTRY: Madagascar

MAIN FOCUS: Rural development, community organisation

PLACE: Fianarantsoa and Morondava

BENEFICIARIES: Rural population

PARTNERS: Agence de Communication, Madagascar
                     (AGECO), Communication pour le
                     Development, Madagascar (CODE),
                     Médiascope

FUNDING: DDC

MEDIA: Radio

SNAPSHOT

At 27 kilometres North of Fianarantsoa, Madagascar, the small village of Akondro in the Ambalakely community is out on a hill overlooking a paradise—a valley full of bright green rice plantations. A few grapevines begin to show their intricate texture over the slopes, wine production is becoming an important economic alternative for Madagascar. Over each smooth hill rises a group of two-story houses, with the characteristic wooden balconies painted bright blue. The houses are solid, made of adobe, with wide walls and small windows. They can be seen over the hills from far away, they stand up with dignity.

These might be poor peasants, but they are not miserable. Their life goes on quietly in harmony with nature, whatever nature is left after decades of bringing down the trees that once covered most of Madagascar. These peasants have their rice, which they sell, they have cattle, and some are growing grapevines. Now they have something else they were lacking only a couple of years ago: a voice.

The peasant association in Ambalakely is one of those that joined *Radio Mampita*. Their concern for education and communication is outstanding: a 2 by 2 metres room in one of the building houses a class with no less than 12 children. They are sitting on the floor, listening and repeating what a very young girl, apparently 17 or 18 years old is teaching them. For teaching tools, she only has a small worn-out blackboard and a sweet smile.

During the meeting with the leaders of the local association, the benefits of *Radio Mampita* are reviewed. They all like the programme on legislation concerning land property the best. They have learned how to defend their rights, and how to settle land disputes among communities. The programmes where local people can send messages to their relatives and friends that are away, come next; after all "mampita" means "message" in the local language. The messages sent through the radio station are helping to build a network of contacts and exchanges. One immediate benefit: the theft of cattle has almost ceased since lost livestock began to be monitored through the station. One long-term benefit: new agricultural techniques have been introduced and production has increased.

DESCRIPTION

NY ATAO RO HITA, NY AMBARA RO RE

Both *Radio Mampita* and *Radio Magneva* aim to cover the rural communities. With a 300-watt transmitter and repeaters, *Radio Mampita* (FM 94 and FM 102) covers a radius of 70 kilometres within the hills surrounding Fianarantsoa, and *Radio Magneva* (FM 94 and FM 102)—at sea level in the west coast of Madagascar—reaches the communities within 100 kilometers from Morondava. Mampita means "message," and Magneva relates to a royal burial place much respected by the rural population.

Radio Mampita went on-the-air for the first time on June 8, 1998, and *Radio Magneva* on May 20, 1998. Both have followed the same path since the inception in 1995 of the Programme d'Appui a la Communication (PACOM), a DDC initiative to support rural development. The PACOM final objective was to raise the consciousness of peasants so they would understand the importance of communication for community development.

Community-based peasant associations were encouraged to send representatives to a general assembly that elected the members of the Conseil d'Administration. These elected officials hired the station manager and technicians, and meet regularly to discuss all issues concerning the radio stations. About 30 correspondents were appointed at the community level and equipped with a cassette recorder, batteries and blank cassettes. The local associations would provide for their travel expenses, though it seems this has not really happened.

Realising that very few families actually own a radio, *Radio Mampita* bought and distributed 500 small FM radios at a reasonable cost. Additionally, some associations received "wind-up" radio sets made in South Africa, though these have not been very popular: they break easily because of plastic components and are much more expensive than the small transistor sets. Also, the plastic ones are not available in the local markets and they do not include a cassette player, in spite of the size.

Both stations are partially autonomously financed through paid advertising, both commercial and institutional. International cooperation agencies buy slots for programming on environmental or health issues. Peasant associations become members by paying 50,000 Francs Malgaches (Fmg) or 60 kilos of rice per year. Individual peasants pay 5,000 Fmg (about US$0.80) for a one-minute message, half of that amount if they are members.

The Ministry of Communication and Culture granted the FM frequencies for both radio stations at no cost, in spite of the fact that there doesn't seem to be specific legislation for community radio stations in Madagascar. Actually, the two stations and a third scheduled to start operating in Antananarivo by the year 2000 will be the first of its kind in Madagascar. The legal status of the stations may become an issue in the future, when the pressure for new frequencies becomes important.

Both stations operate during one or two hours early in the morning, but their main programming starts at 5 p.m. and ends by 10 in the evening. By 6:45 p.m. both stations link with Radio Nationale de Madagascar, the national radio station for the national and international news. Neither of the two stations produce local news, though information on local issues might be part of any other segment.

Programming starts with public announcements and advertising. The main slots feature productions on health, environment, rural security, arts and culture, women and youth. The programme on land property and legislation is still produced by AGECO. A slot is devoted to "exchanges between peasants and technicians on agricultural issues."

BACKGROUND & CONTEXT

Every detail seems to have been designed from the beginning to successfully achieve a process of participatory communication. The strategy devised by the DDC includes four stages that follow a logical path.

At the first stage, 1995 to 1997, PACOM conducted a series of activities at the community level, including productions of street theatre, puppets, songs, comics and tapes for cassette listening groups. The latter was actually the seed for both radio stations; PACOM would produce programmes on health, agriculture and other community issues. The distribution of cassette tapes showed the growing interest of the peasantry towards the installation of a community-oriented radio station. Near Fianarantsoa, 162 peasant associations paid their membership to benefit from the audiocassettes.

The second stage consisted of creating independent agencies, specialised in rural communication, which would continue supporting communication activities on DDC programmes but also on other international cooperation projects. AGECO (Fianarantsoa), CODE (Morondava) and Mediascope (Antananarivo) came to life as private consulting agencies, with staff formerly attached to the PACOM.

The third stage was the creation of the radio stations, the establishment of administrative councils made of elected representatives from the peasant associations, and training the staff and volunteers provided by the communication agencies and independent consultants, such as Bianca Miglioretto, hired by the DDC. For the creation of *Radio Mampita*, 320 associations participated at the general assembly; eventually 240 became members.

The fourth stage, still in the works, is the transfer of the ownership of the stations into the hands of the peasant associations, represented at the Conseil d'Administration through a democratic process of elections. The DDC has decided to phase out support by the end of the year 2000.

ASPECTS OF SOCIAL CHANGE

The programmes that have had more impact among the rural population deal with agricultural issues, legislation on land tenure, and health. Peasants also appreciate the messages, which had a very big impact on helping to dramatically reduce the theft of cattle, one of the main problems. "Thanks to the station, 95 percent of stolen livestock is usually recovered."

"The radio [station] allows us to exchange experiences among peasants, so our skills have improved." A programme on a peasant developing a fish farm was so successful that several associations organised a trip to visit and learn from the experience. "We have introduced new agricultural techniques, our production is better and bigger now."

"We are not afraid of the microphone anymore." Rural folks got used to being interviewed by correspondents and have learned to take advantage of sending messages to family and friends. "Even the political leaders are afraid of us now, because we can say our truth through the station," a member of the Conseil d'Administration pointed out.

"Traditionally, when somebody died only the family would take care of expenses for the burial, now the whole community participates, sharing the costs." Their sense of community has developed and is now stronger.

The most interesting aspect concerning the methodology of the work of these stations is the social structure that has been built to ensure community participation. With all its limitations, the original idea of having the members of the Conseil d'Administration be elected by the general assembly of peasant associations stands as a model of participatory communication.

The organisation of correspondents at the community level, if properly conducted, should facilitate the process of participation by allowing community members to air their voices through the stations.

CONSTRAINTS

The two radio stations are facing problems because of the short period of time that was scheduled for *Radio Mampita* and *Radio Magneva* to become entirely independent from DDC support, and even from the technical guidance initially provided by AGECO and CODE. The objective of having the Conseil d'Administration, made up of peasant associations, run the stations in the short term has been hampered by the lack of real participation and democratic representation.

Only about one-third of the peasant associations existing within the area of influence of the stations are members, and some of those that are not members have expressed their criticism towards a project still perceived as having been "dumped." Even among the associations that joined as members, few pay their dues: in Morondava only 12 out of 147 pay. The very meaning of "association" might be at the core of the problem; small groups of 20 to 30 members become associations, they often represent a single extended family. The Conseil d'Administration in Morondava, moreover, is mainly made up of urban delegates.

On a more technical note, the stations have not yet succeeded in winning the hearts and minds of their potential audience. Their programming is not yet totally responding to the needs of the rural communities. Correspondents are not sufficiently trained or motivated to accomplish their important tasks at the community level; in Morondava only 7 out of 26 stations were operational in March of 2000. Last but not least, very few families, about one in twenty, own a radio. Radio is not, as in Latin America, a generalised feature in rural families. In the Ambalakely area only 12 out of 201 families own an FM transistor radio.

REFERENCES

Field visits to *Radio Mampita* and *Radio Magneva* in March 2000 are the main source of information for this chapter. The former included the visit to a peasant community in Ambalakely, north of Fianarantsoa.

The author held meetings and exchanged information with the Conseil d'Administration, Manager Lucienne Voahirana, and the staff of *Radio Mampita* and of Agence de Communication (AGECO) in Fianarantsoa, as well as with Manager Florentin Razanajatovo and the staff of *Radio Magneva* and of Communication pour le Development (CODE) in Morondava.

Further information was obtained in conversations held in Antananarivo with Mediascope Manager Guy Andrianjanaka, trainer Bianca Miglioretto and the Coordinator of the DDC, Pius Wennubst.

INFODES

BASIC FACTS

TITLE:	Sistema de Información para el Desarrollo Urbano Rural (InfoDes)
COUNTRY:	Peru
MAIN FOCUS:	Community development
PLACE:	Cajamarca
BENEFICIARIES:	Rural and urban population
PARTNERS:	Red de Bibliotecas Rurales de Cajamarca, Universidad de Cajamarca, Servicio Nacional de Adiestramiento en Trabajo Industrial, Peru (SENATI), SONOVISO, Asociación y Desarrollo Forestal, Peru (ADEFOR)
FUNDING:	Intermedia Technology Development Group (ITDG), INFODEV/World Bank
MEDIA:	Internet

SNAPSHOT

We were visiting the Chanta Alta village, talking with people, explaining the advantages of the Internet and the computerised information system, accessible to everyone. When the meeting was over a group of women approached and told us with a soft voice: "Nice, really nice; but do you think there is anything similar for those that do not read and write, the illiterate like us?"

Marisol, a colleague that is involved in education for environmental projects, also visited Chanta Alta and while she was strolling the street of the village she met a woman knitting. Marisol learned that the woman was illiterate and asked her if she would like to read and write. She replied with a tender smile: "What for, my dear? Is there anything to read that can be of use for me?"

We did encounter those reactions when we just started with the InfoDes project, but things have changed since. Now the project offers tailor-made information, which is especially designed for the needs of the community.

In the process of appropriating new technologies the local users have a great capacity to invent their own words to rename the hardware. For example, instead of "ratón," which would be the straight translation to Spanish for "mouse," they opted for "cuy" (a small rabbit), which is a common domestic rodent in the Andes. The mouse is not an animal they would like to be much in contact.

When peasants come to our office and sit in front of the computer, their hands—used to labouring on their land—take the "cuy" and start searching for the information they need on agriculture and livestock. Sometimes the cursor doesn't stop easily on a particular link on the screen they have selected: "This cuy doesn't want to stand still; it keeps running off my hand."—COMPILED BY THE *INFODES* PROJECT TEAM.

DESCRIPTION

InfoDes is an ITDG pilot project that promotes local and rural development by means of effective systems of information and communication. The end objective of the project is to contribute to the subregional development of Cajamarca by increasing the production levels of small farmers and the management skills of local governments, through the provision of information and communication tools.

The project has designed and established a subregional information system that integrates conventional local libraries, research on local knowledge, and the use of modern information technologies. It also aims to test a methodology that can be later adapted to other rural areas of Peru and Latin America.

After a period of two-and-a-half-years the project will be transferred to a consortium of local organisations. *InfoDes* counts on local governments, workers' unions, community-based organisations and NGOs to expand its network.

The Information System is an integrated approach that includes various levels of contact with the local population and the availability of many services. All levels are interrelated as follows:

InfoDes has established a Provincial Coordinating Centre in Cajamarca and several subsystems that are independent from each other. In the immediate subsequent levels are the CIDUR (Centros de Información para el Desarrollo Urbano-Rural) located in district capital towns, and the CIDER (Centros de Información para el Desarrollo Rural) in smaller villages and hamlets. The CIMDUR (Centros de Información Móvil para el Desarrollo Urbano-Rural, Peru), or mobile units articulate both structures, urban and rural.

The Provincial Coordinating Centre maintains the Web server and all external links. Other than coordination, its task mainly consists of building the system database with the information that all local partners are gradually providing. It also promotes the services of the information system.

The CIDUR combines the pre-existent town libraries with the high-tech electronic services: free access to e-mail and the Internet. Each user has its own e-mail account. The CIDUR coordinates the Alforja Rural service for rural librarians, and links with other institutional information initiatives at the local level, on issues of health, social security, legal advice, etc. The coordination of the CIDER in their zone of influence also falls under the responsibility of the CIDUR.

Closer to the rural communities, the CIDER also offers a traditional library service, low-cost video technology, and links to the local information initiatives of other development institutions, but it differs from the CIDUR because it lacks computer technology and access to Web services. On the other hand the CIDER are very important in terms of collecting local knowledge for the database.

The CIMDUR guarantees physical periodic exchanges between the other levels. It is comprised of a traditional library and some books for sale, and facilitates institutional interactions and exchanges of information—including video—between local organisations. It coordinates technical supervisory field visits, training activities, and back up for the rural librarians.

Acknowledging the need to facilitate access to computers and Internet users that may not yet be associated with the CIDUR, *InfoDes* has established telecentres in key areas of Cajamarca. These do not follow the model of the "public cabins," which are spreading in many provinces of Peru. The *InfoDes* telecentres provide services to people of scarce resources and are not commercial ventures.

BACKGROUND & CONTEXT

The Department of Cajamarca contains 15 percent of the total rural population of Peru. Because it is underdeveloped both socially and economically, living conditions are among the hardest in the country; unemployment and insufficient land are constantly forcing people into the cities, where the misery belts that surround urban areas absorb them.

The development of rural areas requires a series of improvements in the way small and medium-sized agricultural projects are managed; these include a rational use of natural resources, the introduction of new technologies, and the enhancement of the quality of products to ensure higher levels of profitability. These measures should be accompanied by decentralisation and an increasing role of local governments in development.

The other aspect that may contribute to bettering the quality of life in rural areas is better information delivery systems. In the provinces of Peru access to information is sporadic and of low quality. Both district capital cities and smaller towns suffer from the same lack of information channels, although community radio has been filling the gap for decades. These stations face the same problem—to get hold of data that can be useful to the rural population. Peasants and small entrepreneurs lack vital information on the prices of their products at provincial markets, on the availability of credit and tools, on technical innovations, on potential external markets, etc.

The Intermedia Technology Development Group is developing a system that may bring important positive changes to rural life in Cajamarca. Based on the traditional rural libraries that were created three decades ago, the ITDG is introducing new information technologies, which will facilitate communication exchanges, diminish isolation and alleviate poverty by propitiating new forms of rural and urban development.

ASPECTS OF SOCIAL CHANGE

The Information System for Urban and Rural Development that *InfoDes* (with support from ITDG) has established in Cajamarca is too new—less than two years in existence—to offer any important results in terms of affecting social change. Most of what has been done up until now is related to organising, setting in place and accumulating information that will be the bases of the services provided by the CIDER and the CIDUR, commonly known as "information centres."

The initial impact can be seen in the way the local governments are operating, improving administration systems and giving more attention to new technologies that can help them to better perform.

In terms of providing the services of the Internet and e-mail, it is too soon to evaluate any impact, although the fact of having generated increased interest among the general population is already a step towards social change. People have shown particular interest in the information on farming techniques that can be obtained through the database that is in the process of being compiled.

The rural population has already been exposed to (and developed an appreciation for) similar approaches to rural development through the use of video in the exploration of cultural values and community identity.

Rather than continuing the fashion of spreading computers and Internet access to rural areas formerly deprived of these gadgets, and which have no conceptual framework to support them, *InfoDes* has opted for a scientific approach. The team incorporates the existing resources, facilitates networking among local institutions and expands the information services on the basis of user demand and community participation.

The methodology that *InfoDes* is gradually developing is comprised of various services and features aiming to stimulate participation of local urban and rural communities.

Apart from the traditional Library the CIDUR offers a number of printed materials to help rural librarians through the Alforja Rural service. The Inforápido is a service that finds quick answers to questions posed by the users, on topics that do not require extensive research. The printed materials available at the CIDER and CIDUR are usually sufficient, however those questions that require further research are channelled through another service, the Preguntón, which uses the computerised database and the Web to answer the queries.

Acknowledging that Internet access will expand gradually but at a slow pace, the Rural-Urban Information System set up by *InfoDes* relies heavily on books and videos to disseminate valuable information among users. A specific service, the Videoclub arranges video shows on topics previously agreed upon by the community.

One of the most promising services is *Saber Campesino* (Peasants Knowledge), which collects traditional knowledge from the peasants on topics related to the areas undertaken by the project.

CONSTRAINTS

In the original structure, the main partner at the central level of the project was the Municipality of Cajamarca. It is at their headquarters that *InfoDes* had initially planned to establish the Coordinating Centre. However after almost two years this institution didn't show any progress, or respect for the agreements that were made or any organisational continuity. Repeated staff changes, often replacing qualified people with friends of the Mayor, and the fact that the libraries were left with no budget, resulted in a rupture of the agreement. *InfoDes* had to find a new place to locate the Coordinating Centre, currently housed at *InfoDes* offices. In order to leave an open door for potential Internet users, *InfoDes* created a telecentre in Cajamarca.

InfoDes has faced a big problem when trying to sell the idea of a self-sustaining Information System for rural development. Most of the programmes and projects in Cajamarca, as in most of rural areas of Peru, are the result of donations and receive continuous support from international or bilateral development agencies. Local institutions, NGOs, and the population-at-large are so used to development driven by external funding, that they are not very enthusiastic about a project that aims to generate funds locally. In response to this, *InfoDes* has decided to establish telecentres that will offer services to the general population.

REFERENCES

Most of the information for this chapter is available at the *InfoDes* Web site <http://www.infodes.org.pe/>.

Additional data provided through e-mail by Luis Fernando Bossio, project librarian.

THE LILAC TENT

(1998) Bolivia

BASIC FACTS

TITLE: The Lilac Tent

COUNTRY: Bolivia

FOCUS: Reproductive health, environment

PLACE: Villages in three geographic areas of the country

BENEFICIARIES: 21 Municipalities

PARTNERS: SERVIR, Project Concern International, USA (PCI), Centro de Promoción Agropecuaria Campesina, Bolivia (CEPAC)

FUNDING: Johns Hopkins University Center for Communication Programs, U.S.A. (JHU/CCP), USAID

MEDIA: Interactive, video, publications, theatre, puppets

SNAPSHOT

People of all ages are lining up outside of a huge lilac tent recently installed at the main square of the village. This is not a visiting circus although it's fun, it is not a school although it's educational, this is something new and different. Everyone is curious about living the experience of learning about sexuality and reproductive health through interactive games, images, audio-visual shows and live music. Groups of ten at at time are allowed inside the tent. Each visit will last less than one hour but there will be plenty to do while it lasts.

Take the giant figures of two men and two women, cut on wood so participants will be able to hold them and improvise a dialogue on the relationship between the two. This is an icebreaker, but it also introduces topics as gender and sexuality. A facilitator will help with pertinent questions before leading the group to the next area in the tent where participants will collectively play with a large puzzle— learning to distinguish bad from good practices on issues related to the environment and reproductive health. If the pieces are correctly positioned, a poster-sized healthy child will appear; if not, the likeness of a sick child will appear.

Discussion, of course, is key to solving the puzzle in the right way. Next is an area where participants will learn about maternal mortality without realising it from the beginning. A number of large tiles are placed on a table. Participants have to distribute smaller tiles that relate to the topics of the larger ones. A collective discussion should lead them to reach an understanding about health care during pregnancy. The group moves to another area where the participants, through the use of fabric dolls that can be placed on a large flannel screen, will develop a problem tree. Various topics will be identified as the causes of maternal mortality: lack of access to health services, women's roles in society, and education and economic constraint among others.

Last but not least, a trip through a dark tunnel of sensations leads participants to the outside of the tent, as a reminder of a birth. In many senses, it is a birth of knowledge and awareness on issues of reproductive health. Later in the day, when the night falls, a live music concert will take place outside of the tent, for all the participants and the community.

DESCRIPTION

The Lilac Tent expanded to the rural areas during the outreach of three previous reproductive health campaigns. From October 1998 to March 1999, three travelling lilac-coloured circus tents reached two hundred thousand people in 21 municipalities of three distinct geographic regions of Bolivia: the highlands, valleys, and tropics. Most attended the activities outside the tent, but 34,710 men and women were active participants inside the tent.

The process that culminates with the installation of *The Lilac Tent* is as important as the tent itself: it ensures community participation and sustainability. It involves advocacy, promotion, training and social mobilisation. A set of about fifty different activities take place in the community before the arrival of *The Lilac Tent*.

In a first stage, NGOs working in a particular geographical region of the country are identified and contracted to be the institutions responsible for coordinating the activities. Actually, three NGOs from the PROCOSI (Programa de Coordinación en Salud Integral, Bolivia) network were identified from the beginning, one for each

region: SERVIR, PCI and CEPAC. A team from the designated
NGO visits the local authorities to request support. The municipal
council, staff from the health centre, schoolteachers and the military,
among others are invited to join a coordinating group. About twenty
people will be trained to become facilitators of *The Lilac Tent*.
Producers from local radio stations receive special training and materials to develop educational programming on reproductive health
issues. A flip chart was developed to introduce topics, questions and
answers to the producers; teachers in the schoolroom can also use it.
Another group is trained on mural painting, an average of six murals
were painted in each of the 21 municipalities.

After three weeks of training activities that contribute to involve
the various institutions of the community, a team of eight people
sets up the three-ton Lilac Tent, while the twenty trained facilitators
prepare to receive the visitors. Guided by the facilitators, groups of
ten participants go inside the tent through different settings, environ-
ments and visual exercises. It is an intense experience. Those that
wait outside can watch video screenings of original Lilac Tent feature
productions, such as *Amanecer* or *Decisiones*, or puppets shows.
Then they may attend the evening shows.

The circuit inside the tent ends with a visit to the library,
publications such as the series of comics *Las Historias de Yoni*, are
given free to participants.

Every evening a platform outside the tent serves as a stage for live
music, dances and theatre. Hundreds of people from the community
gather around for entertainment. Local groups perform along with
young artists from Santa Cruz, Cochabamba or La Paz, brought
specially for the occasion.

By the end of the third day between 1,500 and 3,000 people have
gone inside the tent to a rich learning experience using group
dynamics, toys, images and, above all, participation. The tent will fold
immediately after and move to the next location. Three days may
seem a very short period of activity—sometimes it is extended—
considering that it took about two weeks to organise the whole
thing, to train the facilitators, and to put up the tent. Nonetheless, the
tent is only the culmination of the guided process. After that, the
community will have the materials and the facilitators to sustain the
effort of discussing and debating reproductive health issues in the
school, at the health centre, or within the families.

The cost of operating the tent in each municipality is about
US$7,500. In 1998, US$400,000 were spent, out of the 1 million
allotted to the project.

In 1969 *Yawar Mallku*, a famous feature film by Bolivian Director
Jorge Sanjinés showed a rebellion of peasants against United States
(perceived to be "Peace Corps") volunteers that were sterilising
women. This dramatic statement against United States policies of
birth control in an under-populated country as Bolivia—think about
the population of New York City in a territory almost three times
the State of California—contributed to many years of total rejection
of population issues. It is only through the knowledge of reproductive
health that the topics are back on the national agenda.

According to a John Hopkins University Center for Communication
Programs self-assessment, since 1986 reproductive health strategies
developed with technical support from JHU/CCP and funds from
USAID illustrated "the value of a continuous series of carefully
calibrated campaigns that moved from cautious advocacy to countrywide action."

In ten years the strategy of promoting family planning services in
the main urban areas, evolved to maternal and child health concerns
in rural communities. By 1994 an extensive multimedia campaign was
launched in four major cities. A new logo, radio and TV spots, plus
expanded services partially contributed to wipe away the negative
images associated with family planning. In 1996 the emphasis of a
third campaign was to promote access to services and methods, by
highlighting maternal mortality.

The Lilac Tent is the fourth campaign and takes into account the
lessons from the previous three. It is the first to reach rural areas of
Bolivia. A Technical Committee that included NGOs, the private
sector, government, and international cooperation agencies working
in the field of reproductive health, designed the strategy.

ASPECTS OF SOCIAL CHANGE

The Lilac Tent and the three previous reproductive health campaigns
might not be responsible, but the statistics compiled by DHS
(Demography and Health Survey) and Instituto Nacional de Estadística
(INE) of Bolivia, show that important progress has been achieved in
the last ten years. The Infant mortality rate has gone down from
96/1000 to 67/1000; birth deliveries in health facilities went up from
40 percent to 56 percent; prenatal care went up from 45 percent to
70 percent. The stability of the national economy also has a lot to
do with it.

The family planning objectives of the strategy were also achieved.
DHS statistics show that the knowledge of at least one modern
birth control method went up from 67 percent to 87 percent; the
use of condoms rose to 2.6 percent from next-to-nothing; IUD's to

11.1 percent from 4.8 percent and the pill went up to 3.8 percent from 1.9 percent. The statistics above illustrate that the population is increasingly interested in reducing maternal and infant mortality rates, and not concerned so much about birth control.

The Lilac Tent project is basically addressed to young people that speak Spanish, have a certain level of basic education, and are less resistant to change. The new Bolivian generations have better opportunities to be informed and more chances to make their own decisions.

One important element brought by *The Lilac Tent* is the collective approach. The strategy is no longer aiming only at face-to-face counselling, but also involving the whole community. Its focus is less on "persuasion" and more on promoting discussion and analysis. The community is actively involved, no longer a passive receptor of decisions made by others.

MEDIA & METHODS

The multimedia approach of *The Lilac Tent* is what makes the project so innovative. The tent itself is the environment where things happen, a reference space, and an enabling environment. The methods include interactive games, live music, video-tape, publications, theatre, puppets, etc. Through drawings and brief dialogues, various situations are depicted, leading to counselling and education on the use of condoms, contraceptive devices, STDs, etc. Specially made video productions support similar views.

CONSTRAINTS

The first word that comes to mind when referring to the obstacles is sustainability. Being as it is a project funded and driven by JHU/CCP, it has a period of development with a start-date and an end-date. Once funding is exhausted, who will continue moving the three-ton equipment from one province to another in the vast territory of Bolivia? The largest investment is already completed: the construction of the tents, the acquisition of audio-visual equipment, the training of staff. … Nonetheless, expenditures are in the order of US$7,500 for each time a Lilac Tent is installed at a new place.

Another problem is that the tent only stays three days in each municipality, and often this is not enough time for all the people to go through it. A large number only participate in the recreational activities that take place outside the tent, which are not as effective and educational as those that take place inside the tent.

REFERENCES

The printed information listed below was complemented through conversations held in La Paz (October 1999) with Project Coordinator Marcos Paz, and with video producer Carola Prudencio.

Video productions reviewed: *Diálogo al Desnudo* (1996), *Amanecer* (1998), *Piel de Luna* (1997), *Decisiones* (1998), and *Hablemos en Pareja* (1998). All deal with reproductive health and have been locally produced for this project or for previous stages of the communication strategy.

Publications:

Carpa Lila, as it is called in Spanish, prints its own bulletins and educational materials. Among the later is the series of comics *Las Historias de Yoni*.

Las ONGs y las Carpas Lila by Marcos Paz. In "J & G, Revista de Epidemiología Comunitaria," Julio–Diciembre 1998. La Paz, Bolivia. Pp. 4–8.

La Carpa Lila: Una Experiencia Innovadora en Comunicación para la Salud, por Marcos Paz. In "Opciones, Revista sobre Salud Sexual y Reproductiva," Marzo 1999. La Paz, Bolivia. Pp. 17–20.

Estrategia de IEC para el Área Rural. Subcomité Nacional de IEC, 1997. Pp. 32.

Bolivia's Lilac Tent: A First in Health Promotion. In Communication Impact, John Hopkins University Center for Communication Programs (JHU/CCP), Baltimore. April 1999.

VIDEO & COMMUNITY DREAMS

(**1998**) Egypt

BASIC FACTS

TITLE: Video and the Community Dreams Project

COUNTRY: Egypt

MAIN FOCUS: Reproductive health, women empowerment

PLACE: Beni Rani, El Tayeba, Itsa El'Bellit and Zenhom

BENEFICIARIES: Women

PARTNERS: Communication for Change (C4C)

FUNDING: Centre For Development and Population Activities (CEDPA), Coptic Evangelic Organisation for Social Services (CEOSS), USAID

MEDIA: Video

SNAPSHOT

In only three years, Neama Mohamed, a mother and housewife, has become a health educator, an outspoken advocate for girls and a leader in her community. She is helping to change the attitudes of her neighbours in regard to literacy, girls' education, sanitation and female genital mutilation (FGM) a common practice in her Egyptian community. Once, Neama would have hesitated to confront such issues; however, after gaining communication skills and learning to effectively use participatory video tools, her confidence as a spokesperson has soared.

Neama lives in Tellal Zenhom, a slum area in the southeastern section of Cairo. CEOSS, an Egyptian NGO, has worked in Tellal Zenhom on a range of local development issues for over seven years. Neama became familiar with the organisation as a young mother; later, she was recruited to serve as a nutrition teacher for groups of women. Then, she agreed to lead New Horizons classes, which promote self-empowerment among adolescent girls though training in life skills, education and health.

The New Horizons classes covered a wide range of reproductive health information, everything from the basics of reproductive biology to sexually transmitted diseases, and from breastfeeding to the harmful traditional

practice of female genital mutilation and the proof of virginity. As these are very sensitive issues, the community was briefed about the curriculum and the topics it would cover.

In the 18 months following Neama's video training, levels of participation in the Zenhom project have remained high. Team members have grown increasingly confident in using their technical skills, addressing sensitive topics, and presenting their work for discussion. The team members have a new visibility in their communities as spokespeople and leaders. Community members, the local council and officials are expressing support for the team's work, often suggesting ideas for video programmes. The video team's tapes are being used to spark discussion and promote the search for local solutions.—Edited from "Strengthening the Voices of women," by C4C's Sara Stuart.

DESCRIPTION

In the spring of 1997, Communication for Change (C4C), previously known as *Martha Stuart Communications*—an organisation that has been providing community video training over the past 20 years in India, Bangladesh, Indonesia, China and Nigeria—was selected to carry out a participatory video training programme in Egypt.

The project, which aims at upgrading the status of women, has been sponsored by CEDPA (Centre For Development and Population Activities, a USAID-funded project), in collaboration with the Coptic Evangelic Organisation for Social Services (CEOSS). Communication for Change conducted the training.

During March of 1998, five CEOSS staff and 17 women from three villages in Minya (upper Egypt), Itsa El'Bellit, El Tayeba, Beni Rani and from one slum area in Cairo—Tellal Zenhom—were trained. As in the other communities, four *New Horizons* women leaders from Tellal Zenhom learned to use a home video camcorder and to make simple tapes, about issues in their communities. This participatory video training was intended to strengthen the voices of women at the local level and to extend the reach of New Horizons, an informal educational programme designed to communicate essential information in the areas of basic life skills and reproductive health.

The newly trained video teams in each region evaluated the local problems and used video tools as an instrument to reveal and discuss issues. Often these issues are so embedded in culture, that they are not deeply questioned, except when women collectively reflect on them. The video-training programme addressed a wide range of issues, including financial barriers to marriage, female excision, and local environmental problems.

The programme has been implemented in six villages in Minya and two in Cairo's outlying urban areas. Tellal Zenhom has been singled out as one of the most successful examples. From the project emerged *A Woman of Zenhom*—a video documentary focusing on the importance of women's access to education and work opportunities. "The video encouraged people to let their daughters finish their education before getting married," says Marwa Abdel-Khaleq, an 18-year-old CEOSS facilitator.

Also at Tellal Zenhom, the newly trained women video producers tackled the issue of female genital mutilation through videotaped interviews with a religious leader, a doctor and two girls—one circumcised, the other not.

The problem of financial barriers to marriage was the subject of a video production at El Tayeba, where custom dictates that both bride and groom contribute stipulated amounts of money, gold jewelry and food before a couple can marry. The video team planned a production entitled *I Want to Get Married*. According to tradition, the bride's family is responsible for providing all the food for the wedding celebration. There have been cases of families selling off their land and falling into debt in order to avoid dishonouring themselves at a wedding. "My daughter has been married for two years now and we have not covered the wedding expenses yet," comments Umm Maged, a villager.

In Itsa, local problems of nationwide significance were addressed. Here, it was the environment that provided the subject matter for the first video. The canal that runs through the village, which was meant to channel excess irrigation water away from the fields, is no longer limited to that purpose. Waste from the sugar factory and sewage are being thrown into the canal, which flows directly into the Nile. A copy of the video documentary has been sent to the Minister of Environment, and the villagers were expecting a governmental decree to fill in the canal.

BACKGROUND & CONTEXT

Video and the Community Dreams Project had its starting point at the Beijing International Women's Conference in 1995 where the CEDPA country director and several Egyptian NGO partners had a chance to meet a C4C staff member and to see *Video SEWA*. In 1996 CEDPA invited a group of their Egyptian partners on an exchange trip to Bangladesh and India. They visited *Video SEWA* during that trip. In 1997, CEOSS and Communication for Change were quite successful in convincing leaders of Egyptian Community Development Agencies and young women leaders that participatory video would be valuable in their work.

Communication for Change has established a reputation as a pioneer in participatory video programmes and has demonstrated the possibility of building local leadership through the development of grassroots communication skills.

The video project has not only affected the lives of the target community: the team members have felt the change, too. "The video project has increased our self-confidence. We couldn't be shy when we had to address the whole community," exclaims Neama Mohamed, a 31-year-old facilitator and member of the video team. She feels the team members are now perceived as role models in the community. The team members have a new visibility as spokespeople and leaders.

One taboo that inevitably came under the camera's lens was female genital mutilation. It was discussed with sensitivity, however, through conversations with a Sheikh, a doctor and two girls, one circumcised, the other not. After the video was shown, Rania, the youngest of four daughters, the rest of whom had already been "circumcised," was spared the experience. Her mother and sisters were convinced that it was harmful.

Mohamed also had to put theory into practice a few weeks ago. When her husband insisted that their 10-year-old daughter, Shaimaa, be circumcised like her cousins, she refused. "The most important person involved in this decision is the mother," she asserts. "If the mother is convinced that circumcision is bad, she will be able to influence the husband."

The team feels that its greatest achievement has been promoting the debate on female excision. It is significant that the team took up this issue only after honing their production abilities and gaining general community approbation for their work. There was consensus among team members that the perspective of a religious leader was absolutely necessary, as well as that of a doctor, so that religious views would complement the "scientific" arguments against the practice.

The video productions were shown in church, in the open space in front of the mosque, or in the village's largest homes. Video seems to have played a role in crystallising the debate around extremely delicate cultural issues.

Says Sara Stuart from Communication for Change: "This experience demonstrates the power of media that is not 'mediated' by outside forces, but rather conceived and produced by individuals determined to depict their own reality and effect change. Self-representation is profoundly linked with self-determination. As individuals and communities become self-determining, they gain a greater capacity to obtain social and economic justice. They develop the strength to demand that their governments be responsive and responsible in their policies and decision-making."

In the beginning, the group was afraid to be seen carrying the camera in the streets and videotaping in their community. Although the community agreed to the video activity and the trainees were eager to learn, the support of their parents, husbands, fiancés and in-laws had to be reconfirmed on many occasions. As the women began to gain confidence in operating the camcorder, they progressed from recording inside CEOSS's office and people's homes to shooting in the streets. With each step, individually they overcame fear, and the capacity of the team grew.

Within ten days they began showing their first tapes to members of the community. These tapes were about the importance of literacy, good nutrition, and a local woman who is doing exemplary service as a teacher of disabled children. The screenings allowed the team members to facilitate and lead discussions about the issues the tapes presented.

The video team in Zenhom has shot almost ten productions. Beginning as a group of four women, who were trained for two weeks in basic video procedures, the team has grown to seven as the women teach others in the community. After the training the team members chose to produce a tape about sanitation and garbage issues which plague Tellal Zenhom.

The themes chosen are conveyed to a wider audience at maternity clinics in Zenhom. As the women wait their turn, they watch and have a chance to discuss the productions with the video team. The videotapes are also shown at the monthly classes at CEOSS's Zenhom centre.

CONSTRAINTS

The target communities' initial reaction to the video project was one of rejection. "Do they want to show the problems in our society and exploit our misery to obtain foreign financial support?" one community member demanded. The facilitators explained that the video productions would be exclusively shot by and for the community and would not be shown elsewhere. Certain obstacles proved unavoidable: one 12-year-old girl in the community, who had expressed her strong wish to appear in the video and speak of her experience of being circumcised, was not permitted by her mother to do so. Team members persisted. The final programme includes interviews with one young girl who recalls undergoing the procedure, and another who successfully convinced her mother not to subject her to it.

In Itsa, "at first the problem was in the term 'video' itself. The villagers were reluctant to have their women appear on tape. They would throw stones at us when we walked down the street," recalls

Iman Ibrahim, a CEOSS facilitator. Because the community had previous experience of CEOSS projects, however, and because many of the facilitators are villagers themselves, the video project was accepted gradually.

REFERENCES

Most of this chapter was based on articles received from Sara Stuart from *Communication for Change*, New York.

"Strengthening the Voices of Women," by Sara Stuart, in *Rhodes Journalism Review*, 1999, South Africa.

"Life Under the Lens," by Amira El-Noshokaty, in *Al-Ahram Weekly*, Issue No. 457, December 1999.

VILLAGE
KNOWLEDGE CENTRES

1998 India

BASIC FACTS

TITLE:	Village Knowledge Centres
COUNTRY:	India
FOCUS:	Rural development
PLACE:	Chennai
BENEFICIARIES:	Rural population
PARTNERS:	M.S. Swaminathan Research Foundation, India (MSSRF)
FUNDING:	IDRC
MEDIA:	Information technologies, computers, Internet

SNAPSHOT

In this village at the southern tip of India, the century-old temple has two doors. Through one lies tradition. People from the lowest castes and menstruating women cannot pass its threshold. Inside, the devout perform daily pujas, offering prayers. Through the second door lies the Information Age, and anyone may enter.

In a rare social experiment, the village elders have allowed one side of the temple to house two solar-powered computers that give this poor village a wealth of data, from the price of rice to the day's most auspicious hours. ...

Some months back, Subrayan Panjaili, a round-faced woman who cannot read or write, sat in the courtyard of her small home in the village of Kizhur, in Pondicherry, with the family's only milk cow, Jayalakshmi. For five days and nights, the cow moaned while in labor. Something had gone wrong and she was unable to deliver her calf. Mrs. Panjaili grew ever more fearful that the cow would die.

"This is the only good income we have," she said, explaining that the four gallons of milk the cow produced each day paid the bills.

Word of Mrs. Panjaili's woebegone cow soon spread to Govindaswami, a public-spirited farmer who uses one name. The village's computer, obtained through the Swaminathan Foundation, is in the anteroom of his home. The computer is operated full-time and for no pay by his 23-year-old, college-educated daughter, Azhalarasi, who used it to call up a list of area veterinarians.

*One doctor arrived that night and, by the light of a bare electric bulb,
stuck his arm into Jayalakshmi, pulled out the calf's spindly leg and tied a
rope to it, then dragged the calf into the world.*

*The Swaminathan Foundation has sought to give the four villages
in its network other practical, highly local information, which is distributed
through the village computer network in the local language, Tamil. Generally,
that kind of information is not on the World Wide Web.*—Excerpts from
"Connecting Rural India to the World" by Celia W. Dugger.

DESCRIPTION

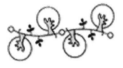 Formerly called "information shops," the
Village Knowledge Centres were established by
the M.S. Swaminathan Research Foundation
(MSSRF) in Chennai to take advantage
of new technologies to provide information to the rural population
on agricultural issues such as: health (availability of vaccines and
medicines in the nearest health centre—preventive measures); relief
information (issue of loans, availability of officials); inputs for agriculture (prices and availability, costs, risks and returns, local market prices
for rural produce); transportation information; micro-meteorological
information (relating to the local area); surface and ground water-
related data, pest surveillance, and agronomic practices for all seasons
and crops (based on queries from the rural families); and the maintenance and update of data on entitlements of the rural families
(vis-à-vis public sector welfare and infrastructural funds).

The village information shops are operated by individuals on a
semi-voluntary basis. Such individuals are identified on the basis of
the following criteria: education (at least high school or 10 years
of schooling); socio-economic status (marginal farmers are given
preference); gender (other things being equal, women will be given
preference); and age (preference is given to the 20-25 age group).

The group mobilisation and credit programme of the biovillage
project is used as a channel for identifying the operators. They are
invited to a brief training session, lasting two days, conducted by the
staff of the ecotechnology centre of the Foundation. The training
session consists of demonstrations of the wireless instruments, training
in its use—PC keyboard and mouse—and use of conditioned power
supply. Based on performance, one person per village will be selected.

The equipment is provided to the operators on the basis of legally
viable non-monetary lease agreements, and the operators are trained
in all the basic operations of a computer—elements of word
processing, spread sheets and HTML, basic operations such as e-mail
and Web browsing, use of the radio modem, and general matters
including basics of upkeep. The training and materials are in Tamil,
the local language.

The "information shops" have been established in four villages: Kizhur, Mangalam, Embalam and Veerampattinam. The shop at Embalam is located on the premises of the village temple, which is owned by the community through an informal trust. In each shop, a Pentium PC with multimedia and a deskjet printer have been installed in a specially designed box to prevent rodent attacks on the instruments. The computer can be connected to the wireless network through a modem and a specially designed interface. The shop volunteers, at their discretion, write in more news from the locality.

The four villages are linked to the foundation's hub at Villianur through an ingenious wireless system. V. Balaji, a graduate of the Indian Institute of Technology at Kanpur, who oversees the project for the foundation, dreamed it up. The value addition centre acts as an exchange point for a variety of local-specific information. Each shop has a board to display bulletins received from the value addition centre. A local area network based on Very High Frequency (VHF) radio has been established with the Villianur office serving as a hub, handling voice communication as well as data.

While the foundation's model is relatively costly and may prove difficult to replicate on a large scale, the government of Pondicherry nonetheless plans to expand the project to 50 more villages. The spread of this approach to more of India's 600,000 villages would ultimately require government money and manpower, with support from NGOs and philanthropies.

BACKGROUND & CONTEXT

Pondicherry, which was the administrative headquarters of the French territories in India, comprises 130 villages and the Pondicherry town, and is spread over an area of 1,100 square kilometres. Tamil is the language spoken with English and French as languages of the administration. More than 60 percent of the population of Pondicherry lives in the rural area. Dominant crops are rice and sugarcane. Approximately 20 percent of the rural families have been officially classified as living below the poverty line.

The Madras-based MSSRF was established in July 1988 as a nonprofit and nonpolitical trust committed to a mission of harnessing science and technology for environmentally sustainable and socially equitable development. MSSRF's research, training, communication, extension and networking programmes, in the fields of agriculture and rural development, seek to link ecological security to livelihood security in a mutually reinforcing manner. The Foundation projects include: *Coastal Systems Research* (CSR), *Biodiversity and Biotechnology, Ecotechnology and Sustainable Agriculture, Reaching the Unreached*, and *Education, Communication, Training and Capacity Building*.

The Pondicherry project was created by the MSSRF with a $120,000 grant from the Canadian government. The foundation provides villages with free technology and information in exchange for the villages' promise to house the computers and staff their operation.

ASPECTS OF SOCIAL CHANGE

India is becoming a laboratory for small experiments that aim to link isolated rural pockets to the borderless world of knowledge. Local governments and NGOs are testing new approaches to provide villages, where no one can afford a telephone, with computers that are accessible to all. A well-placed computer, like an irrigation pump or a communal well, may become another tool for development.

The *Village Knowledge Centre* enables farming families not only to produce more without associated ecological harm, but helps everyone in the village to create a hunger-free area. The villagers themselves identify who are the hungry amidst them; 12 to 15 percent of the families fall under this category. They tend to be illiterate, and they are generally very poor without land, livestock, fishpond or any other productive asset.

Each day, the project's staff downloads a map from a U.S. Navy Web site that shows the wave heights and wind directions in the Bay of Bengal. In the fishing village of Veerampattinam, loudspeakers fixed to tall poles along the broad beach blare out the daily weather report. Fishermen, in loincloths mending nets or repairing homemade wooden boats in the sultry heat, listen attentively.

Though the experience of the *Village Knowledge Centres* is still young, it foresees affecting several social changes: Improved access to markets through the availability of prices and marketing opportunities information; improved access to health infrastructure; increased exposure of rural youth and school students to computer-based networking; an increase in general awareness among youth through multimedia training and local-specific database creation using generic information available on the Internet and other networks; increase in awareness of ecologically sound techniques in agriculture and animal husbandry, leading to enhanced production, income and livelihood opportunities.

MEDIA & METHODS

"From my long experience in agriculture, I find that whenever poor people derive some benefit from a technology, the rich also benefit. The opposite does not happen," says Professor S. M. Swaminathan.

The goal of the Knowledge System for Sustainable Food Security is the empowerment of rural women, men and children with information relating to ecological agriculture, economic access, and biological absorption and utilisation. The Knowledge System aims to create conditions conducive to a healthy and productive life for all.

The project is based upon the understanding that *value addition*, by professionals or trained individuals, to networked information is a key step in enabling rural families to have accessibility. A small office in a centrally located village, Villianur, serves as the value addition centre, where the project staff scans the Internet, especially the World Wide Web, for useful contacts or technologies.

Each shop varies slightly in the way it is operated and supported. In Kizhur the volunteers were chosen by the Village Development Council, which also nominated a 23-member (14 men and 9 women) group to guide the shop's operations. At the shop in Embalam all the volunteers are women in the 21–27 year age group; each of them spends half-a-day at the shop, rotating the schedule.

CONSTRAINTS

The vast majority of Web sites are in English, a language that more than 95 percent of Indians do not speak. Nonetheless, the project has, since its inception, challenged this by translating and producing local contents in Tamil.

Poverty itself is a huge limitation. Only 12 public telephones and 27 private telephones exist in the project area, which covers 19 villages with a population of 22,000. Routine power failures and overloaded telephone lines make connecting to the Internet a frustrating proposition. There are serious questions about whether countries like India, weighed down by high rates of illiteracy and illness, should spend heavily to provide villages, that desperately need schools and health clinics, with what most would consider a luxury.

Project overseer Balaji notes that one immediate obstacle, is that local bureaucrats are often reluctant to give up their monopoly on information, which can be a source of power used to extract bribes.

REFERENCES

Information provided through e-mail exchanges by Raul Roman, Cornell University.

The M.S. Swaminathan Research Foundation (Chennai) Web site <http://www.mssrf.org/>.

"Connecting Rural India to the World," by Celia W. Dugger, *The New York Times*, May 28, 2000.

Success Stories of Rural ICTs in a Developing Country, by Roger Harris, et al. PANTLEG-IDRC December 1999.

LOCAL RADIO NETWORK

1999 Indonesia

....

BASIC FACTS

TITLE:	Capacity Building of Local Radio
COUNTRY:	Indonesia
FOCUS:	Democracy, elections, human rights
PLACE:	Sumatra, Kalimantan, Sulawesi, Maluku, Bali, Java
BENEFICIARIES:	Rural population
PARTNERS:	25 local radio stations, Indonesian Corruption Watch (ICW)
FUNDING:	UNESCO, DANIDA
MEDIA:	Radio, E-mail, Internet

SNAPSHOT

It was a usual morning on the 14th of August 1999 when two uninvited guests came with their Vespa. Without mentioning names or showing their identity, those two men claimed that they're from Police District Office and asked for all the news broadcast by our station, Nikoya. They specifically insisted on having a copy of the news discussion on the "Politic of Violence" held by students of University Ar-Raniry Darussalam Banda Aceh where the chief of Aceh District Police and the commander of Aceh District Military were the speakers.

We refused to give them the copy even though they said it was only for monitoring. In the end we compromised since we remembered that a few months ago two military trucks with the personnel fully armed, had been parked in front of our station, watching us 24 hours per day. We had to "cool down" and stop broadcasting the news. But people called and came to the station asking "why did we stop broadcasting the news." We had not realised people's support until they came to us to discuss the situation and their expectation to be able to listen the true voices of Acehnese. They like our coverage on NGOs, students, and even on the two extremes: Indonesian Military and Free Aceh Movement.

We live a slippery and tricky situation because one of the focal groups in this conflict always disagrees with our news. Some also try to take advantage of the situation; recently several visitors claimed that they were from Free Aceh Movement and asked five million Rupiah from the station to support their movement. It's a very big amount of money for us since there is no income from advertisement. It is also an intimidating situation if we didn't give the money.

On the other hand, the Indonesian military is also ready with their weapons. Meanwhile, we stay put with these different voices and serve it to the public and let them choose since it is their right to determine what they want to be in the future. So far, we know that these millions of innocent people outside the organisations and institutions only have simple expectations: peace and safety.—REPORTED BY ADE GRANDE, UNESCO CONSULTANT.

DESCRIPTION

The "Capacity Building of Local Radio" a UNESCO project funded by the Danish Government, was initiated in early 1999, with a target of strengthening twenty local provincial radio stations in the field reporting capacity, through the provision of equipment and training.

For the first phase of the project, a comprehensive report on local radio stations in the preselected areas was prepared by The Institute of Studies for Free Flow of Information (ISAI). The final selection was done with the guidance of UNESCO. Twenty-five stations have been integrated into the network, all of them benefiting from the same training opportunities, as well as grants and new equipment.

In the isolated islands of Maluku, the stations selected were Istana Bahana Swara and Gema Hikmah; in South Sulawesi: Suara Mesra, Suara Daya Indah, SP FM, and Suara Sawerigading; up north of Indonesia, in Aceh: Nikoya, Gipsi and Adyemaja; in West Kalimantan: Swara Dermaga Ria; in Bali: Guntur and Balisa; in Yogyakarta: Persatuan; in East Java: Bass, Citrawanodya and Andalus; in Central Java: Rona Puspita, Pragola and Ria Female.

Independent, committed local radio stations are carefully chosen under the following criteria:
- These are devoid of sectarian political interests
- Have a wide representation and penetration in different provinces
- Maintain editorial readiness and commitment to catalyse democracy and good governance in the provinces.

Training is the centrepiece of the networking strategy. Journalists from all local stations have been trained in the production of local programmes that foster the democratic process, through participatory approaches. A specific seminar, "Local Media and Democratic Election," was organised in Jakarta for broadcasters of all selected stations prior to the Indonesian general elections.

Other than the workshops and seminars, the project has produced a handbook in Bahasa Indonesia entitled "Guidelines for Election Coverage," originally prepared by the International Federation of Journalists.

An equipment package containing three field recorders, two sets of four-track studios, one portable studio including four microphones, and two computers (one multimedia) is provided to each station. This equipment allows the small local radio stations to face any contingency while recording in rural areas or producing complex live-broadcasts.

The multimedia computer is a key item in terms of facilitating networking among the various stations; it can be used for downloading information from the Internet, as well as for communicating through e-mail. The computer also has capacity for digital sound editing of short inserts, jingles and music. A financial grant of US$2,000 allows each station to employ two additional producers and to ensure Internet connectivity through a local service provider.

The creation of an Internet-based network among participating radio stations is the most innovative aspect of the project. The linking of radio stations across Indonesia is a very powerful tool for allowing access to audio broadcasting materials—particularly concerning democracy and mutual support in the development of field reporting capacity.

BACKGROUND & CONTEXT

Taking into account Indonesia's geographical particularities, radio is the only medium that can reach remote areas. Moreover, Indonesians have a strong, deeply rooted oral tradition and illiteracy levels remain high, particularly in rural settings. With some 769 private commercial stations spread over the archipelago of Indonesia, radio represents the only accessible medium and source of information for a large part of the population. However, during the 32-year-long regime of Suharto, radio stations were not allowed to broadcast local news. It was compulsory for them to broadcast the news bulletins provided by the official broadcasting system (RRI).

The law of Indonesian broadcasting still restricts community radio. Every station has to be a private station with clear company legal status. Most rural radio stations in Indonesia are small structures with modest and often outdated equipment. Computer technology was rarely used except for administration. Broadcasters were not trained journalists, and had no responsibility to produce local news. The lack of qualified human resources is still a major issue.

ASPECTS OF SOCIAL CHANGE

Radio stations that during decades had only aired music and entertainment programmes, have suddenly become information and education tools, capable of producing their own news on national issues. This had an enormous importance before the 1999 elections. For the first time people were offered programming that promoted participation and democracy; for the first time small local stations stood up against censorship and military control.

The networking of radio stations offers the Indonesian population new possibilities for up-to-date information on national topics. The exchange of news among the stations is the most dynamic activity. Each station sends its local news over the network while all stations can freely choose which news to broadcast from all over Indonesia. The exchange of local news is an idea that came from the stations themselves during a project seminar.

The Internet connection has given the stations more sources of information. They now usually broadcast news before other stations. Notable changes are seen in programming. The percentage of information programmes such as news and talk shows are getting broader.

The mere existence of a local radio station in remote areas of Indonesia provides each isolated community with a channel to inform them on local events and to communicate with each other, as if radio were a substitute for the post office. Radio Dermaga in Sanggau (West Kalimantan), for example, is the only station covering an area of 50 kilometres. People use the radio to convene meetings, to send invitations to a marriage, to announce cultural events, and to offer jobs. Radio Citrawanodya (East Java), an AM station covering an area of 70 square kilometres, has been instrumental in denouncing corruption during the elections of the village's head. All three stations in Aceh (Radio Gipsi, Radio Nikoya and Radio Adyemaja) make an effort to broadcast updated information on local political events, often ignored or censored on the national network.

Early in the year 2000 the local radio network embarked on a countrywide campaign against corruption. Each station produces and runs its own programmes. Apart from a short jingle and some ideas, UNESCO didn't take any leadership. Every station managed to run the campaign independently and with its own resources.

The objective of the "Capacity Building of Local Radio" project is to develop human and technical capacity of selected radio stations in rural Indonesia and thereby to enable these radio stations to effectively contribute to the process of national development, good governance, and democracy.

Training is from the methodological point-of-view, one of the key aspects of UNESCO support to the 25 local radio stations that are part of the network. The initial assessment of the stations revealed that they lacked staff with a journalistic background. The successive workshops that were held during 1998 and 1999 in Banda Aceh, Ujung Pandang and Malang, had the objective of providing the basic skills in journalism, news programming and contents from the perspective of the democratic process that Indonesia was going through at that time.

No doubt the other key aspect is the conversion of the individual radio stations to an Internet-based network. Daily contact through e-mail, and daily exchanges of news items among the 25 stations contributed to building a sense of a network in search of common objectives, striving to take on the leadership as examples of a democratic medium, in a country much too accustomed to vertical and authoritarian communication practices.

CONSTRAINTS

Political changes in Indonesia after the fall of Suharto had an impact on liberalisation of media. In spite of this process of democratisation, censorship still haunts some of the local radio stations, particularly in those provinces of Indonesia that have been on the frontline of social upheaval. In Aceh, for example, late in 1999, police were putting pressure on Nikoya Radio to submit a copy of the "news" before it's broadcast.

On a technical note, the quality of phone connectivity is so low, it takes hours to log in and often the connection is suddenly cut. In most areas there is only one Internet provider. Therefore, every time the service is down the stations are not able to send or receive news via the Internet. Internet providers may even voluntarily shut down access to the Internet for political reasons, as has happened in Aceh in times of political unrest.

A crucial challenge, that needs to be carefully assessed, deals with sustainability of the network. The Internet provides tremendous opportunity but the cost is high. Because of the low quality of telephone landlines, a longer on-line time is needed, thus increasing costs even further. Some stations are analysing the possibility of diversifying their income sources through activities such as desktop publishing and advertising.

REFERENCES

Most information for this chapter was provided through personal and e-mail exchanges with Ade Grande, UNESCO Consultant.

"Democracy on Air: Building Expertise of Local Radio" in UNESCO Jakarta Office News, Issue No. 2/1999.

Local Radio Meeting Point <http://www.unesco.or.id/localrad/frontpage.htm>.

NAKASEKE TELECENTRE

1999 Uganda

....

BASIC FACTS

TITLE: Nakaseke Multipurpose Community Telecentre and Library Pilot Project

COUNTRY: Uganda

MAIN FOCUS: Communication and information

PLACE: Nakaseke

BENEFICIARIES: Villagers of Nakaseke and Kasangombe

PARTNERS: Uganda Telecom Ltd., The Public Libraries Board

FUNDING: UNESCO, DANIDA, IDRC, ITU, British Council

MEDIA: Computers, Internet

SNAPSHOT

After the 60 kilometre drive up from Kampala—the last 16 kilometres along a dusty gravel road—it is quite soothing to enter the cool and spacious library hall, the largest room in the Nakaseke Multipurpose Community Telecentre and Library.

A young primary school pupil is writing an exercise in English, equipped with a huge dictionary; a secondary school student is preparing a thesis on agriculture and has borrowed a book on sustainable agriculture in the tropics; a young man has come into the library to read yesterday's newspaper—a few months ago there were no newspapers in Nakaseke at all.

In a corner of the library hall two young women, assistant librarians, are crouched in front of a computer. They keep track of the more than 3,000 books from the library; the service is used by an average of 45 people every day.

There are other computers for the users of the centre. Crammed together in a small room I find three computers and three young persons all very busy practising Microsoft Excel. These young people belong to the group of "volunteers," from the local community who have agreed to train the villagers in computer use after having received free computer training themselves.

Part of the training is in Internet use, e-mail and Web browsing. This training has a slightly "artificial" touch to it, since there is no connection to the Internet. The telephone line, which is supporting the telephone and the telefax machine in the centre, is not of a sufficiently good quality to support data transmission.

As I am talking to the young and ambitious people about the computer training there is a power cut and the computers go "black," the back-up power supply is not yet in place. Thus, my visit to Nakaseke does indeed testify to the necessity of the supporting infrastructure in terms of electricity and telecommunications before a rural community can be adequately equipped with computers.

On my way out through the library hall I notice that the students are still busy working—the books have not stopped providing information, power cut or not!—MONA DAHMS, DISCUSSING A VISIT TO THE NAKASEKE MCT PILOT PROJECT, JULY 1999.

DESCRIPTION

Life has changed in Nakaseke, which is 64 kilometres north of the Ugandan capital Kampala, and 16 kilometres from the nearest town, Wobulenzi. Now a modern telecentre and library, complete with textbooks in English and the local language, Lugandan, serves not only the local people, but also the 24 neighbouring primary schools, four secondary schools, a primary teacher's college and the nearby hospital.

The Nakaseke Multipurpose Community Telecentre started in December 1997 as a project aimed at introducing new information services to the rural areas of Nakaseke and Kasangombe in the Luweero District of Uganda. The project aims to demonstrate that providing information and communication to rural communities catalyses the development process and results in improvement of the quality of life of rural communities. The *Nakaseke Telecentre* is part of a chain of five UNESCO/IDRC/ITU-supported telecentre projects initiated in Benin, Mali, Mozambique and Tanzania.

The services offered by the multipurpose telecentre include computer applications, training, Internet, e-mail, photocopying (the most popular), telephone, fax, a library, video shows, newspapers, audio recordings, and community listening areas.

The Nakaseke MCT and Library Pilot Project is equipped with eight computers, two telephone lines, one fax and a photocopier. A land telephone line was brought from 16 kilometres away. The building was donated by the community and renovated to an acceptable level for project work. Power was never supposed to be any problem if it were not for frequent load shedding; an inverter and a set of deep cycle batteries were, therefore, installed to provide power back up. A generator was not favoured for this purpose because of its relatively high running costs in terms of fuel.

To ensure that the core group of trainees who were selected to learn the computer programs so they could in turn train the rest of their community had the backing of their community, community members were first asked to approve the selection of the 24 people for the free-of-charge programme. The language of instruction was a combination of Lugandan and English. The trainers were a group of very young people from Uganda Connectivity, a group concerned with Internet access.

The telecentre aims at serving the entire communities of Nakaseke and Kasangombe but most particularly the following core user groups: women, youth, children, the medical community, workers, teachers, students, farmers and local leaders. The content and programming for the telecentre is therefore primarily tailored towards meeting the needs and aspirations of its core target groups.

The early users of the telecentre services were teachers and students who wanted photocopy services and a good resource centre; health officers who often need a reference library; business people with the interest of communicating with others in the capital city; women in development groups who wanted to enhance their work by getting information on videos; community members, elders and opinion leaders with the interest of reading newspapers.

Following specific requests by users, other services have been introduced like feature films every Friday afternoon, game facilities in the evenings, functional adult classes and radio listening for particular groups.

In addition, preparations commenced with UNESCO for a pilot telemedicine application within the TeleInViVo project of the European Commission, involving an inexpensive, light and mobile teleconsultancy station able to support a large range of radiological applications. Data collected from the patient by an on-site health worker using such a station will be transferred in compressed form to an expert doctor in the principal hospital in Kampala, who will be able to perform long distance diagnoses.

BACKGROUND & CONTEXT

Nakaseke is located approximately 50 kilometres north of Kampala and 16 kilometres from Luweero. It has a population of 31,004 (1991) out of which 15,617 are women. The Nakaseke town centre itself has a population of 3,000 people.

Most of the people are Baganda, the biggest tribe in the central part of Uganda. The community is largely oral and doesn't have a credible reading culture. Until the telecentre started, there were no newspapers available, they were available at the next town which is 16 kilometres of a rough road away.

Farming in coffee, bananas, livestock raising, small-scale swamp fishing and horticulture is the main economic activity, and Kampala offers the biggest market for local produce. About 90 percent of the farmers use traditional farming methods and techniques.

There are 23 primary schools and four secondary schools in the subcounty. Nakaseke subcounty has a total enrollment of 2,935 boys and 3,329 girls in 79 classrooms according to 1999 local administration records; 59.2 percent of the Nakaseke community is literate which is largely limited to local Lugandan language. Many schools in the area have neither adequate educational facilities nor a library. A Primary Teachers' Training College has been built in Nakaseke.

Nakaseke has 7 health units including a 100-bed hospital, 5 doctors, 6 medical assistants, 23 midwives and 33 nurses. The hospital is connected to other health units by a radio. Access to clean water is possible through a network of 28 bore holes and a protected spring.

ASPECTS OF SOCIAL CHANGE

The Nakaseke MCT and Library Pilot Project has revitalised the life of this rural community in Uganda.

The community (42 villages and 3000 households) is gradually understanding the importance of information, as evidenced by the growing number of people inquiring about a variety of issues. Farmers are now requesting market rates and general trends on crops they grow. The daily newspapers at the telecentre have also helped to keep the community up-to-date with what is going on in the country.

The obvious purpose of the pilot project isn't to test out a new technology but rather to test a new service.

Computers in Nakaseke are no longer strange and mysterious machines. The telecentre has demystified computer communications to some extent through training and general awareness programmes. Over 60 community members have now been trained in computer communication services at the telecentre, which has led to the growth of a core group of skilled people within the local community.

There are a number of lessons learned and documented for future telecentre development. Management systems have been tried and established for sustainable telecentre operations.

The telecentre has proved that MCT in rural areas is useful for development. A good number of development groups have visited the multipurpose telecentre with a view of establishing similar ones in other areas.

The community has been at the centre of the planning and execution of the activities of the multipurpose telecentre. A local steering committee representing each of the core target groups was elected by the community to supervise the telecentre's daily activities, liase with the management committee and mobilise the community.

The telecentre is governed at the top by a management committee chaired by Uganda National Commission for UNESCO; other members include the Uganda Telecom Limited and the Public Libraries Board. The Committee is responsible for overall policy and planning, for staffing and as a liaison with international partners.

Information materials such as brochures and posters, translated in Lugandan to ensure maximum comprehension, were printed and distributed. Traditional communications systems were used during the awareness and consultation process. To ensure that the community opinion leaders send the right message to the community, "A Guide for Community" was developed, complete with illustrations and all the information that a mobiliser should know about the telecentre.

Advertisments were aired at timed intervals on "Radio Nakaseke": a simple combination of an amplifier and two low-watt loudspeakers tied up on a limb of a tree raised a few metres above the host shop.

CONSTRAINTS

The telephone connection was the most problematic component. The landline telephone system stopped 16 kilometres away from the telecentre site. Although the project provided for a special telecom system, it would not be envisaged in a short period. It was decided that a landline be established to run 16 kilometres to the telecentre. The plan provided limited voice connection to the telecentre, but data application has remained difficult to get through because of the poor quality of the telephone line.

Internet and e-mail are the least utilised services at the multipurpose telecentre. People do not use the Internet because it is not yet relevant to their daily life; there is a critical need to develop content specifically for Ugandans. Telecentres should not be looked upon only as places to make a phone call or make photocopies. There is a need to tailor smart attractions for users and get them interested in the new services with a mix of information materials, both print and electronic.

According to Mona Dahms, telephone and photocopying are the only services offered by Nakaseke MCT which can be used by the "target population," the "uneducated" farmers who constitute the majority of the community population. "Thus, a reflection on just who the actual beneficiaries are of the telecentre seems justified," she adds.

REFERENCES

Tracing How Far We Have Come, by Meddie Mayanja, Project Officer, Uganda National Commission for UNESCO.

Nakaseke Telecentre Web site is <http://www.nakaseke.or.ug/index.html>.

Other Web pages on *Nakaseke Telecentre* and ICTs in Uganda include Acacia project <http://www.acacia.or.ug/html/report.html> and Richard Fuchs' *Lemonade Report* at <http://www.futureworks.ca/futureworks/reports/lemon.htm>.

"For Educated People Only. ... Reflections on a Visit to Two Multipurpose Community Telecentres in Uganda" by Mona Dahms, in *Telecentre Evaluation*, IDRC, 1999.

ABBREVIATIONS

ABVP	Associaçao Brasileira de Video Popular
ACPO	Acción Cultural Popular, Colombia
ACT	Awareness Community Theatre
ADB	African Development Bank
ADEFOR	Asociación Civil para la Investigación y Desarrollo Forestal, Peru
AGECO	Agence de Communication, Madagascar
AHI	Action Health Incorporated, Nigeria
AIDS	Acquired Immuno Deficiency Syndrome
AKTC	Aga Khan Trust for Culture
ALAI	Agencia Latinoamericana de Información
ALER	Asociación Latinoamericana de Escuelas Radiofónicas
ALRED	Radios Comunitarias de América Latina en Red
AMARC	World Association of Community Media Broadcasters
AMSCLAE	Autoridad para el Manejo Sustentable de la Cuenca del Lago Atitlan y su Entorno, Guatemala
ANAP	Asociación Nacional de Agricultores Pequeños, Cuba
ANC	African National Congress, South Africa
APC	Association for Progressive Communications
APDESI	Asociación para el Desarrollo Integral, Guatemala
ARPAS	Asociación de Radios y Programas Participativos de El Salvador
ASEP	Asociación Salud por el Pueblo, Guatemala
AusAID	Australian Agency for International Development
AVI	Australian Volunteers International
BBC	British Broadcasting Corporation
BOND	British Overseas NGOs for Development
BRAC	Bangladesh Rural Advancement Committee
C4C	Communication for Change, USA
CAF	Community Assistance Foundation, The Netherlands
CAFOD	Catholic Agency for Overseas Development
CAN	Comisión Nacional del Agua, Mexico
CARIMAC	Caribbean Institute of Media and Communication
CASET	Cassette Education Trust, South Africa
CAT	Community Audio Tower, the Philippines
CBO	Community Based Organization
CCC	Comunidades Cristianas Campesinas, Peru
CCFD	Comité Catholique contre la Faim et pour le Développement, France

CDC	Centre for Development Communication, USA
CDF	Conservation Development Fund, USA
CDTV	Centro de Diagnóstico y Terapia para Varones, Bolivia
CECC	Centro de Estudios para la Comunicación Comunitaria, Cuba
CECI	Centre for International Studies and Cooperation, Canada
CECIP	Centre de Imagem de Criaçâo Popular, Brazil
CEDEP	Centro de Educación Popular, Ecuador
CEDPA	Centre For Development and Population Activities, USA
CEMCOS	Centro y Medios de Comunicación Social, Mexico
CENCIRA	Centro Nacional de Capacitación e Investigación de la Reforma Agraria, Peru
CEOSS	Coptic Evangelic Organisation for Social Services, Egypt
CEPAC	Centro de Promoción Agropecuaria Campesina, Bolivia
CESPA	Centre de services de production audiovisuelle, Mali
CESPAC	Centro de Servicios de Pedagogía Audiovisual para la Capacitación, Peru
CIDA	Canadian International Development Agency
CIDER	Centros de Información para el Desarrollo Rural, Peru
CIDUR	Centros de Información para el Desarrollo Urbano-Rural, Peru
CIERRO	Centre régional de formation à la radio en Afrique de l'Ouest, Burkina Faso
CIMCA	Centro de Integración de Medios de Comunicación Alternativa, Bolivia
CIMDUR	Centros de Información Móvil para el Desarrollo Urbano-Rural, Peru
CINEP	Centro de Investigación y Educación Popular, Colombia
CLAI	Consejo Latino Americano de Iglesias
CMC	Community Media Council, the Philippines
CMCM	Centro de Mujeres Comunicadoras Mayas, Guatemala
CMP	Chiapas Media Project, Mexico/USA
CNA	Comisión Nacional del Agua, Mexico
CNN	Cable News Network
CNR	Coordinadora Nacional de Radio, Peru
COB	Central Obrera Boliviana
CODE	Communication pour le Development, Madagascar
COMNESA	Community Media Network of East and Southern Africa
COMPA	Comunidad de Productores de Arte, Bolivia

ComPAS	Community Public Address System
CORAPE	Coordinadora de Radios Populares del Ecuador
CSIR	Council for Scientific and Industrial Research
DANIDA	Danish International Development Agency
DDC	Développement et Cooperation, Switzerland
DFID	Department for International Development, UK
DHS	Demography and Health Survey
DIAKONIA	A Swedish religious development agency
DSC	Development Support Communication
DV	Digital Video
DW	Deutsche Welle
ECHO	European Community Humanitarian Organization
ELCI	Environmental Liaison Center International
ENA	EcoNews Africa
EPI	Extended Programme of Immunisation
FAN	Forest Action Network
FAO	Food and Agricultural Organization
FAS	Foetal Alcohol Syndrome
FES	Friedrich Ebert Stiftung
FGER	Federación Guatemalteca de Escuelas Radiofónicas
FGM	Female Genital Mutilation
FLASCO	Facultad Latino Americana de Ciencias Sociales
FSC	Forest Stewardship Council
FSP	Foundation for the South Pacific
FSTMB	Federación Sindical de Trabajadores Mineros de Bolivia
FTPP	Forests, Trees and People Programme
GTC	Grameen TeleComm
GTZ	German Agency for Technical Cooperation
HCSP	Historic Cities Support Programme
HIVOS	Humanistic Institute for Cooperation with Developing Countries, The Netherlands
IADB	Inter-American Development Bank
IAMCR	International Association for Media and Communication Research
IBA	Independent Broadcasting Authority, South Africa
IBASE	Brazilian Institute of Social and Economic Analysis
ICRT	Instituto Cubano de Radio y Televisión, Cuba
ICT	Information and Communication Technologies
ICW	Indonesia Corruption Watch
IDRC	International Development Research Centre, Canada
IEC	Information, Education, Communication
IIRR	International Institute for Rural Reconstruction
ILCE	Instituto Latinoamericano de Comunicación Educativa
ILO	International Labour Organisation

IMF	International Monetary Fund
IMTA	Instituto Mexicano de Tecnología del Agua
INE	Instituto Nacional de Estadística, Bolivia
INFODEV	World Bank Program for Information and Development
INGO	International Non Governmental Organisation
INI	Instituto Nacional Indigenista, Mexico
IPDC	International Programme for the Development of Communication
IRDT	Integrated Rural Development Trust
ISAI	Institute of Studies for Free Flow of Information
ITDG	Intermedia Technology Development Group
ITU	International Telecommunications Union
IUCN	World Conservation Union
JHU	Johns Hopkins University, USA
JHU/CCP	John Hopkins University Center for Communication Programs, USA
JICA	Japanese Cooperation Agency
JRS	Jesuit Refugee Service
KCOMNET	Kenya Community Media Network
KCRIP	Kothmale Community Radio Internet Project, Sri Lanka
KCTU	Korean Confederation of Trade Unions
KWASP	Kiribati Water and Sanitation Project
LCU	Local Communications Unit
LGA	Local Government Administration, Nigeria
LNP	Labor News Production, Korea
MACIS	Mamelodi Community Information Services, South Africa
MAF	Mission Aviation Fellowship
MAMWA	Malawi Media Women Association
MCRS	Moutse Community Radio Station, South Africa
MCT	Multipurpose Telecentres
MISA	Media Institute of Southern Africa
MSSRF	M.S. Swaminathan Research Foundation, India
MTC	Media and Training Centre
NCCD	National NGO Coordinating Committee
NEFEJ	Nepal Forum of Environmental Journalists
NET	Network of Educational Theatre, Nigeria
NGO	Non Governmental Organization
NGONET	Non Governmental Organization Network
NIIT	A multinational corporation specialising in information technologies and e-commerce
NIZA	Nederlandse Institute voor Suidelijke Afrika
NNVAW	National Network on Violence Against Women

NOVIB	Netherlands Organisation for International Development Cooperation
NPA	Norwegian Peoples Aid
NPPHCN	National Progressive Primary Health Care Networks, South Africa
NZODA	New Zeland Overseas Development Agency
OECD	Organisation for Economic Cooperation and Development
ÖKO Himal	Society for Ecological Cooperation Alps-Himalayas
OPCV	Overseas Projects Corporation of Victoria
PAAN	Puppeteers Against AIDS, Nigeria
PACOM	Programme d'Appui a la Communication au Madagascar
PAHO	Pan American Health Organisation
PCI	Project Concern International, USA
PIAC	Project for Information Access and Connectivity
PIT	Public Internet Terminals
PRA	Participatory Rural Appraisal
PROCOSI	Programa de Coordinación en Salud Integral, Bolivia
PRODERITH	Programa de Desarrollo Rural Integrado del Trópico Húmedo, Mexico
PRODESA	Proyecto de Desarrollo Santiago, Guatemala
PSI	Population Services International, USA
PVC	Participatory Video Communication Unit
RCP	Red Científica Peruana
RDS	Red de Desarrollo Sostenible
REDESO	Réseau pour le développement soutenible, Tanzania
RFI	Radio France International
RIPS	Rural Integrated Project Support, Tanzania
RTS	Radio Television de Senegal
RWM	Rural Women's Movement, South Africa
SABC	South Africa Broadcast Corporation
SANCO	South Africa National Civic Organization
SARH	Secretaría de Agricultura y Recursos Hidráulicos, Mexico
SCT	Secretariat for Communications and Transport, Mexico
SENATI	Servicio Nacional de Adiestramiento en Trabajo Industrial, Peru
SER	Servicio de Escuelas Radiofónicas, Mexico
SEWA	Self-Employed Women's Association, India
SIDA	Swedish International Development Agency
SKN	Stichting Kinderpostzegels Nederland
SLBC	Sri Lanka Broadcasting Corporation
SNEHA	Society for Natal Effects on Health in Adult life, India

SNV	Netherlands Development Organisation
SSNC	Swedish Society for Nature Conservation
STD	Sexually Transmitted Disease
TELI	Technology Enhanced Learning Initiative
TLA	Textile Labor Association, India
TNSACS	Tamil Nadu State AIDS Control Society, India
TRC	Tanzania Red Cross
TRC	Truth and Reconciliation Commission, South Africa
TRCS	Tracing and Family Reunification, Tanzania
TSKL	Telecom Services Kiribati Limited
TVZ	Television Zanzibar, Tanzania
UCT	University of Cape Town, South Africa
UIB	Unidades Informativas Barriales, Colombia
UNCCD	United Nations Convention to Combat Desertification
UNCHS	United Nations Centre for Human Settlements (Habitat)
UNDCP	United Nations International Drug Control Programme
UNDP	United Nations Development Programme
UNECA	United Nations Economic Commission for Africa
UNESCO	United Nations Educational, Scientific and Cultural Organization
UNFPA	United Nations Fund for Population Activities
UNHCR	United Nations High Commission for Refugees
UNICEF	United Nations International Children's Emergency Fund
UNOPS	United Nations Office for Project Services
USAID	United States Agency for International Development
WACC	World Association of Christian Communication
WCC	World Council of Churches
WFP	World Food Programme
WHO	World Health Organisation
WLL	Wireless Local Loop Technologies
WTO	World Trade Organisation
WWF	World Wildlife Fund

TABLE 1: BY YEAR

YEAR	TITLE	PLACE
1947	Radio Sutatenza	Colombia
1949	Miners' Radio Stations	Bolivia
1965	Radio Huayacocotla	Mexico
1969	Radio Quillabamba	Peru
1975	CESPAC	Peru
1978	PRODERITH	Mexico
1978	Teatro Kerigma	Colombia
1979	Teatro La Fragua	Honduras
1984	Video SEWA	India
1985	Kayapo Video	Brazil
1986	TV Maxambomba	Brazil
1987	Radio Margaritas	Mexico
1988	Aarohan Street Theatre	Nepal
1989	CESPA	Mali
1989	Community Audio Towers	Philippines
1989	Kothmale Community Radio	Sri Lanka
1989	Teatro Trono	Bolivia
1989	Wan Smolbag	Vanuatu, Solomon Islands
1990	La Voz de la Comunidad	Guatemala
1990	Labor News Production	Korea
1990	Tambuli	Philippines
1991	Popular Theatre	Nigeria
1991	Radio Izcanal	El Salvador
1991	Soul City	South Africa
1992	Action Health	Nigeria
1992	EcoNews Africa	Regional, Africa
1993	Nalamdana	India
1993	Radio Zibonele	South Africa
1993	Televisión Serrana	Cuba
1995	Bush Radio	South Africa

YEAR	TITLE	PLACE
1995	Community Media Network	Kenya
1995	Radio Chaguarurco	Ecuador
1995	Radio Gune Yi	Senegal
1995	Radio Kwizera	Tanzania
1996	Púlsar	Regional, Latin America
1997	Moutse Community Radio	South Africa
1997	Radio Sagarmatha	Nepal
1998	Chiapas Media Project	Mexico
1998	Gasaleka & Mamelodi Telecentres	South Africa
1998	Grameen Village Phone	Bangladesh
1998	Kiritimati Radio	Republic of Kiribati
1998	Maneno Mengi	Tanzania
1998	Nutzij	Guatemala
1998	Radio Mampita & Magneva	Madagascar
1998	InfoDes	Peru
1998	The Lilac Tent	Bolivia
1998	Video & Community Dreams	Egypt
1998	Village Knowledge Centres	India
1999	Local Radio Network	Indonesia
1999	Nakaseke Telecentre	Uganda

PLACE	TITLE
Bangladesh	**Grameen Village Phone**
Bolivia	**Miners' Radio Stations**
Bolivia	**Teatro Trono**
Bolivia	**The Lilac Tent**
Brazil	**Kayapo Video**
Brazil	**TV Maxambomba**
Colombia	**Radio Sutatenza**
Colombia	**Teatro Kerigma**
Cuba	**Televisión Serrana**
Ecuador	**Radio Chaguarurco**
Egypt	**Video & Community Dreams**
El Salvador	**Radio Izcanal**
Guatemala	**La Voz de la Comunidad**
Guatemala	**Nutzij**
Honduras	**Teatro La Fragua**
India	**Nalamdana**
India	**Video SEWA**
India	**Village Knowledge Centres**
Indonesia	**Local Radio Network**
Kenya	**Community Media Network**
Korea	**Labor News Production**
Madagascar	**Radio Mampita & Magneva**
Mali	**CESPA**
Mexico	**Chiapas Media Project**
Mexico	**PRODERITH**
Mexico	**Radio Huayacocotla**
Mexico	**Radio Margaritas**
Nepal	**Aarohan Street Theatre**
Nepal	**Radio Sagarmatha**
Nigeria	**Action Health**

PLACE	TITLE
Nigeria	**Popular Theatre**
Peru	**CESPAC**
Peru	**InfoDes**
Peru	**Radio Quillabamba**
Philippines	**Community Audio Towers**
Philippines	**Tambuli**
Republic of Kiribati	**Kiritimati Radio**
Senegal	**Radio Gune Yi**
South Africa	**Bush Radio**
South Africa	**Gasaleka & Mamelodi Telecentres**
South Africa	**Moutse Community Radio**
South Africa	**Soul City**
South Africa	**Radio Zibonele**
Sri Lanka	**Kothmale Community Radio**
Tanzania	**Maneno Mengi**
Tanzania	**Radio Kwizera**
Uganda	**Nakaseke Telecentre**
Vanuatu, Solomon Islands	**Wan Smolbag**
Regional, Africa	**EcoNews Africa**
Regional, Latin America	**Púlsar**

TABLE 3: BY MEDIUM

MEDIA	TITLE	PLACE
Cellular Phones	Grameen Village Phone	Bangladesh
Computers, Internet	Gasaleka & Mamelodi Telecentres	South Africa
	InfoDes	Peru
	Nakaseke Telecentre	Uganda
	Village Knowledge Centres	India
Multimedia	Community Media Network	Kenya
	Soul City	South Africa
	The Lilac Tent	Bolivia
Radio	Bush Radio	South Africa
	Community Audio Towers	Philippines
	EcoNews Africa	Regional, Africa
	Kiritimati Radio	Republic of Kiribati
	La Voz de la Comunidad	Guatemala
	Local Radio Network	Indonesia
	Miners' Radio Stations	Bolivia
	Moutse Community Radio	South Africa
	Radio Chaguarurco	Ecuador
	Radio Gune Yi	Senegal
	Radio Huayacocotla	Mexico
	Radio Izcanal	El Salvador
	Radio Kwizera	Tanzania
	Radio Mampita & Magneva	Madagascar
	Radio Margaritas	Mexico
	Radio Quillabamba	Peru
	Radio Sagarmatha	Nepal
	Radio Sutatenza	Colombia
	Radio Zibonele	South Africa
	Tambuli	Philippines

MEDIA	TITLE	PLACE
Radio/Internet	Kothmale Community Radio	Sri Lanka
	Púlsar	Regional, Latin America
Theatre	Aarohan Street Theatre	Nepal
	Nalamdana	India
	Popular Theatre	Nigeria
	Teatro Kerigma	Colombia
	Teatro La Fragua	Honduras
	Teatro Trono	Bolivia
	Wan Smolbag	Vanuatu, Solomon Islands
Video	Action Health	Nigeria
	CESPA	Mali
	CESPAC	Peru
	Chiapas Media Project	Mexico
	Kayapo Video	Brazil
	Labor News Production	Korea
	Maneno Mengi	Tanzania
	Nutzij	Guatemala
	PRODERITH	Mexico
	Television Serrana	Cuba
	TV Maxambomba	Brazil
	Video & Community Dreams	Egypt
	Video SEWA	India

COMPLETE REFERENCE LIST

	TITLE & PLACE	YEAR	MEDIUM
1	**Radio Sutatenza**, Colombia	1947	radio
2	**Miners' Radio Station**, Bolivia	1949	radio
3	**Radio Huayacocotla**, Mexico	1965	radio
4	**Radio Quillabamba**, Peru	1969	radio
5	**CESPAC**, Peru	1975	video
6	**PRODERITH**, Mexico	1978	video
7	**Teatro Kerigma**, Colombia	1978	theatre
8	**Teatro La Fragua**, Honduras	1979	theatre
9	**Video SEWA**, India	1984	video
10	**Kayapo Video**, Brazil	1985	video
11	**TV Maxambomba**, Brazil	1986	video
12	**Radio Margaritas**, Mexico	1987	radio
13	**Aarohan Street Theatre**, Nepal	1988	theatre
14	**CESPA**, Mali	1989	video
15	**Community Audio Towers**, Philippines	1989	radio
16	**Kothmale Community Radio**, Sri Lanka	1989	radio, internet
17	**Teatro Trono**, Bolivia	1989	theatre
18	**Wan Smolbag**, Vanuatu, Solomon Islands	1989	theatre
19	**La Voz de la Comunidad**, Guatemala	1990	radio
20	**Labor News Production**, Korea	1990	video
21	**Tambuli**, Philippines	1990	radio
22	**Popular Theatre**, Nigeria	1991	theatre
23	**Radio Izcanal**, El Salvador	1991	radio
24	**Soul City**, South Africa	1991	multimedia
25	**Action Health**, Nigeria	1992	video
26	**EcoNews Africa**, Regional, Africa	1992	radio
27	**Nalamdana**, India	1993	theatre
28	**Radio Zibonele**, South Africa	1993	radio
29	**Televisión Serrana**, Cuba	1993	video

TITLE & PLACE	YEAR	MEDIUM
30 **Bush Radio**, South Africa	1995	radio
31 **Community Media Network**, Kenya	1995	multimedia
32 **Radio Chaguarurco**, Ecuador	1995	radio
33 **Radio Gune Yi**, Senegal	1995	radio
34 **Radio Kwizera**, Tanzania	1995	radio
35 **Púlsar**, Regional, Latin America	1996	radio, internet
36 **Moutse Community Radio**, South Africa	1997	radio
37 **Radio Sagarmatha**, Nepal	1997	radio
38 **Chiapas Media Project**, Mexico	1998	video
39 **Gasaleka & Mamelodi Telecentres**, South Africa	1998	computers, internet
40 **Grameen Village Phone**, Bangladesh	1998	cellular phones
41 **Kiritimati Radio**, Republic of Kiribati	1998	radio
42 **Maneno Mengi**, Tanzania	1998	video
43 **Nutzij**, Guatemala	1998	video
44 **Radio Mampita & Magneva**, Madagascar	1998	radio
45 **InfoDes**, Peru	1998	computers, internet
46 **The Lilac Tent**, Bolivia	1998	multimedia
47 **Video & Community Dreams**, Egypt	1998	video
48 **Village Knowledge Centres**, India	1998	computers, internet
49 **Local Radio Network**, Indonesia	1999	radio
50 **Nakaseke Telecentre**, Uganda	1999	computers, internet

ACKNOWLEDGEMENTS

Aside from those who helped provide information on their particular experiences and who have reviewed the draft chapters, most of whom I have mentioned under "References" in each case story, I want to mention the people who supported this venture along its various stages of development.

Denise Gray-Felder at The Rockefeller Foundation understood the importance of the research project and provided the means with which to do it. She and her entire team, in particular Karen McAndrew, Susan Muir and Brian Byrd, were the guardian angels of the process until the book was delivered to the printer.

It was not an easy task getting information on the fifty experiences portrayed in this book, especially on those that I couldn't visit myself. I'm grateful to a number of people who contributed by providing a reference, a logo or a piece of information that I needed. And I am also indebted to those in various countries of Asia, Africa and Latin America who assisted me in getting to the remote communities where many of these participatory communication experiences are rooted.

At the risk of forgetting some names, I would like to mention in alphabetical order: Carlos Andrade, Guy Andrianjanaka, Alonso Aznar, Delia Barcelona, Luis Fernando Bossio, Pamela Brooke, Sylvia Cadena, Manuel Calvelo, Tony Collins, Inés Cornejo Portugal, Mona Dahms, Ron Ehrke, Frank Endaya, Warren Feek, Colin Fraser, Lydda Gaviria, Bruce Girard, Grace Githaiga, Martha Lucía Gutierrez, Lars Johansson, Verena Knippel, Garrett Mehl, Bianca Miglioretto, Don Moore, Lynne Muthoni Wanyeki, Tracey Naughton, Tanya Notley, Farida Nyamachumbe, Sonia Restrepo, Don Richardson, Jose Rimon, Raúl Román, Walter Saba, Federico Salzmann, Jodi Stewart, Sally Stuart, Louie Tabing, Lucila Vargas, Aurora Velasco, Dominick de Waal and Peter Walpole.

If this book were viable through the collaboration of all the above-mentioned people, the communication experience itself—spread over all of Africa, Asia and Latin America—is only possible because people in the communities actively participate and believe that their voices should be heard and that their culture should be valued.

Alfonso Gumucio Dagron is a development communication specialist with experience in Africa, Asia, Latin America and the Caribbean.

He worked for seven years with UNICEF in Nigeria and Haiti, and as an international consultant for FAO, UNDP, UNESCO and other United Nations agencies. He was the project director of "Tierramérica," a UNEP/UNDP regional project on sustainable development and served as communication adviser to Conservation International (Washington, D.C.). Mr. Gumucio is familiar with issues of child rights, indigenous populations, arts and culture, human rights, community organisation, health and sustainable development.

His major country experience also includes Burkina Faso, Bangladesh, Ethiopia, Nicaragua, Costa Rica, Colombia, New Guinea, Mexico, Guatemala and Bolivia, his home country.

He is the author of various studies on communication and has also published several books of his poetry and narrative. His short essays and articles have been printed in more than one hundred publications, mainly in Latin America. As a filmmaker he directed documentaries on cultural and social issues.

Since 1997 he has been part of the Rockefeller Foundation discussion group on "Communication for Social Change."